JAMES BENTLEY

A Guide to
Eastern Germany

VIKING

For Hardi Bharj

VIKING

Published by the Penguin Group
Penguin Books Ltd, 27 Wrights Lane, London w8 5TZ, England
Penguin Books USA Inc., 375 Hudson Street, New York, New York 10014, USA
Penguin Books Australia Ltd, Ringwood, Victoria, Australia
Penguin Books Canada Ltd, 10 Alcorn Avenue, Toronto, Ontario, Canada M4V 3B2
Penguin Books (NZ) Ltd, 182–190 Wairau Road, Auckland 10, New Zealand

Penguin Books Ltd, Registered Offices: Harmondsworth, Middlesex, England

First published 1993
1 3 5 7 9 10 8 6 4 2
First edition

Copyright © James Bentley

Typeset by Datix International Limited, Bungay, Suffolk
Set in 11/13½ pt Lasercomp Bembo
Printed in England by Clays Ltd, St Ives plc

A CIP catalogue record for this book is available from the British Library

ISBN 0-670-84041-6

CONTENTS

_____

LIST OF ILLUSTRATIONS

EASTERN GERMANY

Baltic Sea

Kiel

Darss

RÜGEN

Barth
Stralsund
Rerik · Bad Doberan Grimmen
POEL · Rostock Greifswald
Wismar MECKLENBURGER Anklam.
Lübeck Schönberg Güstrow · Malchin
Schwerin SCHWEIZ
Hamburg Parchim. Müritz Neubrandenburg

G E R M A N Y
Elbe
Ravensbrück
Fürstenberg
POLAND
Neuruppin Ruppin
Stendal. MARK OF Oranienburg
Charlottenburg Havel ■ BERLIN
Köpenick
Plauer Potsdam Spree
Brandenburg FRANKFURT
an der Oder
Magdeburg · BRANDENBURG
SAXONY · Lübben
Halberstadt Wittenberg
Wernigerode · Bode Dessau · Wörlitz
Quedlinburg Köthen
Gernrode ANHALT
Nordhausen Eisleben Halle Görlitz
Mulhausen Merseburg Leipzig Bautzen
Freyburg Meissen Bischofswerda
Eisenach Erfurt Weimar Naumburg SAXONY Dresden
Gotha · Arnstadt Jena SWITZERLAND Pirna
Schmalkalden THÜRINGER WALD Freiberg
Meiningen Karlmarxstadt Neisse
Odra
Labe

N

C Z E C H O S L O V A K I A

0   50   100 km
0 10 20 30 40 50 miles

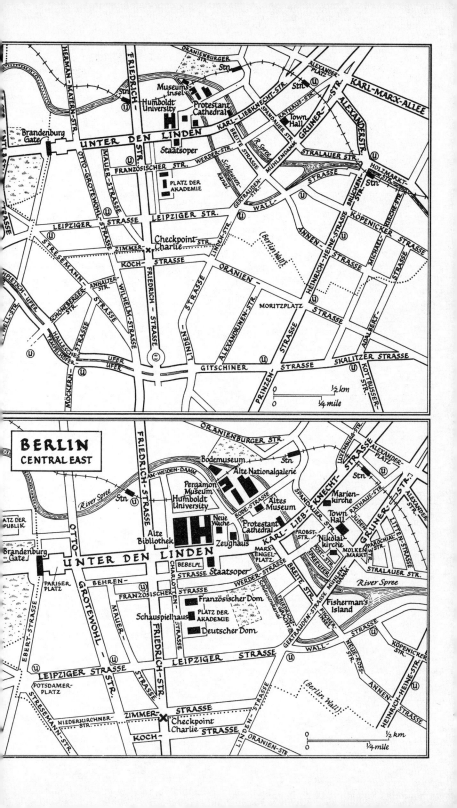

INTRODUCTION

Two paintings by Bernardo Bellotto, the nephew and pupil of Canaletto, hang in the City Art Gallery, Manchester. Commissioned in 1748 by Augustus II of Saxony as part of a series displaying the castles in his domains, they romantically depict Schloss Königstein, which rises on a 360 m high rock in the part of eastern Germany known as Saxony Switzerland. Often besieged, never taken, this fortress was the country retreat of the rulers of Saxony and their refuge in times of war. Here they would hide the royal treasury and their magnificent collection of art. These two paintings never joined that collection. Bellotto failed to deliver them to Augustus because of the Seven Years' War.

Until autumn 1989, when the infamous Iron Curtain which stretched from the Elbe to the Oder collapsed, I often feared that Manchester's City Art Gallery was the nearest I should ever be to this magical Schloss Königstein. Looking back, it seems to me intolerable that for so long after the Second World War countless West Germans and travellers from other lands should have been denied the joy of visiting a superb part of Germany which has contributed enormously to Europe's cultural heritage.

In fact, in those years you were allowed to visit East Berlin, and even Dresden and Leipzig, provided you booked in advance a room in a ridiculously overpriced hotel. Even then, insolent border guards would often make your crossing a misery. Friends warned you not to take along any possibly subversive literature. Once in 1972 my wife and I were driving our car through Checkpoint Charlie into East Berlin to visit the then Bishop of Berlin-Brandenburg, Albrecht Schönherr (who, like his postwar predecessors, insisted on preaching the Christian Gospel in the Communist-ruled part of the city). The ban on books meant that we could take with us no literary present for the bishop. As usual the guards held us up, more or less ripping the car apart, looking underneath it with mirrors on poles. They confiscated one journal I had not supposed would offend anyone, a copy of the *Oldham Chronicle*.

It seems scarcely believable that in the so-recent past our West German friends were obliged to cross at a different checkpoint, so that having, for instance, sweated in a crowded, miserable room in Friedrichstrasse station, waiting to be let out into what is one of the finest urban ensembles in the world, we had to languish in some café till our friends could join us before exploring that ensemble.

All that harassment has been swept away. Westerners once more flock to the Hoppengarten racecourse on the eastern edge of Berlin. Today you can walk freely past the Brandenburg Gate and down Unter den Linden, and soon maybe those hateful memories of sullenly impertinent border guards will be forgotten.

For nearly half a century most visitors were totally denied access to this exquisite part of Europe, apart from Berlin, Leipzig and Dresden. When the Iron Curtain was breached all of it was suddenly opened up. Five new provinces (*Länder*) were restored to the German people of the West. In each of them, a resurgence of vitality has restored buildings and striven to eliminate the industrial pollution which marred the former East Germany, setting out to attract tourism into a hitherto closed world.

Berlin, now no longer a divided city, begins and ends this book. The ensemble at the heart of what was formerly East Berlin is primarily the work of one man, Karl Friedrich Schinkel (1781–1841), his mark on the city as distinctive as that of Haussmann on Paris. Schinkel was a multi-talented genius. He painted dreamy Romantic landscapes comparable with those of Turner. He designed theatre sets and bridges. Patronized by King Friedrich-Wilhelm III and a close friend of the crown prince who was to become Friedrich-Wilhelm IV, he produced elaborate jewellery for the Prussian nobility and royal family, who appointed him their supreme director of public buildings (or *Oberlandesbaudirektor*).

His most famous building, the Altes Museum in Berlin, modelled on Smirke's British Museum and (I regret to say) infinitely finer, has characterized him as an architect of the classical revival. As we shall see, Schinkel was much more. In 1826 he spent three weeks in Paris, before coming to Britain and exploring England, Scotland and Wales for three and a half months. Sketching factories and warehouses in Manchester, cottages on the Scottish coast and the Conway suspension bridge a mere nine days after its opening, he also absorbed the Gothic revival. And on his return, Berlin above all, but also the rest of Prussia, benefited from what he had learnt.

Mention of Schinkel is also a reminder that reunited Germany consciously decided to come to terms with the uglier aspects of its past. In 1813 Schinkel designed the Iron Cross, Prussia's highest military medal, for which all ranks were eligible. Twenty-two years previously a statue of Nike, the goddess of victory, had been designed by Johann Schadow to top Berlin's Brandenburg Gate. Napoleon Bonaparte stole the statue in 1806, and Nike returned to Berlin only in 1814, now to be decked out with the Prussian eagle as well as Schinkel's Iron Cross. Nike was badly damaged in the Second World War, and when the East German government restored the statue in 1958, the Prussian eagle and the Iron Cross were left out, deemed unsuitably warlike.

On the anniversary of the fall of the Berlin Wall souvenir hunters again damaged the statue. A year later she returned, once more restored and this time with the eagle and the Iron Cross, a symbol to me that the Germans have exorcized some unhappy ghosts. In the pages of this book we shall recall others of these ghosts, visiting concentration camps, now memorials to those who died at the hands of the Nazis. As for exorcism, the Jewish quarter of east Berlin, whose Jewish inhabitants had been reduced to some 200 by the 1980s, has revived. Yiddish songs are once more heard in the cafés around Tucholsky Strasse. The Byzantine-style synagogue inaugurated by Kaiser Wilhelm I in 1866 was smashed by the Nazis on the Kristallnacht of 1938 and was further damaged in the Second World War. The Communists reluctantly started rebuilding it only in 1988. Today its restored dome once again carries the gold star of David.

Its size sets Berlin apart from all the other cities of eastern Germany. Leipzig and Dresden are major cities and yet infinitely homelier, even though the former has nearly 600,000 inhabitants and the latter nearly 500,500. (Lest one mistakenly supposes, admiring the Brandenburg Gate, that only Berliners defeated Napoleon, there is an even more megalomaniac memorial in Leipzig, the 91 m high Völkerschlachtdenkmal, with a colossal statue, commemorating the defeat of the French by the Prussians, Austrians and Russians in 1813.) As for other great cities, the population of Eisenach, with its baroque Schloss and the historic Wartburg, is annually swollen by 300,000 tourists. Still in Thuringia, Erfurt competes in attracting visitors, for the old city is breathtakingly beautiful. The major centres of the north, such as Rostock, Schwerin, Wismar and Güstrow, boast huge medieval churches, built of brick. On the eastern border of Germany the baroque houses and

Gothic churches of Frankfurt-an-der-Oder are surpassed in splendour only by the city's magnificent Gothic Rathaus. On the western border of the former East Germany, Magdeburg has a cathedral which matches the Gothic masterpieces of north-west France — not surprisingly, since it was built by French master masons. In this book I have set out to describe these cities in detail, as well as drawing attention to the delights of the smaller towns and villages of eastern Germany.

Each chapter focuses on a major city before taking the reader on tours through the surrounding countryside, itself delightful and astonishingly varied. The Baltic coast offers a series of stunning chalky rocks and cliffs. Further south the *Land* of Mecklenburg is dotted with lakes and splendid castles. Around Berlin, Potsdam and the Spree forest are equally lapped with streams, rivers and lakes. The environs of Dresden, the supreme baroque city of Germany, include moated castles and the town of Meissen, which rises on a hill beside the Elbe. The industrial city of Dessau, whose charms I shall prise out, is surrounded by the finest parks and some of the most beautiful palaces of the country, as well as by Wittenberg, the cradle of the Protestant Reformation. The Harz mountains, described by Heinrich Heine in the book which made his name, is washed by the bubbling River Bode. And Bautzen is the capital of a people whose traditions are so remote from the rest of Germany that the people speak an entirely different language, greeting you with the cry *Wutrobnje witacjce*, which means 'Welcome to our country.'

Alongside its exquisite towns and cities, eastern Germany is also a land of forests, grassy meadows and tree-lined roads. Long avenues of limes and chestnuts flank the roads, especially in the northern part of the country. Clumps of trees shade lakes. The tree-lined Unter den Linden in Berlin is famous. Not generally known is that Frederick the Great wanted the whole of Prussia to resemble it. He achieved his aim.

Some spots are entrancing above all because of their setting. Almost at the southernmost tip of eastern Germany, the town of Steinach is one. Its neo-Romanesque church dates from around 1900. A Saturday market sets itself up in the wide and handsome Marktplatz. From here narrow cobbled streets twist to hidden quarters of the town. Steinach nestles amongst the wooded hills of the Spessart forest, the highest of its peaks reaching 844 m. Sometimes in winter up to 5 m of snow can fall, and there is a slalom run at Steinach.

The sturdy houses are covered with slate from the neighbouring quarries (and the town has a slate museum which I have so far neglected to visit). Here I fell in with Herr Heinz Stefan who, in a factory designed much as a barn, manufactures the hooks for clothes hangers. Steinach, he said, once possessed five breweries and still has two, brewing Anker and Gessner beers. Then he kindly took me up to his weekend house (a prized possession of many eastern Germans), overlooking the town. Here he sits of an evening, he said, taking a drink with his friend the moral philosopher Professor Ernst. Regretfully I explained that I had some distance to go and could not share the discussion that evening, at which Herr Stefan took me to the Anker brewery, bought twenty-eight bottles of Anker Pils and placed them in the boot of my car.

The lush landscape and seascapes, as well as the lake-strewn forests, match the setting of such towns. In 1776 Goethe wrote from Ilmenau in Thuringia, 'the countryside is superb, superb.' At the age of eighty-two when on 27 August 1831, he looked down for the last time on the Thuringian forest, he once again exclaimed 'Superb, superb!'

Goethe is not the sole genius to have flourished in this region. In the market square of Arnstadt is a modern statue entitled 'Bach as a young man in Arnstadt'. After Martin Luther had enrolled at Erfurt's university in 1501, he observed that the other universities he had known seemed by comparison 'little schools for archers'. Not far away from Erfurt, the fortified medieval town of Mühlhausen was from 1524 the headquarters of the revolutionary Anabaptist and peasants' leader Thomas Müntzer, who was executed by his religious enemies in May 1525. Leaving aside these passionate Protestants, eastern Germany is also the land of Schiller and Herder, of Theodor Fontane, Gerhart Hauptmann and Bertolt Brecht.

Equally rich and varied is the artistic heritage of this part of Germany. Along with the treasures of Berlin and the collections of great princes such as that of Augustus the Strong of Saxony, eastern Germany boasts masterpieces by Lucas Cranach the Elder. The misty landscapes and seascapes of Mecklenburg have been memorably captured by Caspar David Friedrich. I warm to mad oddities, such as the sculptor and painter Max Klinger (1857–1920), now almost forgotten in spite of his influence on the Surrealists, his works occupying the top floor of the Leipzig art gallery. Amongst them is a statue of Beethoven, made of patterned and white marble, amber, ivory, mother-of-pearl, jasper, agate, alabaster and bronze, which was first exhibited in Vienna in 1902, when a wind ensemble conducted by Gustav Mahler played parts of the Ninth Symphony. (The exhition drew 600,000 visitors.)

Dresden was where, in 1919, Otto Dix founded a society of avant-garde artists (Die Gruppe) who laid the foundations for the Neue Sachlichkeit (or 'new objectivity') school. The city's Gemäldegalerie Neuer Meister contains some of the most startling of his works, *Salon I* of 1921, with four intensely vulgar, bored tarts and a momentary return to kindliness in his 1923 portrait of the family of the lawyer Dr Fritz Glaser. Dix was professor at the Dresden Art Academy from 1927 until the Nazis dismissed him in 1933 (for depicting too realistically the horrors of the First World War), whereat Dix responded with a painting of the Seven Deadly Sins (now in the Staatsgalerie, Stuttgart) depicting Hitler as 'Envy'.

In the words of Francis Bacon, 'Travel, in the younger sort, is a part of education.' He added that in the elder sort, it was 'a part of experience'. In addition to the enthralling education provided by all these galleries and this artistic patrimony, I have also had some memorable meals at eastern Germany's rustic dining tables. As we shall see, food in this land is as varied as the countryside and the art. Wherever you eat, typical local food is hearty. East Berliners tuck into a *Pökelkamm mit Mostrichstippe*, that is a pork chop from the pig's fatty neck served with a mustard dip, or *Eisbein mit Sauerkraut und Erbsenpüree*, which is a knuckle of pork accompanied by sauerkraut and mashed peas. On the Baltic coast fish reigns, sometimes much disguised. Here herring fillets (*Matjesfilets*) can be served with beans, gherkins, cucumber, capers, herbs and fresh cream. In this part the locals drink beer with their meals, downing a *Koem* (a cumin liqueur) to aid their digestion. In Saxony meals begin with a vegetable soup known as *Leipziger Allerlei* and end with succulent cakes, and Radeberger Pilsner accompanies the food from start to finish. The Thuringians work wonders with the potato, serving it as *Kartoffelnklösse*. The Spreewald is pre-eminently the region of gherkins and horseradish, serving *Spreewälder Gurkenfleisch* (beef with gherkins and onions) and *Karpfen blau mit Sahnemeerrettich* (blue carp with a sauce made from horseradish and cream).

As for one's daily needs (such as in my case wine, food and books), the eastern Germans still tend to close down their shops at weekends, unlike the bustling westerners who are used to setting out their stalls for weekend visitors. Yet I soon noticed that some enterprising easterners were changing. Beside the exquisite Pfaffenteich lake at the heart of Schwerin, I discovered a cheery couple running a kiosk which traded every day of the week, and where for a mere 16 DM I could buy myself a couple of litres of dry white wine, four Schwerin beers and a can of orange juice. (You can also buy alcohol at petrol stations, since the former East German régime forbade drinking and driving.) The eastern Germans also turn out to be delightfully reluctant to rip off their visitors. At the Weimar Ratskeller I once tried to order *pommes frites* with my farmer's omelette. The waitress counselled me not to – 'You'll never manage to eat both' – and she was right.

Initially I shared the common misconception that eastern Germany is a land of austerity and shortages. The first time we ever ventured into the eastern part of newly unified Germany my wife suggested that we ought to take with us a fair stock of picnic food, just in case there was nothing in the shops. So we took tins of salmon, some jars of *pâté*, even a pack of cheese. These emergency rations travelled to Leipzig, lived in the boot of a car for a while, and then came back to Britain uneaten. It was then I first realized that the supposed shortcomings of eastern Germany had been much exaggerated.

Eastern Germany, I discovered, had made a cleaner break with its Communist past than I had supposed. Even the names of streets, once dedicated to Soviet heroes, had been changed. At Rostock the former Ernst Thälmann Platz, named after the inter-war Communist leader who perished at Buchenwald, was once more called the Neuer Markt. At Dresden the Georgij Dimitroff bridge, dedicated to a Communist worthy, speedily reverted to its original name, the Augustusbrücke (in honour of Elector August the Strong, who became King of Poland and is said to have fathered at least 365 children). So rapidly did street names change after reunification that the joke was you went to bed one evening and woke up the following morning somewhere else.

Another myth soon exploded was the notion that the hotels of eastern Germany, even if you could find them, were ridiculously expensive. Heinz Stefan told me that before the division of Germany his home town of Steinach was happily welcoming tourists from the former West. As he pointed out, its *Gasthäuser* were still intact, and its citizens planned to welcome tourists once again. In 1992 he recommended to me a new, inexpensive hotel, the Gaststätte Schöne Aussicht, set on the side of a hill. There I stayed, and I confirm that the lovely view from its rooms and restaurant fully justifies its name.

On my first stay there I began most meals with *Soljanka*, a beneficent legacy of the Russians, consisting of an extremely spicy soup, more or less a mixture of every available ingredient, sometimes on a meat base, sometimes on a fish base. When I next reached Steinach the menu had a new, delicious hors-d'oeuvre, namely baked Camembert with cranberry sauce. This second time around, Herr Stefan's hopes of a revival in tourism seemed to be coming true, for the hotel was full and I had to stay at the even cheaper Steinacher Hof down in the village.

Eastern Germany boasts more expensive hotels than this, some of them of international standards. At Dresden I have stayed at the Maritim-Bellevue hotel. With its eight restaurants, three kitchens and sixteen apartments, as well as a casino and fitness centre, the Bellevue gave and still gives the lie to eastern German austerity. It also blends sympathetically with a baroque wing which survived the fire-bombs of February 1945 (though, but for a popular protest, the Communists would have pulled it down). The Maritim-Bellevue is idyllically sited. Just around the corner across the Augustusbrücke rises Dresden's undulatingly baroque cathedral whose interior is exquisite.

There are, of course, cheaper hotels in Dresden, especially near the main railway station. But on my first visit after reunification Thomas Püttjer, marketing head of the tourist board, told me that Dresden already had too few hotel rooms for those who were flocking to the city. So he took me to explore one imaginative response to the problem: the hotel-ship *Elbresidenz*. The *Elbresidenz* belongs to a shipping line which has twenty-five boats on the Rhine and now three on the Elbe. The ship boasts no fewer than ninety-seven cabins and 200 beds, as well as a swimming-pool, conference room and sauna. Naturally, this being super-efficient Germany, there is a business centre with its telephones and fax machines. Often the *Elbresidenz* treats its guests to trips along the river, but I found it entrancing simply to eat on board, with virtually the same view of Dresden as Bellotto painted. As regards the food, although Yves Belzacq, the director of this floating hotel, happened to be French, his cuisine was Saxon and the wines he served were the delicate and rare ones from nearby Meissen.

After the fall of the Communist régime, Dresden soon conquered the air pollution which once disfigured its buildings. Not far away, Weimar in 1990 had yet to solve this problem. But at least the nasty taste failed to penetrate the Weimar Hilton, a hotel superbly placed for the tourist since it stands on the way to the rococo Schloss Belvedere and directly opposite the romantic park which Goethe himself caused to be laid out in the English fashion. In the Goethehaus in this park is a portrait of his wife, painted in 1800. She is a pensive-looking lady, but, after all, she had to put up with a lot from her philandering genius of a husband.

Like Dresden, Weimar was keen to develop more tourist facilities. Joachim Vogel, press agent of the city, told me that the Bürgermeister was setting his mind particularly to creating middle-range hotels. I discovered that you could find rooms for thirty or so Deutschmarks in the *Gasthäuser* of the villages surrounding Weimar, but they tended to fill up before midday, often with those West Germans who were here to help rebuild the land of their eastern neighbours.

Visiting the northern regions of eastern Germany I stayed at a quite different and utterly charming hotel, the Strandhotel at Schwerin. Under the blue awnings of its windows appears a superb view over a little sandy beach and across the Schwerin lake, with its ducks, swans and tree-clad islands. Over to the left of the lake you can see the old centre of Schwerin, with the Chambord-style Schloss and the spires of its brick-built Gothic church. While the hotel has its banqueting room for weddings and conferences, one of its most pleasing features is that in summer some 150 people can eat on the balcony outside.

Many local tourist offices offer the service of finding bed and breakfast for visitors in a *Privatzimmer*. At Dessau I was offered one for 45 DM. Spotless, it included a television set and its own shower and toilet, as well as providing the typically massive German breakfast. That evening, as I sat reading and drinking my own bottle of wine, the owner knocked on the door with the cry 'Allo'. Then she asked why I wasn't taking advantage of her sitting-room, for that was (she said) a much homelier spot. And so it was.

As for the new capital of the new Germany, whenever in the past I have visited Berlin I have roomed with an old friend in the West or stayed at the inexpensive Hotel Bernhardt in Bernhardtstrasse. But with reunion I seized the chance to stay in the Hotel Stadt Berlin, which towers 137 m over Alexander-platz. This monster, with 880 rooms and 1540 beds, was one of the showcases of the old eastern régime. In the old days nearly 50 per cent of its rooms were taken up by Russians, and the hotel employed Russian-speaking staff. Its other guests, paying in hard currency, helped to prop up Erich Honecker's lifestyle.

According to Jürgen Wittig, who became its director of marketing after reunification, hardly anything was done in the old days to improve it. Today its outrageously well-planned conference rooms display the latest technology, while three kitchens cope with its numerous restaurants. The raciest of these is the remarkably inexpensive Zillestube, named after one of Berlin's raunchiest caricaturists, and decorated with some of his more decorous pieces. (We shall later in this book discover some juicier ones.) Its finest cuisine is served on the thirty-seventh floor, in a restaurant which overlooks the red town hall, the churches of St Nicholas and the Virgin Mary, the hideous television tower and the Protestant cathedral. Its Bierpub has thirty-nine seats and serves thirty-nine different beers. 'Our philosophy is to make this the leading three-star hotel in Berlin,' declared Herr Wittig.

In my view Herr Wittig and the eastern Germans will achieve most of their ambitions, especially with regard to tourism. Everywhere the people have seemed to me welcoming and helpful (even in traditionally truculent Berlin). Thomas Püttjer, who came from Frankfurt-am-Main to work in Dresden, illustrated this courtesy with a neat tale. One day by error he took a bus going the wrong way. At the terminus the driver comforted him with the promise, 'I'll drive faster on the way back.'

As well as those mentioned above, I am particularly grateful to Herr Harold Henning and Frau Agatha Suess of the German National Tourist Office in London, and to Mr H. S. Bharj for coming with me to photograph eastern Germany. May I also thank David Oliver, Sales Manager of Dan-Air, whose courteous airline daily flies from the UK to Berlin.

James Bentley

Note
We have used 'ss' instead of the German *Eszett* (ß) throughout.

THE SEA AND ITS HINTERLAND

Wismar is an astonishingly rich and beautiful city. Stand on the corner of Lübsche Strasse, Hegedestrasse and Krämerstrasse to drink in the charm of little curving streets flanked by delicious gabled houses, built in varied styles between the fifteenth and the eighteenth centuries. Some of these houses have pulleys, which in past times lifted merchandise to the loft, for Wismar flourished as a trading city. The chemist's on the corner where we are standing is a pink and white gabled house whose façade carries the date 1621. Opposite stands a green-gabled house, this one with the date 1584.

The city's history goes back further, to the 1220s. Wismar was founded by pioneers from Lübeck, Flanders and Lower Saxony, and along with Lübeck, Rostock and Stralsund was a principal founder in the fourteenth century of the prosperous Hanseatic League, set up with the aim of protecting and mutually supporting trade on land and sea. Her merchants traversed the known world and brought back, especially from France and Flanders, new architectural ideas which inspired the town's fabulous churches. Wismar also profited as a brewing town, its beers renowned in the fifteenth century (and still exceedingly acceptable today).

As every other fine city and town in this region, Wismar suffered during the wars of the seventeenth century and the invasions of the eighteenth. At the peace of Westphalia in 1648 the town became Swedish and her new masters proceeded to make Wismar into a fortress. In the next century the Danes vied with the Swedes over her. In 1767 Prussian troops ravaged and set fire to the town. Only in 1803 did Wismar become German again, when the Duke of Mecklenburg leased her for one hundred years at a cost of 1,250,000 Thalers. And in spite of the depredations of the Second World War, the town's architectural patrimony retains memories of all these turbulent years.

In the spacious, cobbled and irregular market square (known as Am Markt, and one of the largest in Germany) the triple-gabled house at no. 20 is known as the Alter Schwede (the Old Swede), though it long pre-dates the Swedish invasions. The Alter Schwede was built out of brick in the Gothic style in 1385, and above its porch is a bust of a swaggeringly moustachioed Swede. Today the building serves as a restaurant (opened in 1878, when it was baptized Alter Schwede), with models of sailing ships hanging from the ceiling. In a piquant contrast, the building next door is also a restaurant, also gabled, painted green and white, but this time built in the Jugendstil, which the British dub by its French name art nouveau.

In front of the Alter Schwede rises a twelve-sided Renaissance pavilion, the Wasserkunst, which was built in the late sixteenth century by the architect and sculptor Philip Brandin of Utrecht. Often besieged, Wismar drew water from the spring which it shelters. The pavilion is covered in gilt inscriptions, praising its water, detailing its history and proclaiming those times when it was the salvation of the city. The Wasserkunst supplied Wismar's water until 1897.

When they ruled Wismar the Swedes used the double-gabled house at no. 15 as their headquarters. At the opposite side of Am Markt the Rathaus stands out from the rest, a classical building of 1819, painted pale green with its date picked out in gilt. From here you can see, rising above the houses, the 81 m-high tower of the Marienkirche, built in the thirteenth and fourteenth centuries and modelled on the Marienkirche of Lübeck. Underneath its clock the date 1981 records the completion of its restoration after the Second World War. To reach the church follow Sargmacherstrasse from the south-east corner of Am Markt to the Marienkirchhof, passing the quaint, glazed brick and gabled Archidiakonat, which was built in the fifteenth century.

South of this church stands the Renaissance ducal palace, the Fürstenhof of 1555. This is an entertaining building, decorated with limestone and terracotta, created by Gabriel von Aachen and Valentina von Lira to celebrate the engagement of Duke Johann Albrecht to a princess of Brandenburg. They modelled the palace on the Palazzo Roverella in Ferrara. But what makes this notable is that both architects clearly liked an architectural joke. The sculpted porch is flanked by four grotesque female and male beasts, linking each other backwards, so to speak, their hooves cloven. Three storeys high, the Fürstenhof has rows of windows on either side of which are caryatids and Samsons. A row of portrait medallions, depicting figures from antiquity, is matched by a frieze depicting heroes of an idealized Trojan war. Go through the porch and archway at the centre of the Fürstenhof to discover on the other side an equally bizarrely sculpted doorway. Here the frieze is more homely, depicting pigs and a swineherd, musicians, soldiers, knights on horseback with their ladies and Renaissance feasting. I find it hard to comprehend that this jolly frieze is supposed to represent the story of the Prodigal Son. Above this is another row of portrait medallions. Look out for the statues of David and Goliath and Samson and Delilah. You can also visit the Fürstenhof, which contains the city archives.

A few paces further west, alongside the remains of an earlier wing of the palace built in 1512, is the brick basilica of St George, built in the flamboyant Gothic style in the fifteenth century. Its massive flying buttresses and gables were severely damaged in the Second World War, but today the Georgenkirche is being meticulously restored.

Walk north from here along Grosse Hohe Strasse to reach the hospice church of the Holy Ghost, a fourteenth-century Gothic building, whose treasures include a medieval stained-glass window, Gothic reredoses (brought here from the Georgenkirche) and above all a ceiling of 1688 carved with acanthus leaves. This Heiliggeistkirche, was restored between 1964 and 1978. From here Lübsche Strasse, with its beguiling sixteenth- and seventeenth-century houses, run west to Ulmenstrasse, where you turn right to find the Arsenal built by the Swedes in 1699. Continue along Am Hafen to discover the fifteenth-century Wassertor, which once belonged to Wismar's medieval fortifications. Here turn right along eighteenth-century Spiegelber, and take the second right to find the Nikolaikirche. This buttressed, three-aisled basilica was begun in 1380 under the direction of Heinrich von Bresme, to whom we owe the ambulatory, which was finished in 1415. His successor was Hermann von Münster, who built the nave between 1435 and 1460. The belfry dates from 1487, and at the beginning of the seventeenth century the church was frescoed with (amongst other paintings) a gigantic St Christopher.

St Nicholas bristles with gables. And inside is a font of 1335, sculpted with scenes from the life of Jesus and carried by three kneeling men. The 1430 winged reredos of the high altar is lovely, devoted to the coronation of the Blessed Virgin Mary. Do not miss the altar of the Grocers' Guild, created in Lübeck in the mid fifteenth century and depicting the Virgin Mary between the archangel Michael and St Maurice, nor the bronze funeral plaque of Duchess Sophie, who died in 1505. Fine chandeliers light the church and – to my mind – its finest reredos, Christ crucified between his mother and St John. From Wismar's baroque age come the retable of the choir altar, created in 1772 (with a copy of a *Deposition* by Rubens), the pulpit of 1708 and the organ console of 1719.

Crossing a stream which runs through the city on the south side of the church, you come upon the Dutch Renaissance Schabbelt-Haus, built in 1570 with a gable and decorated doorways. It houses Wismar's local-history museum. And from here you can make your way back to the Markt through Krämerstrasse, with its sixteenth- and seventeenth-century houses, and the pedestrianized Hegedestrasse.

A garland of delights surrounds Wismar. Fourteen kilometres north is the island of Poel with its beaches, which you can visit by boat from Wismar's animated old port. Kirchdorf, the island's main port, has a late-Gothic town church. Close by this island are two others which are reserved for birds. Twenty-four kilometres north-east of Wismar is Klütz, with a mid-thirteenth-century church, half-Gothic, half-Renaissance. This three-aisled basilica, dedicated to Our Lady, has a square west tower which transforms itself higher up into an octagonal one. Inside are fourteenth-century choir-stalls. In a suburb of Klütz stands the baroque Schloss Bothmer of 1726. Inspired by Vanbrugh's Blenheim Palace, the architect Johann Friedrich Künecke built it for the imperial count Johann Kaspar von Bothmer. Like Blenheim, it boasts elongated wings, and a park, which was transformed into the English style only in the twentieth century. The staircase hall and main room of the building were stuccoed by Italian rococo masters between 1726 and 1732. The Schloss today houses fortunate old folks. Only 3 km further on is the seaside resort of Boltenhagen, whose Kurpark (hydro) is the venue for summer concerts.

To the east of Wismar you reach Neukloster, which lies along the old Hanseatic trading road from Lübeck to Danzig.

Neukloster boasts a church of 1220–45 which once belonged to Cistercian nuns and has three remarkable (and rare) contemporary stained-glass windows in the east of the choir. Its freestanding belfry dates from 1586, its winged altarpiece (depicting the Blessed Virgin Mary in the rays of the sun) from the sixteenth. You can hire boats on the Neukloster lake. Brüel lies further south, by way of the Warin lake, and has a thirteenth-century Gothic church. And to the west of Wismar on the way to Lübeck is Grevesmühlen, also boasting a thirteenth-century Gothic church (though its neo-Gothic choir dates from 1872). The town hall of Grevesmühlen dates from 1715.

But our major route now takes us south from Wismar, through Mecklenburg-Dorf to the superb Schwerin. The village of Mecklenburg-Dorf has an early-fifteenth-century brick church whose furniture includes a pulpit of 1619 carved with the four evangelists and the Crucifixion, and an altar of 1622 carved with scenes of the Passion. Through a countryside of lakes and forests the route reaches Schwerin, the old capital of the Grand Duchy of Mecklenburg-Schwerin until the dukes abdicated in 1918. An ancient city, its outskirts were certainly peopled in the seventeenth century BC, and its name derives from that of a Slavonic fortress, Zuarin (meaning 'region of many animals').

In spite of industrialization and its two satellite towns of Weststadt and Lankow, old Schwerin is delicious. Founded by Henry the Lion in 1160 and the oldest city in the Land of Mecklenburg-Vorpommern, Schwerin has trams, beaches, French-style houses, a sports and congress hall, and a symphony orchestra whose origins as the Mecklenburg Staatskapelle date back four centuries. The city is washed by lakes which press into its very centre. Lake Schwerin itself (the Schweriner See) has a surface area of 65.5 km² and reaches a depth of 52 m. Schwerin's Altstadt lies between two other lakes, the Burgsee and the Pfaffenteich. The citizens have taken these lakes to their heart, endowing the Pfaffenteich with a fountain. It is also flanked by a huge, white, comically pseudo-Gothic arsenal, built in 1844 by G. A. Demmler (whose capacious architectural tastes here encompassed a Germanic mock-Tudor style).

The cathedral stands just beyond the southern end of this lake, brick, Gothic, dating from the fourteenth and early fifteenth centuries and the only medieval survival in this city. Henry the Lion laid the foundation-stone of an earlier, Romanesque building on this spot. Inevitably, Schwerin cathedral has been much modified over the centuries, though its Romanesque Paradise Door remains. Its windows have ogival tracery; its tower (dating only from 1892, the work of Georg Daniel) reaches 118 m. In the 1330s a master came from Lübeck to fresco its Chapel of the Assumption with a portrait of the enthroned Virgin Mary surrounded by symbols of the four Evangelists. A couple of bronze funeral slabs remain from the fourteenth century. Another tomb came here from Nuremberg, from the workshop of the Renaissance genius Peter Vischer the Younger. Robert Coppens of Mechelin made the funeral monument of Duke Christoph and his wife in 1595. Today the late-Gothic cloister (which has not withstood the ravages of the centuries well) houses the library of the Land of Mecklenburg.

South of the Dom across Am Markt is the classical Neues Gebäude, which was new when Johann Joachim Busch created its twelve Doric and Attic columns in 1783. The nearby Rathaus seems to be authentically Gothic, but it has been much ravaged by fire and its present façade dates only from 1835, the work of G. A. Demmler. More authentic are the four gabled eighteenth-century houses behind it. In front is a gilded rider, with a sort of old-fashioned policeman's helmet on his head, somehow representing the equestrian figure of Henry the Lion which is now part of the coat of arms of this city.

Schelfmarkt is north-east of the Rathaus, and here is an earlier town hall, paradoxically that of the new city. The Neustädtisches Rathaus of Schwerin was built in the mid eighteenth century. Surrounded by late-eighteenth-century gabled houses, it stands opposite the baroque Schelfkirche, dedicated to St Nicholas, the patron saint of sailors, begun in 1708 by the engineer and architect Jakob Reutz and finished in 1713 after his death by Leonhard Christoph Sturm. Brick and baroque seem to go ill together to those of us who have relished Bavarian baroque, so that this fine church seems to me an excellent introduction to the quiddities of eastern Germany's native architectural styles.

A stroll south of Schwerin's town hall is even more rewarding. The city is dotted with half-timbered houses, and many of its cobbled streets are traffic-free. In Schlachtermarkt they shade an open-air market. In Puschkinstrasse one of them bears the inscription O HERR ERBARME DI UNSER SUNDE WES UNS GNEDICH 1574 ('O Lord, have pity upon us and be merciful to us, 1574'). No. 17 in the same street has a sinuous Jugendstil door.

Schusterstrasse runs south from the Markt to the Catholic church of 1792, where J. J. Busch's hand can be seen in the characteristic pilasters. Turn left here along Schlossstrasse to find amongst the handsome official buildings the classical college built by Georg Adolph Demmler between 1825 and 1834.

Beyond it is Schwerin's loveliest ensemble. In the square called Alter Garten rise two other classical buildings, Mecklenburg's national theatre and, at an angle to it, the Staatliches Museum, both of them dating from the 1880s. The former is the more elaborate of the two, with caryatids and Atlantes and rich swags. The latter reveals the Italian Renaissance reminiscences which were the passion of its architect Willebrand. A flight of steps flanked by sculpted lions leads up to the Doric pillars of its portico, whose pediment depicts the gods and goddesses of Olympus.

The Staatliches Museum also houses a tremendous collection of Dutch art, with masterpieces by Jacob Jordaens (including a stunningly bulky nude, painted from behind) and pastoral works by Adriaen Brouwer. Amongst the works by Lucas Cranach the Elder is a pensive portrait of a young man in a floppy red hat. An exquisite picture by Jan Lievens depicts St Luke as an old man with silver filigree hair and beard, about to write his gospel with a quill pen. Jan Breugel is, unusually, represented here by a satyr in hot pursuit of a half-dressed and understandably distressed woman.

British visitors seek out Thomas Gainsborough's portrait of Charlotte von Mecklenburg-Strelitz, who in 1761 became the queen of George III – in this painting she seems unhappy about her fate. A more remarkable series of regal portraits here are some forty done for the Mecklenburg-Schwerin family by the Huguenot refugee Georges-David Matthieu, who was born in 1737 and lived here from 1762 till his death in 1778. Another Frenchman, Jean-Baptiste Oudry, satisfied the passion for hunting of the ducal founder of this gallery by painting a series of gruesome dead animals and livelier hunting scenes.

These are not the only treasures of Schwerin's Staatliches Museum. The twentieth-century Berlin masters Max Liebermann, Lovis Corinth (with an amazing *Rückenakt* that matches in virtuosity that of Jan Jordaens) and Otto Nagel are well represented, along with some late medieval treats and rococo, Empire and Biedermeier porcelain.

The buildings surrounding Alter Garten form an even more exquisite ensemble when they are illuminated after dusk. Eastwards stand the four aisles and pavilions of the ducal stables of Schwerin, built by Demmler between 1838 and 1842. Boats are moored in the little harbour. A stele commemorates those who died in the Franco-Prussian war of 1870–71. To the south of Alter Garten you cross over the water connecting the Schweriner See and the Burgsee and arrive at Burg island, with its mid-nineteenth-century garden, and a Schloss – modelled in part on the Château de Chambord in France – by Demmler and Friedrich August Stüler (who also incorporated some Renaissance elements, including the chapel of the earlier ducal castle, which was built by Johann Baptist Pahr in the mid sixteenth century). Over the Schloss entrance is an equestrian statue inscribed NIKLOT LOBE SAN, 1160. The reference is to Duke Niklot who lived here in an earlier castle till Henry the Lion defeated him in that year. The rider looks very heroic, most un-French.

The lakeside-setting of this Schloss is unforgettable, with an artificial grotto and an orangery whose tree-lined inner courtyard adds piquancy. Cross a bridge over another stretch of water to reach the baroque garden with its canals, the work of the Frenchman J. Legeay, who laid it out between 1748 and 1756. Many of the statues were designed by the baroque genius Balthasar Permoser. To the south-west, reached by Jäger Weg, is the Berliner Tor – created from a couple of Doric temples designed by Demmler in 1844.

Twice a week you can enjoy a *Kaffee Konzert* in the Schloss at Schwerin. Here I often feel myself to be in eastern Europe, perhaps Vienna, perhaps even further east along the Danube, rather than in Germany. In the Café Prag a pianist plays 'Smoke Gets in Your Eyes', while ladies in felt hats eat cream cakes, drink coffee slugged with cream and deplore their increasing girth. On the bar are newspapers for the benefit of the whole company. An idealized portrait of the city of Prague adorns one wall. I eat my *Hühnerkraftbrühe* and my *Champignon-Steak* with potatoes and then am unable to resist a so called *Maria Theresia Kaffee*, coffee with a dash of orange liqueur topped by a huge dollop of cream.

Schwerin, like Wismar, is surrounded by pleasant, sometimes

delightful little villages and towns. Half an hour away to the west is Gadebusch, with its Gothic town hall of 1330 (in part rebuilt in 1618) set in a triangular market square. Brick-built, with curving gables and two arches on the ground floor, this was originally the headquarters of the merchants' guild.

Here the magnificent late-Romanesque, partly Gothic church has a bronze font of 1450, carried by three angels and depicting scenes of Jesus' Passion, wall paintings and an impressive rose window. The town's three-storeyed Renaissance Schloss of 1570 rises on a hill. If its terracotta decoration reminds one of the Schloss at Wismar, this is because it was built for the brother of the prince who commissioned that one. Although the Schloss of Gadebusch is Italianate in style, its architect Christoph Haubitz came from Mecklenburg.

At Rhena, 11 km north-west, the late Romanesque church, which formerly belonged to the Benedictines, has fifteenth-century choir stalls and Gothic frescos of 1338 showing scenes from the life of Jesus and prophets and saints. Drive a further 11 km along the F104 and you find at Schönberg another brick basilica, this one from the fourteenth century and housing a bronze font of 1357.

To the south of Schwerin are more delightful spots, still watered by lakes and sometimes at the foot of forest-clad mountains. Wöbbelin and Ludwigslust are due south. At Wöbbelin, beside the oak-shaded park, is buried the poet Karl Theodor Körner, who wrote passionate, patriotic lyrics and died fighting Napoleon's troops near Gadebusch on 26 August 1813. Though born in Dresden, he himself chose this spot for burial, and his tombstone is adorned with a lyre (for his poetry) transfixed by a sword (for his military ardour). Oaks shade his heroic, curly-haired bust. A less heroic memorial near Wöbbelin commemorates five thousand victims of the Nazi concentration camp at Reiherhorst.

Ludwigslust, 13 km further south, is a rare survival, a

perfect German baroque and classical town. It was created by the court architect J. J. Busch and his successor Johann Georg Barchim from 1746 onwards on behalf of Duke Friedrich von Mecklenburg-Schwerin. Seen across its lake, Busch's gleaming white, late-baroque Schloss, built between 1772 and 1776, is breathtaking. The allegorical sculptures and vases are by the Bohemian sculptor Rudolf Kaplunger. Barca added the classical fire-station in 1814 and stables in 1821.

The dukes lived here until 1837. In the nineteenth century they employed the brilliant Peter Joseph Lenné, Germany's finest creator of Italian landscape gardens, to lay out the park, with its canal and cascade. The park incorporates a bridge of 1760, Duke Friedrich's 1785 memorial, a 'Swiss House' of 1789, and a neo-Gothic church by Barca. Here too are classical mausoleums for Crown Princess Palowna, who died in 1806, and Duchess Luise, who died in 1809. Although the town itself has classical houses (especially in Schweriner Strasse and Kanal-strasse) it also rejoices in a barrel-vaulted baroque parish church which Busch created in 1770.

The F191 runs north-east from here to Parchim. On the way you pass through Neustadt-Glewe. Neustadt-Glewe was forti-fied in the fourteenth century. The crenellated walls date from the next century. Its early-fourteenth-century fortress is the oldest secular building in Mecklenburg-Vorpommern. Its Neues Schloss was begun by the Dutch Renaissance architect Ghert Evert Pilot in 1619 and finished in the baroque style by Leonhard Christoph Sturm in 1717. Inside, the stucco was done by the Italian Giuseppe Mogia. The parish church of this little town dates from the fourteenth century and has a vaulted wooden ceiling of 1565. Ten kilometres north stands the late-baroque hunting lodge of Friedrichsmoor, which was built in 1780.

Half-timbered houses set beside chequerboard streets and two Gothic hall churches add allure to Parchim, while ducks swim on its little lake and the citizens enjoy its tree-shaded park and beaches. The church of St George (which serves the Altstadt) was begun in 1290 and finished in 1307 and shelters Gothic carvings of 1421 on the altar, as well as a pulpit of 1580 by Johann Grantzin of Lübeck and a stone font of 1620. In the mid fifteenth century the citizens decided to add a Gothic choir and ambulatory. In the three-aisled Marienkirche, which was begun in 1280 to serve the Neustadt, is a font, borne since 1365 on the backs of four sculpted men, and a late-Gothic altar made around 1500. The early-seventeenth-century organ console is superb. Parchim also has a long, two-storeyed brick town hall whose windows have upper mullions that perfectly match the ogival curves of its gable. This little spot gained the right to call itself a city as early as 1225, but apart from its churches its present beauty dates from the Renaissance and also from the early-nineteenth-century houses which are nearly all the work of Johann Georg Barca.

Before driving the 40 km from Parchim back to Schwerin I suggest a small excursion eastwards. Through rolling farm-lands 13 km further along the F191 lies Lübz, with its Gothic church (with a vaulted wooden ceiling of 1565) and a fortified stone tower, late Gothic in style and decked with coats of arms. This is an industrial town, enlivened by a brewery pouring out Lübzer Pils. Seven kilometres due north, Passow has a mid-thirteenth-century Romanesque church with late-seventeenth-century choir stalls and a pulpit from the same era. On the way back to Schwerin from Parchim, pause at Crivitz, another town set out in chequerboard fashion. Here the parish church was begun in the late fourteenth century (its imposing tower dating from around 1370) and has a fifteenth-century crucifix, a winged altar carved in the late-Gothic style at the beginning of the sixteenth century and a fine Renaissance pulpit of 1621.

The tree-lined, undulating and lake-strewn road to Rostock

from Schwerin takes in the fine city of Güstrow. (Here I must mention that in Mecklenburg one does not pronounce the final W of any noun. My German master – himself a German – used to cry to us pupils, 'In German you pronounce every single letter.' Not in Mecklenburg-Vorpommern you don't.) Güstrow is partly surrounded by a sunken park, which I guess must derive from its former defences but is now peaceful enough.

Leave Schwerin by Spieltordamm, passing between the Pfaffenteich and the Ziegelsee. Driving through marshland and beside the Schweriner See, you reach Brüel, whose thirteenth-century Gothic church has an impressive gable, and then Sternberg, on the Grosser Sternberger See. The thickset tower of its brick hall church dominates the town. Begun in the thirteenth century, this parish church has a fourteenth-century choir fresco depicting Jesus judging the world.

Turn south-east here to find Dobbertin, set alongside its lake. Here is a church with a fourteenth-century cloister, formerly belonging to the Benedictines, the church restored (and altered) by the great Berlin architect Karl Friedrich Schinkel between 1828 and 1837. Schinkel was canny enough to preserve the 1586 font and some mid-eighteenth-century pews.

This is a region of delightful lakeside villages and marshes, and the city of Güstrow, due north of Dobbertin and at the heart of Mecklenburg, is surrounded by no fewer than three lakes. A sunken park delineates, I think, its former defences. Set amidst Renaissance houses, its cathedral was founded in 1226, but owes its present Gothic aspect to rebuilding in the fourteenth century and the 1860s. Today the oldest surviving parts are the choir and the finely sculpted transepts. Its chief treasure consists of twelve statues of the Apostles, carved in wood by Claus Berg of Lübeck around 1530. A Crucifixion carved in Rostock at the beginning of the sixteenth century is also splendid, and the powerful high altar was made in the workshop of Hinrik Bornemann of Hamburg around 1500. Profoundly rivalling the Lübeck apostles here is Ernst Barlach's swooping angel of 1926, a bronze masterpiece which the Nazis destroyed and which was re-founded after their defeat. As we shall later see with another Barlach masterpiece in Magdeburg cathedral, art usually triumphs over brutality – though only in the long run and often after the artist has suffered.

The rectangular Markt is charming, its gabled Renaissance houses contrasting in style with the classical façade of the Rathaus. This façade was created by D. A. Kufahl in 1797 to unite four gabled houses. Here the Gothic parish church of St Mary was restored in the 1880s, though its belfry, apart from the baroque dome, dates from the sixteenth century. Inside are a reredos of 1521 depicting the life of Jesus, the work of the Brussels sculptor Jan Bormann, and a group representing the Triumph of the Cross, carved in Rostock in 1516. And Güstrow's classical theatre of 1828 happens to be the oldest in the province.

But here devotees of Ernst Barlach will make their way to the Gertrudenkapelle, a fifteenth-century chapel which has served as a Barlach museum since 1963. The leading sculptor of the German expressionists, Barlach lived at Güstrow from 1910 until shortly before his death in 1938. As well as this comprehensive exhibition of his sculptures, many of Barlach's manuscripts and drawings can be seen in his former home, at no. 15 Heidberg, close by the Inselsee.

Another notable resident of Güstrow was the early-seventeenth-century warrior Wallenstein, who was Duke of Mecklenburg and lived for a time in the Renaissance Schloss which dominates the city. To my mind, its western façade is the finest, with its asymetrical towers and overhanging doorways. This once ancient building was razed by a fire and rebuilt between 1558 and 1563 by an architect from Lombardy who took the Germanic name Franziskus Pahr. In subsequent years the interior was sumptuously decorated by, amongst others, the stuccoist Christoph Pahr (brother of Franziskus); after a second fire Philipp Brandin rebuilt the north wing.

Before driving on to Rostock, make a short excursion west to Rühn to see the early Gothic church (built in the second half of the thirteenth century by the Cistercians) with its fourteenth-century tombstones, its fifteenth-century crucifix and above all its Renaissance reredos of the Last Supper. Carved around 1560 by the Flemish master Cornelius Crommeny, amongst its portraits are Duke Ulrich I and his duchess Elisabeth. A little further to the north-east stands the Gothic parish church at Bützow, inside which is a bronze font of 1474, a sculpted pulpit of 1617 by Hans Peper of Rendsburg and a Lübeck reredos of 1503 which depicts the death and coronation of the Virgin Mary.

It was on the way to Rostock that I first spotted the myriad little holiday homes, each with its allotment and tiny terrace, which the eastern Germans much relish and call *Blockhäuser*.

First heard of in recorded history in 1160 as 'Roztok', Rostock was created by a judicious union of three hamlets. By the mid thirteenth century this woodland-garlanded city was surrounded by fortifications encompassing no fewer than twenty-two gateways, and was playing a powerful commercial role as a member of the Hanseatic League. Situated on two arms of the River Warnow only 12 km from the Baltic coast, during that time the city had flexed its economic muscle and bought from the poverty-stricken Princes of Mecklenburg much of the surrounding countryside. In 1323 Rostock acquired the village of Warnemünde on the coast itself, guaranteeing its access to the sea. Today fishing boats berth peacefully at Warnemünde close by the verandas of the port's houses. You can climb the 135 steps of its lighthouse or enjoy a sandy beach. And from here ferries ply to Gedser in Denmark.

At the Reformation, Rostock opted for Protestantism, forbidding Catholicism within its bounds. In consequence the city became a prize target of both sides during the Thirty Years' War. The Danes blockaded the port; Wallenstein occupied the city; and in 1631 Rostock was even annexed to Denmark. In the next century, during the wars of 1700–1721 and during the Seven Years' War of 1756–63, the city was again much besieged and her fortunes at an ebb. Recovering for a short while, her citizens rose up against the French in 1799 during a period of shortages, objecting to food being transported from their land to France (in particular butter, so that the insurrection became known as the Rostock Butter War). Yet more suffering was caused during the continental blockade against Napoleon, who in turn responded by closing the port of Warnemünde.

Liberated, the citizens turned to shipbuilding, creating their own fleet of sailing ships and in the 1880s becoming major builders of steam vessels. In building fishing vessels, Rostock is still the world leader, with two dockyards (Warnow-Warnemünde and Neptun-Rostock). Its skills cost the city dear in the Second World War, for Rostock had also turned to the production of planes, in particular the deadly Heinkel III. The Allies hit back savagely in 1942 and again in 1945, when 40 per cent of the city went up in flames.

The massive postwar rebuilding programme, though vital to house the citizens with some decency, has disfigured parts of the city – though other judges, whose architectural opinions are not mine, have aggressively lauded the new satellite towns (Reutershagen I and Reutershagen II, built between 1953 and 1965 to house over 16,000; Lütten Klein, built in the second half of the 1960s and housing some 30,000; and the subsequent expansions of Südstadt, with 23,000 inhabitants, and Eversahen, with 29,000 inhabitants). These functional suburbs also contain Rostock's international fair, and are enlivened by its zoo, which was founded in 1910, covers 16 hectares and shelters around 2,000 animals of some 300 different species.

The city's sports hall in Kopernikusstrasse seats 30,000 spectators, and its botanical gardens in Hamburger Strasse comprise 8 hectares in which 8,000 types of plant grow.

To me the old city is infinitely more seductive than these treats, though outside summer chill winds can blow from its harbour. Once when I was there with two companions the wind was so savage that they chose to stay in a little café on Neuer Markt while I explored the city. The café itself was of course centrally heated, and when I returned, freezing, I discovered they had been eating ice-creams.

Of Rostock's four brick Hanseatic churches, of a quality matched but not surpassed in Rostock's sister Hanseatic city of Lübeck, the finest is the Marienkirche. This Gothic masterpiece began life as a hall church of the 1280s. It fell down in 1398, and rebuilding began. Only in the mid fifteenth century did it achieve its present form: a Latin cross with a nave and two aisles. The slender belfry was finished only in 1796. Miraculously, while bombs fell all around it, Rostock's Marienkirche went unscathed.

Though massive, the Marienkirche is rendered elegant, not simply because of its graceful windows, but also because of the delicately coloured and patterned brick which surrounds them. The treasures inside include an astronomical clock, created in 1470 though rebuilt in 1640 (and still in its Renaissance case), which is programmed to give the date of Easter until the year 2017. The bronze font, carried by four men and depicting scenes from the life of Jesus, dates from 1290. A late-Gothic reredos, dedicated to St Roch, depicts not only that saint but also St Antony and St Sebastian. The high altar is baroque, created in 1720, and the organ case was built in an even more refined baroque style some fifty years later. The Renaissance pulpit drips gilt like candle wax. Finally, the Marienkirche shelters handsome eighteenth-century tombstones.

It stands in Bei der Marienkirche, most of which was entirely demolished in the Second World War and has been decently restored, with some modern buildings and others built in brick in the traditional Gothic fashion of this region of Germany. To the south of the Marienkirche in Am Ziegenmarkt rises a building that speaks of the ancient importance of Rostock. The city gained the right to mint its own coinage in 1260, and this former mint (the Alte Münze), whose Renaissance portal was built around 1620, is where the coins were produced from 1325 to 1864. Notice the little carving of a man striking coins with a hammer.

Walk along the south side of the church to reach the Neuer Markt, whose war-damaged buildings have all been sensitively restored or rebuilt and include the delicious town hall, which is in fact three buildings rolled into one. The first two gabled ones date from the late twelfth century, and the third (the southernmost) was added around 1310. The splendid façade was added shortly afterwards, with its seven pink and white turrets separated by little Gothic arcades. A further baroque addition dates from 1727. The Ratskeller serves Rostocker Pils. And beside the town hall is a lovely Renaissance doorway created around 1600.

On the opposite side of Neuer Markt stands the oldest Renaissance gabled house of Rostock (according to its plaque it was rebuilt in 1965), with a lion on its gable. Older Gothic gables much enliven this square and much of this part of the old town, especially in the street behind the town hall which is (logically enough) called Hinter dem Rathaus. Two of the most delightful are at no. 1, the Walldienerhaus, which was built in the fourteenth century, and at no. 5, the Kerkhofhaus, which now houses the city archives, and is a splendid relic of the flamboyant Gothic style, save for its Renaissance terracotta embellishment and doorway. It sports green and brown glazed bricks, wild faces in its roundels and the Crucifixion depicted in the topmost gable. Take Grosse Wasserstrasse eastwards from the Kerkhofhaus to reach Kleine Wasserstrasse, in which, at no. 30, is the late-fifteenth-century gabled Giebelhaus.

Steinstrasse leads west from Neuer Markt to the Steintor, dating from 1270, though it was given its present Renaissance aspect between 1574 and 1577. Built of brick, this defensive gate has stone arches (hence its name, the Stone Gate), a tall pointed cap and a porch dated 1576. The three coats of arms on the gateway represent the three towns from which Rostock was created. In case its sturdy aspect were not enough to repel invaders, it is also defended with fierce carved lions. This gate was the gift of Duke Johann Albrecht, who also rebuilt the city walls. Taking care not to be mown down by tramcars, you can follow these walls left from here to reach the Lagebuschturm of 1575, and then the earliest of Rostock's medieval gates, the Kuhtor of 1280, which was in part rebuilt in 1575.

A few paces further west rises the Nikolaikirche, a massive early-Gothic church built with two tall aisles in the mid thirteenth century. In 1450 the church was given a tower and a choir. The city wall continues along the River Warnow to reach the church of St Peter in the Alter Markt. This brick-built Petrikirche remains the hall-type basilica typical of north German Gothic and was built in the mid fourteenth century. Its belfry pokes 117 m up to the sky, and inside is a bronze font of 1512.

If instead of turning left you turn right at the Steintor you walk beside the Rosengarten and a second watered garden called the Wallanlagen. Before the end of the Rosengarten I suggest you turn left along Rungestrasse to see the third of the city's medieval brick churches, the Michaeliskirche of 1480.

The pedestrianized Kröpelinerstrasse, a busy and beguiling shopping street, also leads off from Neuer Markt. Off to the right, in Klosterhof, is the regional library, housed in another splendidly gabled building, this one formerly the hospice of the Holy Spirit and built in the late fifteenth century, though it was founded around 1270 by Queen Margaret of Denmark.

Halfway down Kröpelinerstrasse the Jugendstil Deutsche Bank is sculpted with men and women assuming exceedingly sad postures, as if they have just seen the state of their bank accounts. A sparse collection of baroque houses in this street also escaped the ravages of the Second World War.

Kröpelinerstrasse runs on to Universitäts-Platz, in which stands Johann Gottfried Schadow's 1815 statue of Marshal Gebhard Leberecht von Blücher, who was born at Rostock on 16 December 1742. It was Blücher who entered Paris on 31 March 1814, having several times routed the armies of Napoleon. But for him Wellington's outnumbered infantry would probably have lost the battle of Waterloo (though Wellington took a different view, of course, observing, 'By God, I don't think it would have been done if I had not been there'). It seems to me Blücher well deserves the commendation, by Goethe himself, on his statue, which reads:

> *In Harren*
> *Und Krieg*
> *In Sturz und Sieg*
> *Bewusst und Gross*
> *So riss er uns*
> *Von Feinden los.*

(In time of alarm and in time of war,
In disaster and in victory,
Confident in himself and great,
He thus delivered us from the yoke of our enemies.)

Reliefs on the plinth of the statue symbolically depict his battles, watched over by angels.

Universitäts-Platz is also blessed with an entertaining modern fountain, in which bronzes of naked men, women and children disport themselves, at peace with equally playful beasts and birds (with even a wild boar lying on its back, feet in the air).

A restaurant at no. 32 has a thirty-two-bell *Glockenspiel*. As for the university, its main building was built in the Renaissance style in the late 1860s, but earlier work is incorporated in the whole: a neoclassical building of 1825 by C. T. Severin; an even older Palais of 1714, once a home of the Dukes of Mecklenburg and enlarged by the Saalbau of 1750 by Jean-Laurent Legeay; and a fine late-baroque hall which the city proudly uses for concerts and exhibitions.

Behind the university stands the Heilig-Kreuz-Kloster, which once belonged to the Cistercians. Today the church serves the university. This three-aisled hall church has an extremely impressive Gothic central ceiling, dating from the first half of the fourteenth century. Inside is a flamboyant Gothic reredos of the Crucifixion, with two wings.

Walk on to the Wallanlagen, to discover more remains of the medieval fortifications (known as the Dreiwallbastion, or Bastion of the Three Walls) and to the right Rostock's stateliest gateway, the Kröpelinertor. Fifty-five metres high, its lower part dates from around 1290, while the upper storeys and the tower were added around 1400. The Kröpelinertor houses the city museum, with Rostock's charter of 1252, models of ships and the old city, and of course a section devoted to the Napoleonic wars and the heroic Blücher.

Sixteen kilometres south-west of Rostock, by way of the seaside resort of Nienhagen, is Bad Doberan, a spa famous in the middle ages for its Cistercian monastery, which flourished here from 1186 to the Reformation. However pressed one is on a short holiday in this part of Germany, Bad Doberan should on no account be missed. The monastic church still stands, a magnificent brick building in the high Gothic style, whose nave measures 10 × 75 m and is 25 m high from the ground to its richly ornamented ogival vaulting. Begun at the end of the thirteenth century, it was consecrated in 1368. Tall and spare, it makes one smile with glee at its elegance.

One evocative wall remains from the monastic buildings, and elegant bridges cross the streams in its former garden. Inside, the church is vividly frescoed, while the stone Gothic vaulting contrasts with white walls. The radiating chapels of the choir are as richly ornamented as the vault. Exquisite foliage consoles support the five arcades of the nave. A very early fourteenth-century winged reredos over the high altar depicts scenes from the Old and New Testaments, while the church also possesses other fine reredoses, dating from the fourteenth and fifteenth centuries, as well as a Gothic tabernacle.

Though those who created the high-altar reredos took the Bible literally in a fashion few would follow today, their work is none the less exceedingly subtle. Here their slender Gothic sculptures draw lovely comparisons between Old and New Testament scenes and episodes. The main scene is the birth of Jesus (with a couple of animals peeping shyly into the stable). Immediately below it is the bush which attracted Moses on Mount Sinai because it was on fire without being consumed. The connection is this: like the bush, Mary bore the divine in her body, and it would have consumed anyone else, but not her.

In the middle ages the laity and the monks worshipped in separate parts of many great monastic churches. At Bad Doberan they provided themselves with separate altars, and in my view the laity got the better bargain. The reredos of the lay altar is superb, and like the church, massive. On one side it is topped with a crowned Virgin Mary; under her you discern amongst a plethora of biblical scenes an eagle (symbol of St John), the Old Testament heroine Esther in the king's palace; a Madonna and Child flanked by a lion (symbol of St Mark), and a bull (symbol of St Luke), Judith with the head of Holofernes, God (in a tree) talking to Gideon, the birth of Jesus, the presentation in the temple and the flight of the holy family into Egypt.

The crucifix is not depicted as a dead tree but as a living plant, bearing grapes and leaves, as if to proclaim that the death of Jesus has brought life to doomed humankind. On the other side of this crucifix are sculpted more symbolic tales, with parallels from the Old and New Testaments. Here Job is tormented by Satan, as is Jesus by soldiers. Isaac is about to be sacrificed by his father just as Jesus is indeed sacrificed on his cross.

Another ornament of this exquisite church is a hanging lantern in which is a statue of the Virgin Mary, created around 1290. She stands on a horned moon, which was added in the early fifteenth century, as was her twelve-starred crown. The reference is to chapter 12 of the Revelation of St John the Divine: 'A great sign appeared in heaven: a woman, adorned with the sun, standing on the moon, with twelve stars on her head for a crown.' The text continues that this woman shall bear a son who was destined to rule all the nations with an iron sceptre.

Bad Doberan's monastery church has sculpted Renaissance stalls and rich Gothic altars. It was also one of the chief burial chambers of the Dukes of Mecklenburg and other local notables. Their princely seat in the stalls of the lay choir is naturally finer than all the rest. Their portraits, both men and women, hang on the walls. The oldest sarcophagus in this church cherishes the mortal remains of Queen Margaret of Denmark, who died in Rostock in 1282. This wooden tomb carries her statue. An elaborate Renaissance chapel, built around 1640 and reached by a flight of stairs, is a memorial to Duke Adolf Friedrich and Duchess Anna Maria. Her statue gazes cheekily out, while she carries a fan in her left hand and seems even in death to glory in her rich clothing. And against one pillar are two early-sixteenth-century statues of dead dukes, Balthasar and Erich von Mecklenburg.

More touching and today more meaningful than these is a

simple plaque commemorating those who suffered at the hands of Nazi Germany between 1933 and 1945. Inscribed on it are the names ROTTERDAM, COVENTRY, LIDICE, STALINGRAD, MONTE CASSINO, HAMBURG, DRESDEN, RAVENSBRÜCK and HIROSHIMA.

The religious order eventually departed from Bad Doberan (and today the church serves Lutherans), but in 1793 the town became the principal seat of the Mecklenburg court. The dukes brought with them as principal architect Carl Theodor Severin. He proceeded to surround the Kamp – a park laid out in the English style – with pleasing late-baroque and classical buildings, beginning with what is now a baroque hotel and continuing with a school, a palace and the so-called Salongebäude. He added two pavilions in the chinoiserie stye in 1813, and today the Grand Pavilion is the local-history museum. In 1825, at what is now no. 5 Severinstrasse, he designed the Medini house for the duke's chief chef.

North-west of Bad Doberan is Heiligendamm, which was developed for the ducal family in 1793 and is thus the oldest bathing resort in Germany (today visited by 40,000 holiday-makers annually). The jolliest way to visit the resort from Bad Doberan is to take the Molli, a steam train which puffs its way along a line (with a gauge of 900 mm) built in 1886 to connect the two. At Heiligendamm the Kurhaus and other spa buildings are the work of C. T. Severin, all in the neoclassical style. The largest seaside resort in eastern Germany, due west, is Ostseebad-Kühlungsborn. In 1910 the miniature railway was extended to reach here. The resort has a flowery promenade, 4 km of beach and a swimming hall, and is surrounded by woods and hills. And not far away at Nienhagen is a 24 hectare nature reserve, with beeches and rare plants.

Culture-vultures will seek out the resort of Rerik, further south-west along the coast on the Salzhall lake (which opens out into the sea), because of the late-thirteenth-century Gothic church with its eight-sided tower. As well as the baroque furnishings and ogival vaults rising from powerful pillars, the vaults and walls were decorated in 1668 with frescos which were rediscovered only in 1970. For sunbathers and swimmers, Rerik is also blest by the peninsula of Wustrow.

Drive south-east from Rerik and you reach the F105 at Kröpelin, to turn right for one of two round trips which I recommend, based on Rostock (though I do not suggest that everything I am about to describe – as well as the lake-strewn scenery – can be enjoyed in one day, especially if you make diversions to entrancing villages).

The drive from Rostock to Stralsund along the F105 is 72 km. Less speedy but far more picturesque is to leave Rostock by the Mühlen Damm in the direction Neubrandenburg–Demmin and then follow the F110 to Sanitz, where you turn left for the spa of Bad Sülze. Once again you find a splendid late-Gothic church (with a pulpit of 1770), as well as a salt-museum. Ten kilometres further on is Tribsee, where two gates from the former fortifications still stand. Here the late-Gothic parish church, which has a fifteenth-century reredos, is dedicated to Archbishop Thomas à Becket of Canterbury. Drive 14 km north-east to find at Franzburg an abbey church which shelters an *Immaculate Conception* of 1420, depicting Mary on the crescent moon, and a huge crucifix of 1720. And then drive on to Stralsund through Richtenberg, where you will not be surprised to see another thirteenth-century church, this one with an altar carved around 1700 and depicting the Passion of Jesus.

Another alternative and picturesque route is to drive through the seaside resorts of this part of the Baltic coast. Such spots as Graal-Müritz and especially Ahrenshoop, with its excellent sandy beach and fishermen's cottages, are prized by the eastern Germans, and in 1880 the latter also became a nest of artists, whose successors still work here. One of their early leaders was Paul Müller-Kaempf, who settled at Ahrenshoop in 1892. He and his friends created the thatched 'art cottage' here in 1909. The most celebrated Ahrenshoop artist of the twentieth century is probably Gerhard Marcks.

Another attraction of this part of the coast is the nature reserve on the peninsula of Darss. In the village of Prerow is the Darss regional museum, devoted to sailing, fishing, geology and local art. Prerow also boasts a baroque seafarer's church, built in 1728, which houses model sailing vessels. And from here you can also sail yourself. A short way further east is Zingst, from where you can make an excursion to the island of Hiddensee, where no vehicles are allowed and where in the hamlet of Kloster is a museum dedicated to the dramatist Gerhart Hauptmann, who made it his home each summer until his death in 1946. The church here was built in 1862 by F. A. Stüler.

Darss is partly covered by a 60 km² forest, while its bird life includes eighteen different types of duck as well as herons, cranes, geese, ravens, sea eagles and mute swans. Nearly all its beaches are nudist ones.

Barth, south of Zingst, is another attractive spot, which you enter through the fifteenth-century Dammtor, a powerful, 35 m high defensive gateway with a pointed hat which was once part of the town fortifications. The 85 m high tower of the Marienkirche has an even more pointed spire and a thirteenth-century choir, while the rest dates from the fourteenth century. Its chief treasure is the *Barther plattdeutsche Bibel*, a Bible translated here into low German in 1588 and decorated with ninety-nine woodcuts by the Hamburg goldsmith Jacob Mores. And Barth has another tower surviving from its fortifications, the sixteenth-century Fangelturm.

Though I prefer these routes, the fast road to Stralsund is not without interest. Twenty-seven kilometres from Rostock is Ribnitz-Damgarten, pleasantly situated at the end of the Ribnitzer See and the Saaler Bodden. As at Barth, you enter Ribnitz-Damgarten through the remains of a medieval gate, this one the fifteenth-century Rostock Tor. Ribnitz-Damgarten is also blessed with two fine churches, the lesser the hall-type parish church of St Mary, begun in the thirteenth century, finished in the next, but rebuilt after a fire in 1790 (and with a west tower dating from 1840). Follow Neue Klosterstrasse from the Markt to find the former abbey church, built around 1400. Its attractions include fifteenth-century Gothic Madonnas and six paintings on wood, done in the early sixteenth century, depicting scenes from the life of Jesus and his mother. Ribnitz-Damgarten also has a regional museum which, apart from the usual maritime collection of this part of Germany, displays the particular local industry – jewelry made from yellow amber. Nearby at Klockenhagen is an open-air museum of rural life.

Between Ribnitz-Damgarten and Stralsund you pass through Löbnitz and across the dyke known as the Triebseer Damm. Ahead you can see the towers of three of Stralsund's churches. Prince Jaromir von Rügen founded this Hanseatic city in 1209 on a site virtually surrounded by water. In spite of the historical vicissitudes which the city shared with the others in this region (in this case passing at various times into the hands of the Swedes, the Prussians and Bismarck's Germany), and in spite of industrialization and the ravages of the Second World War, Stralsund has retained numerous fine gabled houses and three splendid parish churches whose spires beckon.

Make your way to the Alter Markt, with the late-Gothic, brick-gabled Wulframhaus, built in the fifteenth century, and the Swedish baroque Kommandantur of 1746. These fine buildings pale beside the Rathaus and the church of St Nicholas. The former, consisting of two wings separated by a street, was built in the thirteenth century when the merchants of Stralsund were approaching the height of their prosperity, but its gabled façade was added a century later, and the wooden arcades of its courtyard date from 1680. The north façade in particular proclaims the ostentation of the medieval patricians. On another side is a Renaissance staircase with the date 1579; on another a baroque portal dated 1715. The finest room inside, the Achtmannskammer, is also baroque.

The brick Gothic Nikolaikirche with its massive flying buttresses has a baroque lantern of 1667 and a baroque north entrance. Begun in 1265, modelled on the great Gothic churches of northern France, and finished in the mid fourteenth century, it boasts a south tower 105 m high. St Nicholas has preserved works of art dating from its own beginnings, in particular a limestone group of St Anne, the Virgin Mary and the Infant Jesus of 1290. In the north chapel is an altar donated by the Junge family in the fifteenth century, carved out of hazel wood and depicting an exquisite Madonna known as the *Junge Virgin*. The church is also decorated with medieval wall paintings, some of them on the pillars of the nave, others in the chapels on the south side. These, like the limestone statue, are the work of Lübeck artists, and the finest, in the second chapel, is an early-fourteenth-century painting of the Crucifixion, with St Peter, St Paul and the church's patron, St Nicholas. These medieval masterpieces contrast with the baroque high altar of 1708, which was created by Andreas Schlüter. The pulpit dates from 1611.

Badenstrasse, which runs on the south side of the Nikolaikirche, undoubtedly contains Stralsund's finest ensemble of houses, Gothic, Renaissance, baroque and classical. One of them, the early-eighteenth-century baroque Landständehaus, is decorated with the coat of arms of the provincial estates of Pomerania, whose capital Stralsund once was. The street ends at the classical Looshaus, designed by the Swedish architect Cornelius Loos in 1730 as the palace of the Statthalter. Half way down Badenstrasse, you meet Jacobiturmstrasse, which leads to the Gothic church of St James, damaged and repaired countless times since it was built in the fourteenth century, its last indignity conferred by bombs in 1944. Its tower rises 68 m above the west façade, and inside is a late-baroque high altar of 1786 by J. H. Tischbein.

At the other side of the Nikolaikirche, follow Külp Strasse north from the Alter Markt, passing two baroque gabled houses (known collectively as the Doppelgiebelhaus) built in the mid seventeenth century and in 1700, to reach the thirteenth-century Johanniskloster, which now houses the town archives. Apart from its choir, the Gothic monastery church was burned down in 1624. Turn left here to find the late-thirteenth-century Knieper Gate, and walk on past the Knieper lake to turn left again by way of Mönchstrasse to enjoy the old houses of Mühlenstrasse, built between the fifteenth and eighteenth centuries. At the end of this street rises the Küter Tor, a town gate of 1446, and the former town water-tower, the Wasserkunst. Beyond it, by the lake, is a little zoo, in the Küter Bastion.

Walk on south from the Küter Tor to find in Mönchstrasse Stralsund's local-history and maritime museum, imaginatively housed in the medieval Katarinenkloster, which was once a Dominican monastery. Further on down Mönchstrasse, across the Neuer Markt, stands the huge Gothic Marienkirche, built between 1384 and 1473. Its western tower rises to 105 m and its nave, carried on powerful octagonal pillars, is 95 m long and has ogival vaulting rising to 32 m. This church makes a splendid venue for concerts, in part because of its organ, built by the Hamburg master Friedrich Stellwagen and restored in 1959. Picturesque Frankenstrasse leads east from here past the Catholic church towards the three-aisled Heiliggeistkirche with its fifteenth-century ogival vaulting.

If you leave Stralsund by the Frankenwall and cross the lake called Frankenteich, taking the 2,550 m long Rügendamm dyke, you reach the island of Rügen. (If you want to get back the same day, note the times when the Ziegelgraben bridge is closed.) The largest island in Germany, Rügen is 926 km² in area, and has three celebrated seaside resorts (Göhren, Sellin and Binz) and granite and chalk cliffs which sometimes plunge a hundred metres down to the sea. The most spectacular, at the far end of the island, is the Stubenkammer, which derives from the Slavic for rocky steps.

From its main town, Putbus, you can take a trip on another narrow-gauge railway, pulled by a train called 'Running Roland', which travels east alongside hills and lakes via Binz, Sellin and Baabe to the farming and fishing village Göhren on the Mönchgut peninsula. The Mönchgut local-history museum is in a pretty, half-timbered and thatched cottage.

Rügen's charms also derive from its hilly, sometimes forested landscape, its lakes, its prehistoric sites (such as the Hertaburg, a 10 m high rampart built by the Slavs) and the views from its summits, especially that from the Königstuhl, which rises 133 m above sea level. Beeches, dwarf pines, peninsulas, lakes and fishing villages add to the charms of Rügen. The island continually throws up unexpected delights, some of them connected with the princelings who once disported themselves here. Just beside the lake known as the Grosser Jasmunder Bodden, for instance, stands the Renaissance Schloss Spyker of 1560. Again, at the south-east corner of the island at Granitz is a hunting pavilion of 1844 with a tower designed by Schinkel. Situated on the highest part of the island, the 100 m Tempelberg, the cast-iron winding staircase which leads to the top of the tower, promises superb views.

Rügen's three major towns are each well worth visiting, for different reasons. Garz, the first as you arrive from the direction of Stralsund (6 km south of the main route), was the home of the poet and polemicist Ernst Moritz Arndt, who was born at nearby Gross Schoritz in 1769 when Rügen was Swedish. In 1803 his *History of Serfdom in Pomerania and*

Rügen led to the abolition of serfdom here. Four years later, as professor of history at Griefswald, he virulently attacked Napoleon, following up his polemic with patriotic poetry. Not surprisingly, he was obliged to flee to Stockholm after Bonaparte's victory at Jena. He also lost his job (as professor of history at Bonn) in 1819 for supporting democracy, and only got it back in 1840. Eight years later Arndt was elected a member of the German National Assembly. This admirable man died in 1860 and is celebrated at Garz in the Ernst Moritz Arndt museum. Garz's other delight is its Gothic church with its early-eighteenth-century furnishings.

Putbus, north-east of Garz, owes its existence to the King of Sweden who in 1808 created the town as a bathing resort. For his Schloss, now demolished, he commissioned an immense 'English' garden which still survives. The classical theatre of 1821 is by W. Steinbach; the stables date from 1825; the orangery was designed by the great Schinkel; and the presbytery, built by F. A. Stüler in 1845, was subsequently transformed into the parish church. Another treat here is a circular Platz surrounded by late-classical houses.

Bergen, at the centre of the island, is notable chiefly for its former abbey church of St Mary, a hall church built in the Gothic style in brick. It stands imposingly on a hill. Late-twelfth-century frescos in the choir (in part restored in 1900) depict Heaven and Hell; a chalice of 1275 was made in Lübeck; the church houses a twelfth-century tomb slab; and the pulpit was made in 1775.

From Rügen (as from Stralsund) you can take a ferry to the island of Hiddensee, where cars are forbidden. Eighteen kilometres long (and in places only 125 m wide) it has a dune heath which has been designated a protected nature reserve. The University of Greifswald has an ornithological station at Kloster, which is also notable for Haus Seedomm, the former holiday home of the dramatist and novelist Gerhart

Hauptmann (and now a Hauptmann museum). He died in 1946, and in the local cemetery is his grave, marked by a simple slab of rough stone which bears only his name.

South of the islands and south-east of Stralsund is Greifswald. Instead of driving directly there from Stralsund, it is well worth taking the F194 south to Grimmen, with its three fifteenth-century Gothic gateways, the Mühltor, the Stralsunder Tor and the late-Gothic Greifswalder Tor. The Stralsunder Tor is a particular treat, topped by a three-storeyed pierced gable. Grimmen's fourteenth-century Rathaus is even finer, with its splendid gable and a little baroque tower. The Marienkirche is a three-aisled basilica, begun around 1280, inside which is a pulpit of 1707.

From here drive east to Greifswald, passing through Griebenow, with its baroque Schloss and half-timbered village church. Greifswald is a city of gabled houses as well as a sprinkling of classical ones (many signed by the architect Johann Gottlieb Quistorp). The city is set on the River Ryck and the Greifswalder Bodden. A member of the Hanseatic League, Greifswald has a university founded in 1456. The present university buildings in Rubenowplatz are baroque, the mid-eighteenth-century work of the architect A. Meyer of Augsburg. In the square opposite stands a statue of the founder, Heinrich Rubenow (erected in 1856 and sculpted by Stüler), a radical thinker who upset the authorities of the time and was mysteriously assassinated in 1462. Opposite the university rises the Jakobikirche, a Gothic hall church with a thirteenth-century, late-Romanesque font, and near by is the hospice of the Holy Spirit. Founded in the thirteenth century, the St Spiritus Hospital today offers its inner courtyard with its half-timbered houses for summer concerts.

Greifswald's gabled town hall was once Gothic, though a fire destroyed much of the original building in 1736 and it was rebuilt in the Renaissance style. Its present bronze doors (with their reliefs, by Joachim Jastram, depicting the defeat of fascism) were added in 1965. Inside, the council chamber is gilded and decorated with mid-eighteenth-century tapestries. Two other gabled houses in the town hall square date from the fifteenth century, the finest at no. 11.

Another of Greifswald's glories is its brick cathedral, dedicated to St Nicholas. A Gothic building begun in the thirteenth century, it is notable for a tower that rises to nearly 100 m and is topped by a lantern of 1635. Purists have objected to the restoration of the interior by Schinkel's disciple Gottfried Gieses in 1833, but I think he did a good enough job; he also uncovered some medieval frescos. In addition, the cathedral shelters a flamboyant Gothic painting of the Virgin Mary with the Doctors of the Church, the gift of Heinrich Rubenow.

An even nobler church, the Marienkirche (known unkindly to the citizens as 'fat Mary' in contrast to the much more slender tower of the cathedral), rises in Brüggstrasse. Built out of brick in the thirteenth and fourteenth centuries, it displays ogival vaulting rising from chased pillars. Fifteenth-century frescos, and a pulpit sculpted in wood by Joachim Mekelenborg of Rostock in 1587 complete the furnishings. Here lies the unfortunately murdered Heinrich Rubenow. The chapel of St Anne, added in the fifteenth century, is a jewel designed by Hinrich von Brunsberg.

To round off a visit to Greifswald, visit the city museum, which is housed in what remains of a former Franciscan monastery. As well as a section devoted to Ernst Moritz Arndt, the museum is principally notable for its collection of paintings, engravings and drawings by Germany's greatest romantic artist, Caspar David Friedrich. Four kilometres east at Eldena are the ruins of a Cistercian monastery which often feature in his moody paintings.

Wolgast is less than 35 km east of this melancholy spot. *En route*, at Kemnitz, make an excursion left for 3 km to discover near the spa and cure centre of Loissin the Renaissance Schloss Ludwigsburg, which was partly restored in the nineteenth century and shelters half-timbered houses. To the north is the seaside resort of Lubmin, reached by the so-called Hohe Berg which is in fact no more than 48 m above sea level.

Although Wolgast was founded in the twelfth century, the Dukes of Pomerania-Wolgast enhanced the town whose name they adopted, and Wolgast today is noted for its two Gothic churches. Inside the late-fourteenth-century Petrikirche is a Dance of Death, depicted in a cycle of twenty-four paintings done by Caspar Sigmund Köppe in 1700. Here too is the tomb of Duke Philipp II who died in 1660. The other church is the fifteenth-century, vaulted cemetery chapel of St Gertrud. In the Markt Platz, with its pretty fountain, rises the Gothic town hall, which was given a baroque aspect in 1725. The local-history museum next to it houses the paintings of Otto Runge, who was born at Wolgast in 1777 and like Caspar David Friedrich exulted in painting romantic landscapes.

Wolgast is also the best jumping-off place to visit the island of Usedom, which nestles in the estuary of the Oder. An area of 445 km² (of which 91 are Polish) encompasses dunes and beaches, lakes and forests of conifers. At Peenemünde on this island Wernher von Braun directed the rocket research station which developed the V-2 rockets which were launched against Britain in September 1944. At Heringdorf, Maxim Gorki worked on the third volume of his autobiography in the summer of 1922, and the Villa Irmgard in which he lived is now a Maxim Gorki museum.

South-west of Wolgast, join the F109 and turn left to make for Anklam. The baroque Schloss which shortly appears at Karlsburg (and is now a hospital for diabetics) was built in 1732 and stands in gardens laid out in both the English and the French fashion. As for Anklam, its most imposing building is the hall church of St Mary, raised in the thirteenth and fourteenth centuries and frescoed at the end of the fourteenth century. Anklam also boasts an early-fifteenth-century, late-Gothic stone gate, very tall and gabled at its peak. It is big enough to house the local-history museum. This was the birthplace in 1849 of Otto Lilienthal, the pioneer aviator (hence the Lilienthal memorials in the local-history museum and in Peenestrasse) who plunged to his death at Berlin in 1896.

To enjoy a succession of extremely well-preserved medieval fortications, make an excursion of 24 km south-west from Anklam along the F197 to Friedland, whose museum is in a fifteenth-century gateway-tower. Its Gothic Marienkirche has eighteenth-century furnishings, including the altar, pulpit and organ. Otherwise continue south-east along the F109 to Pasewalk, which was founded in 1239 by Slavonic tribes (who called it 'Posdowic'). Pasewalk is still protected by the massive stones of its mid-fifteenth-century wall and by four towers. They shelter the fourteenth-century Marienkirche and the thirteenth-century Nikolaikirche.

From Pasewalk the F104 runs west to Strasburg, whose late Gothic church has preserved a twelfth-century choir, and on to Woldegk, where you turn right along the F198 to Neubrandenburg. Founded in 1248, the old city is circular, and surrounded by a string of remarkably well preserved walls and gates built around 1300 and considerably strengthened later. The first gate to appear is the fifteenth-century Neues Tor with its blind arches. Turn right here for a tour of these walls, some 7 m high, to find the complex Friedländer Gate, built in the early fourteenth century and enlarged a century and a half later. The next gate, the Treptower Tor, guarded the western approach to Neubrandenburg. Its archway is curiously offset, its gables profusely decorated, and as the largest of the four it today houses the local museum. Finally appears the loveliest of them all, the fourteenth-century Stargarder Tor.

Much of the city was destroyed in 1945, but rebuilding has wisely kept to the old urban plan (with the addition of the two satellite suburbs of Oststadt and Südstadt). Inside the walls two contrasting monuments flank the street which runs from the Stargarder Tor. The first is the monumental Marienkirche, which was badly damaged in 1945. The base of the tower dates from its foundation in 1271, while the rest of the building displays every one of the various developments of German medieval Gothic. On the same side of the street rises Neubrandenburg's Haus der Kultur und Bildung, built in the mid-1960s, with a 56 m high eight-storey tower which does not at all impress me. Infinitely more at home in Neubrandenburg is the Johanniskirche, founded in 1260 by Franciscan monks and transformed into a late-Gothic hall church in the fourteenth century. Inside is a pulpit of 1588.

Rostock is 117 km away, and the road to it leaves from the Treptower Tor. On the way, at Reuterstadt-Stavenhagen, you find a baroque Schloss, church and Rathaus. The first half of its name is that of the low-German poet Fritz Reuter, who was born here in 1810. An extremely witty writer, he studied law at Rostock and Jena, and also passionately embraced the corporations of liberal students known as the Burschenschaften. In consequence, in 1833 he was arrested in Berlin for supposedly seditious talk and sentenced to death, a sentence commuted to thirty years' imprisonment. Released after four years in Prussian fortresses, he profited from the experience to write an account of his imprisonment (*Ut mine Festungstid*) which made him famous. The Prussian authorities gave out that Reuter's health was ruined and that he had become an alcoholic. None the less, he continued to produce a steady stream of popular humorous tales (the finest, his two-volume *Läuschen un Rimels*), and a tragic poem *Kein Hüsung*, until his death at Bisenach in 1874. Naturally at Reuterstadt-Stavenhagen the late-eighteenth-century town hall is also the Fritz-Reuter-

Literaturmuseum, and outside it, in a bronze armchair, sits the writer's contented statue.

At Malchin, 13 km nearer Rostock, two gateways – the Kalensches Tor and the Steintor – have survived from the fifteenth-century fortifications. They guard a brick parish church, a three-aisled late-Gothic building with ogival vaulting and a pulpit of 1570. In the south aisle, on what was once the high altar, is a polyptych of 1425 depicting the coronation of the Blessed Virgin, accompanied by apostles and saints. Hans Boeckler created the pulpit in 1571, and a Crucifixion group dates from around 1500.

Because of its lakes and forest-clad hills, the region beyond Malchin is known as Mecklenburger Schweiz, or Mecklenburg Switzerland. This region stretches from Neubrandenburg as far as Güstrow. The lake 3 km north of Malchin is called Lake Kummerow, after the village at its southernmost point, which boasts a Gothic church and a baroque Schloss. Fourteen kilometres nearer Rostock the route reaches Teterow. Lying close by the Teterow lake, the concentric old town is still protected by the fifteenth-century Malchin and Rostock gates. The brick basilica which serves as its parish church dates from the late thirteenth century (though the wooden ogival vaulting was not added till 1850). The frescos of the life of Jesus in the choir were painted in 1345. For me Teterow ceases to be magical at Whitsun, when its 1,887 m racecourse is the venue of wild motor-cycle races; but for others, I know, this is the finest aspect of the town.

Before returning to Rostock, Laage is the last stop, to admire its transitional-style hall church, built in the thirteenth century but, like the parish church of Teterow, with ogival wooden vaulting of 1850. It lies a mere 20 km from the city where we began this long tour, whose incidental treats as we have driven between city, village and town have been thatched windmills and half-timbered thatched cottages.

2

DRESDEN AND THE TREASURES OF SAXONY

At Dresden the meandering River Elbe is some 130 m wide, and on either side parks and gardens add to its beauty. Dresden is a green city, and some of its suburbs are lovely (and often neglected by the visitor). Hellerau to the north, for instance, is celebrated as the first German garden city, laid out between 1909 and 1914 at the instigation of the founder of the German Craft Workshop movement, Karl Schmidt, with a Festspielhaus of 1912 built by Heinrich Tesserow. Dresden's finest and largest park, the Grosser Garten, laid out in 1676, is traversed by a little train, and houses a zoo (with some 2,000 animals of 450 varieties), a baroque palace of 1683 and a couple of lakes.

Further afield, Dresden is surrounded by castle-topped hills and mountains. The wide river winds its way below slopes covered in vineyards and the Elbhänge hills. This is a shallow river, but when there is enough water such lovely hotel-ships as the *Elbresidenz* and its sisters the *Clara Schumann* and the *Theodor Fontane* cruise to Saxon Switzerland or as far as Magdeburg or Prague. At night, as you eat on board, the great black river is streaked with gold from the lights of great cities.

At the heart of Dresden itself, a mixture of Renaissance and baroque architecture makes this city one of the pearls of the Elbe, enhanced by an astounding collection of art galleries,

Above: Schwerin's theatre and opera house.

Below: The inner city of Schwerin, both classical and half-timbered.

Above: In the former monastic church at Bad Doberan this Madonna, carved around 1290, is housed in a hanging shrine made in the early fifteenth century.

Below: Christmas celebrations at the Rathaus, Wernigerode.

Above: The cobbled Marktplatz at Wismar centres on the town's impressive Renaissance fountain.

Below: At Wismar the Ducal Palace boasts this bizarre Renaissance porch.

Old houses on the bridge, Erfurt.

Above: Gottfried Semper's 1847 Renaissance art gallery, Dresden.

Below: A ship of the White Fleet sails on the River Elbe near Dresden's Augustus Bridge.

Above: An equestrian statue of the reclusive King Johann of Saxony stands in front of Gottfried Semper's Dresden Opera House.

Below: The inner courtyard of Pöppelmann's Zwinger Palace at Dresden, looking towards the baroque Wall Pavilion.

Above: An intimate corner of Meissen.

Below: The late-Gothic and gabled Rathaus of Meissen was built between 1472 and 1478.

Above: At Radebeul the Schloss Pavilion of 1713 stands in its formal garden, surrounded by stepped vineyards.

Below: On the lake at Moritzburg, with its fake lighthouse, Saxon princes would stage mock sea battles.

rich in the pickings of the dukes and kings of Saxony who made this city their capital from 1270 to 1918 – all this notwithstanding the murderous bombardment inflicted by the Allied air forces in 1945.

The name Dresden in the ancient dialect of the Sorabes means the people of the forest (the *Drezgajan*, a reference to the Slavs who first peopled the spot in historical memory). By 1216 Dresden was a city, and a dependency of the bishops of Meissen. Fifty-nine years later the first bridge was thrown across the Elbe. Eventually the Margraves of Meissen wrested control of the city from the bishops, and in 1270 Heinrich the Illustrious chose the spot for his principal residence, flinging walls and defences around it. His first wife brought a fragment of the true cross, which soon attracted pilgrims (and their wealth) to her husband's capital.

Their successors were invested with the title Dukes of Saxony by the Emperor Sigismund in 1427. Two years later the Hussites attacked the city, pillaging and sacking parts of it. Dresden recovered, and when in 1485 Saxony was divided in two, the first of the Albertiner line of the Wettin dynasty, Moritz of Saxony, became first elector and then duke, once more making the city his chief residence. His line continued uninterrupted until 1918, his successors becoming Kings of Saxony in 1806.

They also became Protestant in 1539, when Heinrich the Pious was elector. However, his successor, Moritz, initially supported the attempts of the Holy Roman Emperor Charles V to stem the swelling tide of Protestantism in Germany. When Moritz became disillusioned with what he saw as the emperor's bad faith, he intrigued against Charles V with the King of France, and together in 1522 their armies drove the Holy Roman Emperor from Germany.

Medieval Dresden had meanwhile been ravaged by fire, especially in 1491, but its rulers were rich, for they controlled the silver which had been discovered in 1168 on the border of Czechoslovakia 60 km or so to the south. This region became known as the Erzgebirge, the Ore Mountains, for next iron, gold, tin and copper, as well as a string of semiprecious stones were dug from here – all under the control of the Wettin rulers of Saxony.

Their wealth enabled the city to recover from the fire of 1491, but Dresden was yet to see its greatest architectural age. Under the first Duke Augustus, who died in 1605, the foundations of Renaissance Dresden were laid, and the city continued to embellish itself with superb buildings until the outbreak of the Thirty Years' War.

A second Augustus (dubbed 'the Strong') ruled from 1694 to 1733 (becoming also King Friedrich Augustus I of Poland in 1697 and renouncing Protestantism to do so). Augustus was fond of saying that 'princes acquire immortality from what they build' (though he also sought another form of immortality in siring seventeen legitimate children and in the region of 365 others). He gave the city its baroque face. Augustus was in the habit of making temporary about-faces, allying first with Prussia against Austria and then, during the Seven Years' War, with Austria against Prussia. The Prussians remembered this betrayal, and in 1756 Friedrich II took Dresden, firing one of its suburbs.

Friedrich did yet more damage when he bombarded the city four years later, destroying five churches and four hundred houses. One victim was the Kreuzkirche in the Alt Markt – in a sense to our benefit, for the church was rebuilt in the baroque style between 1764 and 1792. It is the home of the celebrated Kreuzchor, a boys' choir with a 750-year-old history.

Next Napoleon Bonaparte left his mark, demolishing the fortifications of the city in 1810. Three years later the Grande Armée took on and defeated the Russians and the Austrians around Dresden. Napoleon's eventual fall did not extinguish the republican ideals which he had preached, and on 9 September 1830 the citizens of Dresden rose in revolt and gained a measure of constitutional reform. A yet more radical revolt in May 1849 forced the monarch into temporary refuge in the fortress at Königstein, but the Prussians came to his aid, the revolt was put down and the King resumed power. Amongst the revolutionaries had been the young Richard Wagner (having been musical director of the city, as was Carl Maria von Weber before him), who was obliged to flee to Paris.

As the second half of the nineteenth century progressed Dresden prospered on tobacco, metallurgy and the chemical industry. The Dresdner Bank became one of the most powerful in Europe. In the sixty years from 1850 to 1910 the population grew fivefold to 550 thousand, and many of the citizens passionately espoused the Social Democrats and the trades union movement. (The Social Democratic congress was held here in 1871.) In consequence, at the end of the First World War the citizens of Dresden joined in the revolution of November 1918, and their sovereign, Augustus, abdicated with the vulgar remark *Mach euch euren Dreck alleene* (Dresden slang for 'Now you can make your own dirt'). Similarly, during the Kapp Putsch of 1920, Dresden had little time for the right-wing extremists and the legitimate government several times retreated there from Berlin. The citizens rejoiced at the Weimar Republic. Dresden was now the home of Richard Strauss and the centre of German music-making and dance. Here too the Brücke movement gave birth to German Expressionism.

During the Second World War the citizens blithely considered themselves deliberately spared from the worst effects of the war. They welcomed refugees, evacuees and the wounded. Then on the night of 13 February 1945, RAF Lancaster bombers and USAF Flying Fortresses turned the city into a fire bomb. As *The Times* bleakly reported, 'In two attacks on Tuesday night the RAF sent 800 of a force of 1,400 Bomber

Command aircraft to Dresden, on which they showered 651,000 incendiaries together with 8,000 lb high-explosive bombs and hundreds of 4,000 pounders. The night assault was followed by day attacks, in which 1,350 American heavy bombers and 900 fighters took part.' Perhaps 60,000 people died, perhaps 130,000; 60 per cent of the city had been destroyed. For two days after the bombing the heat remained so intense that survivors dared not emerge from their cellars. The Frauenkirche (built by Georg Bähr between 1726 and 1743), whose 95 m high baroque dome was part of the characteristic silhouette of Dresden and the city's symbol, remained standing. But inside the eight columns supporting its roof were melting, and after two days the church collapsed.

What was saved was cherished, even under Communist rule. After the Russians withdrew (and on 2 January 1991, after an absence of forty-five years, the Dresdner Bank reopened its Dresden office), the pace of restoration quickened. The Communist régime decided to preserve the Frauenkirche as a ruin, as a memorial of the infamous bombing. Now Dresden plans to restore it to its original baroque splendour.

On the bank of the Elbe, at no. 15 Grosse Meissner Strasse, a delicious baroque palace of 1723–7, though badly damaged, remained standing. Bizarrely enough, the palace began as a result of another conflagration, in 1685. On this spot in 1654 Bürgermeister Elias Jentzsch had built a combined home and brewery, which perished in the fire. The court architect Matthäus Schumann was commissioned to rebuild. He died in 1709, and Johann Georg Gebhard took over. Eventually, paid for by a court treasurer named Franz-Johann Hoffmann, the planned brewery and stables were completed in an exquisite, rhythmical ensemble.

This palace, at no. 15 Grosse Meissner Strasse, is an excellent spot to begin a tour of the city. In a baroque shell on its façade you can make out in dog Latin the name of its sometime owner, 'FranCIsCVs IohannIs HoffMan'. Next to it is an inexpensive restaurant in the Gaststätte Blockhaus, which also dates from the 1730s and was rebuilt after 1945. Then around the corner, across the Augustusbrücke, appears the view of Dresden's Altstadt made famous by Bernardo Bellotto (who was the nephew of Canaletto and was sometimes so called), a view which gained the city the title of the Florence of the Elbe. Still on this side of the river, a few paces east at no. 1 Grosse Meissner Strasse, stands Dresden's oldest Renaissance building, a wing of the Jägerhof, the elector's hunting lodge, now a museum of folk art.

With its long arches and bastion-like refuges where you can pause to admire the river, the Augustusbrücke is a treat, named after Augustus the Strong who had it built. Across from it is Augustus' sinuous court church, Catholic, as he was (though most of his subjects remained Protestant). He commissioned the Roman architect Gaetano Chiaveri to build it between 1739 and 1751 in the Italian late-baroque style. The interior glitters, especially the ceiling frescos, the pulpit and above all Gottfried Silbermann's 3,000-pipe organ. The church also incorporates the royal mausoleum. Augustus' heart is here, in an egg-shaped bronze container. It is said to flutter whenever a pretty woman passes by.

West of the church stands Dresden's greatest treasure, the Zwinger palace. This too was built because of the conflagration of 1685. Amongst the architects brought to rebuild the inner city by Augustus the Strong was Wolf Caspar von Klengel, whose most celebrated pupil was Matthäus Daniel Pöppelmann. Pöppelmann was born in Westphalia in 1662 and died at Dresden in 1736. When von Klengel died Pöppelmann took over his work for Augustus, taking sole charge in 1691. Augustus made him sculptor-architect to the court in 1704, and he now produced a succession of drawings for rebuilding the royal palace in Dresden.

Work began on the Zwinger in 1709. Initially Pöppelmann intended a much larger palace. What he left is an outdoor theatre. Here would be mounted dances, tournaments, opera, indeed any form of royal entertainment. This elaborate building has a simple basis: a square court, with the transverse axes extended in U shapes, each closed by glass pavilions. Pöppelmann then brilliantly alleviates the severity of this design with luxurious curves, balconies, sinuous staircases, urns and statues.

No one ever lived in this palace. Its purpose, quite simply, was to serve as a royal playground, its orangery to store in winter the plants which in summer would grace the grounds. Go through the archway of the town pavilion (Stadtpavillon) and immediately turn round to spy a *Glockenspiel* whose bells are made of Meissen pottery. Augustus commissioned it, but no one managed to create it successfully until the twentieth century. The crossed swords carved above the *Glockenspiel* are the symbol of Meissen porcelain.

Over on the left of the main courtyard rises a triumphal archway, the *Kronentor* (or Crown Gate). The copper dome on top of its double arcade supports four eagles who bear the Polish crown. Here, as elsewhere on the palace façades, you can (just) make out the letters ARP. They stand for AUGUSTUS REX POLONIAE – Augustus, King of Poland.

At the other side of the lawns and fountains (later additions to the central courtyard), at the right-hand corner you climb the steps to the Nymphenbad, a fountain of three nymphs set between rococo grottoes. This is the best example of Pöppelmann's remarkable good fortune in having the cooperation of the Bavarian sculptor Balthasar Permoser, who created the classically inspired statues of the fountain. Born in 1651, Permoser had studied in Salzburg, in Rome, in Venice, Genoa and Florence before coming to Saxony to work with Pöppelmann. The statues of the Four Seasons on the Kronentor, as well as the drummer sculpted on its internal face, are his work. So are the diaphanously clad nymphs of the fountain.

Since in winter the water would freeze, it had to be turned off. To cope artistically with this Permoser and his assistants carved on the basin seaweed, moss, fishes and stones which appear to drip with water even when none is flowing.

If you look from here over the wall which supports the Polish crown you spot the art deco court theatre of 1911. If you look the other way across the river you see what appears to be a mosque. In reality it is a late-nineteenth-century tobacco factory (now converted into a hotel, and illuminated at night).

Like Permoser, Pöppelmann had travelled. From 1710 he could be found in Prague, Vienna and Italy, familiarizing himself with contemporary baroque masters. In 1715 he visited the Grand Trianon at Versailles, and the long galleries which stretch from the gate of the Zwinger palace to the pavilions were almost certainly inspired by what he saw there.

Yet in spite of this foreign influence, the Zwinger palace remains the ultimate masterpiece of German baroque. The pavilion to the north-west rising by the ramparts of the palace is known as the Wallpavillon and is superb. Columns elaborately carved with Atlantes carry the upper storey with its clouded glass windows. Above this is sculpted Augustus' coats of arms (Polish and Saxon), the letters ARP and the Polish crown. For its pinnacle Permoser created a celebrated statue of Hercules carrying the world. Seen from the other side of the moat, the Wallpavillon resembles a garden orangery, as Pöppelmann intended.

Pöppelmann planned to create what he himself described as 'a stroll in the middle of the city which would delight the most refined ladies and gentlemen of the court'. But he never finished the Zwinger palace. His style fell out of favour, and work ceased in 1732. The north-east wing, the picture gallery, was added only in 1847 by the classical architect Gottfried Semper.

Today it houses one of the most important collections of old masters in Germany.

The core of this collection, some hundred masterpieces, was bought in 1745 by Augustus the Strong's son Augustus III almost as a job lot from the Dukes of Modena at the cost of a million Zechinen. Nine years later he bought from the monastery church of San Sisto in Piacenza Raphael's Sistine Madonna.

Fortunately the collection was dispersed throughout Saxony in 1942 and thus escaped conflagration in the air raid three years later. Works by Rubens (including copies he made of Michelangelo and Tintoretto) reach their apogee in his *Bathsheba* seated by the fountain. Rembrandt is represented here by superb portraits of his wife Saskia and a self-portrait in which, after her death, he seems close to despair. Van Dyck painted the children of the doomed King Charles I of Britain several times, but the picture displayed here is masterly. The Cranachs, Hans Holbein the Elder and the Younger and Frans Hals are represented by portraits, including two by Lucas Cranach the Elder of Heinrich the Pious and his wife Katharina von Mecklenburg, painted in 1514. Though the faces are realistic, like all Cranach's work these paintings are filled with symbolism. The rich garments of the couple clearly proclaim their exalted status. The carnations in their hats refer to their marriage two years previously.

The Italian origin of the collection means that in spite of these superb works, its greatest strength lies in Italian masters: Quercino, Dominichino, Pintoricchio, Botticelli, Raphael (including the Sistine Madonna with its cheeky little cherubs), Canaletto, and above all Correggio, Giorgione (with a famous Venus) and Titian.

Five other collections fill the rest of the Zwinger palace. Harness and armour, porcelain, pewter and automats. Of these the porcelain, in the gallery at the south-west corner, is to my mind the most enchanting. As well as gems from China and Japan, there are exhibited Saxon works collected and commissioned by Augustus the Strong. As we shall shortly see, his reign coincided with the work of Johann Friedrich Böttger, who reinvented the skills of making porcelain in early-eighteenth-century Saxony, creating his first successful dish in 1708. On display in the Zwinger palace are some of his earliest essays in the rediscovered genre. Here too are the entertaining porcelain animals and curiosities created in the 1720s by the sculptor Christian Kirchner (a pupil of Permoser) and in the 1730s by Johann Kaendler. By the former is a rhinoceros (taken from a painting by Albrecht Dürer) and an elephant; by the latter are Harlequins and a porcelain statue of a giant Turk. On no account miss a 1713 statue of Augustus the Strong himself, by Johann Kretzschmar (another pupil of Permoser). Kretzschmar has got away with portraying the king as at once ugly and arrogant.

In the square beyond Gottfried Semper's Renaissance addition to the Zwinger palace stands his Opera House. He built it between 1838 and 1841, and it was here that Wagner produced his *Rienzi, Flying Dutchman* and *Tannhäuser*. In 1869 the Opera House was gutted by fire. Semper designed another one in the high-Renaissance style, and his son built it in the 1870s. It saw the first performance of Richard Strauss's *Der Rosenkavalier* in 1911. Destroyed on 13 February 1945, it was meticulously restored and opened again on 13 February exactly forty years later. The venue of ballet as well as opera, it is also graced by Dresden's Staatskapelle and Philharmonic orchestra.

In the same square is the Ionic Guard House which Karl Friedrich Schinkel designed in 1832. The square centres on an equestrian statue of King Johann (who reigned from 1854 to 1872). Johann was a scholarly monarch, and translated, under the pseudonym Philalethes, Dante's *Divine Comedy*, which appears on the plinth of the statue. He also disliked company and preferred living in a little Schloss at Moritzburg to living in his capital.

At the other side of the Catholic church (which became a cathedral in 1980) rises the Residenzschloss, the former royal palace, its interior begun in 1537, though the massive pseudo-medieval gateway which you first see was built only in 1901. Its oldest part, the fourteenth-century tower (the Haus-mannsturm), was all that remained standing after 13 February 1945, and then only a truncated 52 m of it. Soon it will be restored, its gilded weather-vane once more rising from the cupola to a height of 100 m. The city has announced that the palace will be completely restored by 1999.

Walk from here along Augustinerstrasse, where on the wall of an extension to the Schloss known as the Johannaeum is another intriguing survivor of the last war: a 101 m long series of portraits depicting the family tree of the Wettin dynasty and created out of 25,000 Meissen tiles to the 1876 designs of Wilhelm Walther. It replaced an earlier one designed in the late sixteenth century, and looks like a tapestry, as the prince-lings ride and strut their way along it. Walk around to the other side of the Johannaeum wall to discover the 'Lange Gang', with its rails that once delineated the fields for jousting matches. Built in the Renaissance style around 1590 and given baroque decorations in the eighteenth century, the arcade overlooking this princely playground is adorned with escutch-eons and the sculpted heads of horned animals, as well as an accurate sundial.

Our tour shortly reaches the Albertinum, a massive art gallery, built in the 1880s by Carl Adolf Canzler. Its rarest works of art are displayed in the Grünes Gewölbe (Green Vault), and comprise the Wettin collection of jewellery. Pride of place goes to a crazed baroque creation depicting the birthday of a contemporary Indian ruler named Aureng Zeb, which is studded with more than 5,000 diamonds and 160 rubies amongst the other precious stones. The court goldsmith Johann Dinglinger and his two brothers took seven years to make it. The Albertinum is also the home of Dresden's collection of nineteenth- and twentieth-century paintings, including some stunning paintings by Lovis Corinth. Amongst works by Die Brücke group on display here are paintings by Erich Heckel, Karl Schmidt-Rottluff and Max Pechstein. The expressionists include Max Beckmann and there is a terrifying painting of war by Otto Dix.

Beside the Albertinum, in Georg-Treu-Platz, you can (save on Sundays) make a fascinating, underground tour of the former sixteenth-century fortifications of Dresden (the 'Festung Dresden'), by way of great stone arches and tunnels. Here, I was told, the Elector Augustus II imprisoned the alchemist Friedrich Böttger until such a time as he might find a way of transmuting base metals into gold. Instead he discovered how to make china.

Climb the steps from the Platz on to the Brühlsche terrasse, which overlooks the Elbe and was described by Goethe as the balcony of Europe. It takes its name from the gardens which once belonged to a family named Brühl. At the top of the steps is a statue of Gottfried Semper, unrolling plans. At the other side of the river are handsome government buildings, and on our side the façade of the Akademie der Kunst. Here in summer you can sit in the open air and drink coffee. As you walk back towards the Augustusbrücke you pass the baroque Brühl palace and a statue of the Dresden sculptor Ernst Rietschel, who died famous in 1861 and is virtually forgotten today. Then a garden in front of the imposing Saxon Land Library takes us back to the Augustusbrücke. Just by here, in Münzgasse, is a little bar, the Kleppereck, where you can sit outside, resting after the tour, sipping a beer 'Frisch vom Fass' and watching the ships go by through an archway.

Across the bridge and past the Hotel Maritim-Bellevue is the gilded equestrian statue of Augustus the Strong, which is here known as the 'Goldener Reiter'. On one side golden letters describe him both as FRID AVGVSTVS I (Duke Friedrich August I of Saxony) and AVGVSTVS II (i.e. King Augustus II of Poland); on the other the inscription tells us that his successor placed the statue here in 1736. Augustus and his prancing steed look along pedestrianized Hauptstrasse, which leads into his Neustadt and is flanked with a startling number of bookshops, as well as food shops, clothes shops and restaurants. Trees shade statues of artists, gods and goddesses. On the left is the nineteenth-century market hall. On the right are some surviving houses of the original street.

One of them, the Kügelgen Haus, takes its name from a distinguished Saxon family which included the painter Gerhard von Kügelgen. He came here in 1808 and was murdered by a deserting soldier. History does not record what his bereaved family thought of the inscription outside this house: IN GOTTES SEGEN IST ALLES BELEGEN ('In God's sight all is blessed'). Now his home is a restaurant serving powerful local dishes, such as spicy shredded beef and onions wrapped in red cabbage and bacon. Its paintings depict old Dresden, numerous members of the Kügelgen family, and prints of people walking in the parks, taking coffee and skating on the Elbe.

Ahead on the left rises the tower of Pöppelmann's massive Dreikönigenkirche, now a concert hall. Along the street by the church (An der Dreikönigenkirche) signs hanging outside the shops indicate the various businesses (a boot for the shoeshop, curly bread for the bakers). Turn left here to return to the Elbe, and (I suggest) on your way find in Rähnitzgasse, with its eighteenth-century houses, the Café Donnersberg (whose name derives from a radical faction in the first German National Assembly of 1848). Here a monthly literary salon is held. Once the novelist Günter Grass was presiding over one when I was there, and he signed the visitors' book. A few days later, I sat where he had sat, and explained to the owner's wife that I too, in a humbler fashion, was a writer. Since she knew of my biography of Pastor Martin Niemöller, she kindly allowed me to sign the book, on the very page following that used by Grass.

Finally, to the west, find the Japanisches Palais. In spite of its name, this palace was begun in the Dutch style by Pöppel-mann, and the herms in the courtyard are carved in the chinoiserie fashion. Augustus the Strong intended to house his porcelain collection here, but today it is a museum of folk art. In front of it stands Ernst Rietschel's 1843 memorial to King Friedrich Augustus I.

An entrancing excursion from Dresden takes in Schloss Pillnitz and then makes a tour of Saxony Switzerland. The way to Pillnitz from Dresden crosses the Elbe by the Loschwitz suspension bridge (known as the 'Blue Miracle', since it is painted in blue), which was flung across the river in 1893. Nearly 3,000 tonnes of steel went into its lattice-work, and it stretches 141.5 m over the Elbe. You can also walk or cycle to Loschwitz along the river's banks, while a boat trip as far as Pillnitz takes half an hour.

In the suburb of Loschwitz, at no. 19 Schillerstrasse, stands the house in which Schiller wrote his *Don Carlos*. This is hilly country, with a cable car taking tourists up to the belvedere of Loschwitzhöhe, with its splendid panoramas. A second easy way to see the panoramic views is to take the funicular railway which, built in 1895, is one of the oldest in Europe. Another fine view is from the local television tower, with its café some 250 m above the ground. Here too is a museum (at no. 44 Dresdner Strasse in the suburb of Hostewitz) dedicated to the composer Carl Maria von Weber, who lived in this small house from 1818 to 1824.

Soon, through vineyards, the route reaches Schloss Pillnitz, with its superb park. Augustus the Strong bought the grounds and a Schloss here in 1718. On behalf of his mistress the Countess Cosel, he rebuilt it as a summer residence and transformed the spot into a French garden, with parterres running down to the riverside. (They later quarrelled, and the countess was imprisoned in the Schloss at Stolpen.) Spread amongst the gardens are wings and outbuildings, some of them designed by Pöppelmann, others by Zacharias Longue-lune, all of them faithful to Pöppelmann's vision (including the partly ruined Neues Palais, built to the designs of Christoph Schuricht in 1826, the Bergpalais of 1723 and the 'Chinese' water palace of 1723, both designed by Pöppelmann). Turreted dormer windows enliven roofs. As well as a museum of handicraft, the Schloss at Pillnitz has an exhibition of Italian art, including views of old Dresden by 'Canaletto' (actually Bellotto, Canaletto's nephew).

On the other side of the river is Pirna where there is another 'Canaletto scene' comprising the parish church of St Mary, the fifteenth-to-seventeenth-century Festung Sonnenstein and the Rathaus, which has a porch of 1612 and a baroque tower of 1718. The Marienkirche has a Gothic belfry of 1480, against which Peter Ulrich built the rest of the church in the first half of the sixteenth century. The Gothic vaulting becomes quite deliri-ous in the nave, and retains its colouring of the 1540s. The font of 1561 is decorated with sculpted children; the late-Gothic pulpit dates from 1525; and the high altar was created in 1615.

Pirna's town museum is housed in a former Dominican monastery, whose church was built in the fourteenth century and decorated with late-medieval frescos. Its late-Gothic winged altar was carved in Thuringia around 1510. And 5 km west of Pirna is the fifteenth-century Schloss Weesenstein, partly rebuilt in the nineteenth century, rising on a rock over the River Müglitz. Nowadays a museum, its main hall has a stuccoed ceiling of 1619 and displays rococo wall-paintings, French tapestries and chinoiserie. We are also close to a baroque garden, that at Heidenau designed by Pöppelmann, Johann Christoph Knöffel and Zacharias Longuelune in the 1720s, with Knöffel's orangery and a monumental staircase decorated with putti musicians and known as the 'Stille Musik'.

Schloss Pillnitz is a good place from which to start exploring 'Saxon Switzerland', though a comprehensive tour of this superb climbing country would take at least a week (and that is without climbing). Saxon Switzerland comprises 368 km² of sandstone mountains beside the Elbe. You can see how they inspired Carl Maria von Weber's wolf's glen scene in *Der Freischütz*. Here are some 1,000 registered climbing peaks, and 1,200 km of entrancing footpaths.

By way of Graupa (4 km south-east of Pillnitz), where Richard Wagner worked on his *Lohengrin*, and of Lohmen, the tour reaches the celebrated Bastei, a bastion of fantastically shaped rocks overlooking the Elbe. The intrepid perch on top of them, while the rest of us wonder at them from the ancient bridge. Near by is the ruined thirteenth-century fortress of Felsenburg Neurathen, and to the north is the half-timbered village of Hohenstein, with a massive sixteenth-century fortress and a baroque church built by Georg Bähr in 1725.

In Lausitz, east of Saxon Switzerland, the signposts are written in two languages. This is the home of the Sorabes, a tribe of Slavs originating west of the River Elbe, whose sixty thousand or so descendants, though they and their ancestors have lived side by side with Germans for centuries, still cling fiercely to their traditions and have preserved their own culture. In this region lies Görlitz, the easternmost town of Saxony, where more Renaissance and baroque houses are said to be found than in any other German city or town, in part the result of a fire of 1525 which destroyed much of the medieval town.

Görlitz lies on a slope whose foot is washed by the River

Neisse. Its Untermarkt, as well as being bordered by Renaissance and baroque houses (some of them betraying Gothic origins), has stone Gothic arcades borne on sturdy pillars. It also houses the Rathaus, which first saw the light of day in the fourteenth century but was rebuilt by the architect Wendel Roskopf the Elder after the fire of 1525. He retained a Gothic doorway, added a Renaissance one and linked them by a staircase with a pulpit from which the councillors could address the people. Other fine Gothic, Renaissance and baroque houses, a candelabra column (with the arms of Matthias Corvinus I of Hungary), a Neptune fountain and Roskopf's towered Schönhoff add to the ambience of the Untermarkt.

West of the Untermarkt rises the Gothic Oberkirche, in front of which is a statue of Roland of 1590. Dedicated to the Holy Trinity, the church once belonged to a Franciscan monastery and possesses sixty-four superb Gothic stalls of 1484, as well as a sandstone *Entombment* of 1492. The vaults have preserved their fifteenth-century frescos, and a late-Gothic winged altar enshrines a *Golden Maria* of 1510.

A baroque building at no. 30 Neissestrasse (which runs east from the Untermarkt) serves as the town museum, while next door at no. 29 is the Biblisches Haus of 1570, whose reliefs represent scenes from the Old and New Testaments. The birth of Eve is paralleled by the Annunciation; original sin by its remedy, the birth of Jesus; the sacrifice of Abraham by Jesus' baptism in the river Jordan; Moses receiving the Ten Commandments by the scene of the Last Supper; and Moses raising the serpent in the desert by Jesus raised on the cross. In the same street, no. 27, the Golden Anchor, is a Renaissance inn of 1545.

Peterstrasse (running north from the Untermarkt) is just as attractive, with its baroque and Renaissance houses, and it leads to the Peterskirche (properly dedicated to St Paul as well). Five-aisled, the Peterskirche began life in 1230 but ended as a flamboyant Gothic church. Its crypt, begun in 1423, was vaulted in 1497 by Conrad Pflüger, and the church had to wait until 1891 before receiving its 85 m high concrete towers.

Behind the church you can see bastions known as Wick-häuschen, the remains of the town's mid-sixteenth-century fortifications, while to the south of its apse is the Renthaus, which was begun in the thirteenth century. Follow Nikolai-strasse west from here to reach the fourteenth-century Nikolai tower, which has a baroque hat. North of the tower is the Nikolai cemetery, with a flamboyant church dedicated to St Nicholas. Built between 1452 and 1520, in 1925 it became a monument to the fallen of the First World War. The cemetery boasts some impressive tombs, including that of the philo-sopher Jakob Böhme, who died at Görlitz in 1624.

Another of Conrad Pflüger's architectural gifts to Görlitz is the church of the Holy Sepulchre (Heiliges Grab), built between 1481 and 1504 as a supposedly faithful reproduction of the original on the Mount of Olives. It was paid for by Georg Emmerich, son of the mayor of Görlitz, who had made the mistake of falling in love with the daughter of a political enemy and was forced as a penance to make a pilgrimage to Jerusalem.

Grüner Graben leads south from here to two of the town's former defences. The fourteenth- and fifteenth-century Reichen-bacher gate has a baroque top added in 1782 and is now the home of a collection of arms from the middle ages to the eighteenth century. The powerful late-fifteenth-century bastion known as the Kaisertrutz is now the Görlitz museum. It displays some fine medieval sculpture, but my own favourite exhibits are the paintings by Corinth and Slevogt. Close by, a few paces south-east, stands the last of Görlitz's medieval churches, the Frauenkirche. Built between 1449 and 1486, its finest feature is the double doorway decorated with the scene of the Annunciation.

Before leaving Görlitz, take time to wander in the park which Lenné laid out. Its concert hall dates from 1912, and the meridian stone, which marks the fifteenth meridian, was placed here after the first successful space flight by the Russian cosmonaut Yuri Gagarin. The town of Reichenbach, 12 km south-west of Görlitz along the F6, is not the spot where, in his short story 'The Final Problem', Sir Arthur Conan Doyle sought to kill off Sherlock Holmes and Professor Moriarty, but it is worth a visit for its flamboyant Gothic church, which shelters an altar of 1680 and a pulpit of 1690.

From here return south-east to rejoin the Polish border at Hagenwerder. Now our route curves south alongside both the River Neisse and the border through Ostritz to Zittau. At Ostritz is a Cistercian convent whose church dates from 1685 and abbey buildings from 1744. The square, domed chapel of St Michael of 1756 was decorated with frescos depicting the Adoration of the Cross and a bronze serpent by Giovanni-Battista Casanova, who spent his working life based in Dresden.

At Hirschfelde, between here and Zittau, is a Gothic church with paintings of 1726 by N. Prescher. Zittau, like Görlitz, is a town of the Renaissance and the baroque, with Gothic churches and also a leavening of neoclassical architecture. All this piquant mix is seen in the Johanniskirche, the last architect to have a hand in its transformation being Schinkel himself. Schinkel also designed the town hall (which was not built till 1845, after his death), this time flexing his considerable architectural muscle in the Italian style. The fountain in the market square is topped with the god Mars and dates from 1585, and the west side of this square boasts merchants' houses of the seventeenth and eighteenth centuries.

Nearby are the former stables of the town, a late-Gothic building of 1511 with a mansard roof of 1630. The Samaritan Fountain, created in 1679, stands to the south of them, while to the north are the Hercules Fountain of 1708 and the Swan Fountain of 1710. The citizens evidently took no chances with their water supply, for another fountain of 1679, the Grüne Born ('Green Spring') with wrought iron by M. Fröhlich, gushes in front of the town museum in Klosterstrasse. The finest offerings in the museum's collection are examples of local earthenware, and as the name of the street in which it stands indicates, it is housed in what was once a Franciscan monastery. The monastery church, dedicated to St Peter and St Paul, began as a Gothic building but was altered in 1680. Its pulpit dates from 1668, its tower points 70 m towards heaven.

The town is overshadowed by the Zittau mountains, with their health resorts, in particular Johnsdorf, and winter-sports centres such as Obyn (with a fourteenth-century fortress and a former monastery), the charming Gross-Schönau, Hörnitz (with a Renaissance Schloss), Oberwitz (with its classical church of 1818) and Waltersdorf. At Obyn you can see where the cliff fell down in 1681, leaving both town and monastery in ruins. Leaving Zittau and driving north-west, you reach Eibau, many of whose gabled houses date from the eighteenth century, as does its large baroque church of 1797. Ten kilometres later appears Ebersbach, with a baroque church built in 1682 and enlarged in 1733, whose organ console dates from 1685.

A succession of surprisingly rich towns and villages rapidly appears as you drive on. The market square of Löbau, north-east of Ebersbach, is surrounded by baroque houses, and its baroque town hall of 1711 has a battlemented tower; while at Kittlitz, 4 km further north, is a baroque church of 1775 by A. Hüningen.

Herrnhut, close by, is a spot redolent with Protestant history. Here you can still see the baroque buildings on the domain of Count Nicolaus Ludwig von Zinzendorf, who was born at Dresden in 1700 and lived till 1760. After completing his studies at the University of Wittenberg, Zinzendorf became a government official at Dresden. In 1722 he invited the followers of the Bohemian Brethren, a group of much persecuted Christians (whose most famous bishop was the educationalist Johannes Amos Comenius), to join him at Herrnhut. Zinzendorf himself was subsequently persecuted and forced into exile between 1736 and 1748, when he visited both Britain and America; but the Herrnhut Christians flourished, often under the name of Moravians, after the chief seat of the former Bohemian Brethren. They influenced John Wesley profoundly. And as zealous missionaries, they sent two of the brethren to the West Indies in 1732 and began another mission in Greenland the following year – activities commemorated and recorded here in their museum at no. 1 Goethestrasse.

Take the E40 north-west from Löbau to reach Bautzen, on the rocky banks of the River Spree (whose source is near by). Bautzen, which the Sorabes call Budysin, is stunning. Founded by these Slavs and in alliance with its neighbours, it remained a powerful force throughout the middle ages, and the King of Bohemia granted it city rights in the early thirteenth century. Dominating Bautzen is the fortress overlooking the Spree which is known as the Ortenburg. Built around 1000, the fortress was transformed into a Gothic Schloss in the early 1480s and was later humanized with Renaissance gables. Its tower was sculpted by Briccius Gausks in 1486 with a couple of angels crowning the King of Hungary.

The city suffered grievously in the Thirty Years' War and by 1620 a good deal had been razed. One of Wallenstein's lieutenants set fire to some of the rest (incinerating several citizens as well) in 1634. A memorial of that act of viciousness are the ruins of the flamboyant Nikolaikirche.

Another savage battle took place here on 20–21 May 1813, when Napoleon's troops slaughtered eight thousand Russians and Prussians, but lost twelve thousand of their own men. (Technically, the French claimed it as a victory.) Yet in spite of these depredations, some of the old defences are still here: the early-fifteenth-century Lauenturm with its baroque roof; the Mühlbastei of 1480; the late-fifteenth-century Reichentorturm, a tower-gateway with a massive baroque lantern, the whole leaning slightly; the Gerber-Bastei of 1506; the Schülerturm with its fifteenth-century relief of the Crucifixion.

Another ancient survival is the water tower of 1558, near to the Gothic church of St Michael. Still in use, the water tower also has a museum displaying models of its inner workings. Another of Bautzen's museums (in Postplatz) is devoted to Sorabian literature, known in Sorabian as the Serbski Dom. Here is a German–Sorabian Volkstheater. At Bautzen too is the Domowina, seat of the Sorabian national organization. And a third (the Stadtmuseum) contains paintings from Cranach to Max Liebermann and Slevogt, with a fine Jugendstil section.

Bautzen's Hauptmarkt delights in a baroque town hall designed by J.-C. Naumann in 1732. The Ratskeller has a fine façade of 1882, while the vault inside rises from a single pillar. Two other baroque houses complete the ensemble of the square, to the north of which, across Fleischmarkt with more baroque houses, rises the cathedral, the Petridom.

A late-thirteenth- and mid-fifteenth-century Gothic house of God, in 1524, following a pattern found elsewhere in Germany, it became a shared church, the Catholics worshipping in the choir and the Protestants in the nave, the two congregations separated by a grille, part of which still remains. Since the eighteenth century the Catholics have centred their worship on a marble and sandstone altar of 1724 created by the baroque masters G. Fossati and J.-B. Thoma, an altar embellished by paintings by Pellegrini. Their crucifix was sculpted out of wood in 1714 by the pupils of Permoser and their stalls date from 1725. In the Catholic sacristy is a rococo altar of 1782. An older altar, with a wooden reredos of 1644 depicting the Crucifixion, serves the Protestants.

Take the F6 from Bautzen to Bischofswerda, with its harmonious classical market square and a late Renaissance church of the Holy Cross in which is a powerful sandstone crucifix of 1535 or so, carved by Christoph Walther the Elder. The three-storeyed classical Rathaus was built in 1818. Three kilometres north-east, in the hamlet of Rammenau, was born the radical philosopher Johann Gottlieb Fichte. In 1794, at the age of thirty-two, the became a professor at Jena, where his disquisitions on the nature of humanity seem to many to make him one of the first existentialists. But what made Fichte famous – even notorious – were his passionately nationalistic *Addresses to the German Nation* of 1807 and 1808, inspired by hatred of Napoleon Bonaparte. Two years later he was appointed the first rector of Berlin University. His wife's benevolence killed him. She nursed wounded men and women in the Berlin hospitals, caught an infection and gave it to her husband, who expired in 1814. Rammenau remembers him with a museum in part of its baroque, ochre Schloss of 1725, which was probably designed by J. C. Knöffel and sits in an orderly green garden.

Certainly worth a visit is Kamenz, 19 km north-west of Bischofswerda, whose late-Gothic parish church of St Mary has early-eighteenth-century baroque furnishings. The dramatist and man of letters Gotthold Ephraim Lessing was born here in 1729 and his museum is in Lessingsplatz. There is a fine view of the town and its surroundings from the 294 m high Hutberg to the west. And 16 km west of Kamenz is Königsbrück, with its baroque Schloss of 1700 and baroque church. Begun in 1682, the church shelters an altar of 1693 and a late-Gothic altar painting of 1475 depicting the flagellation and crucifixion of Jesus.

Amongst the many delightful towns, spas and villages of this region, two towns on the way back to Dresden from Bischofswerda ought not to be missed. Stolpen's main square has eighteenth-century houses, but its chief attraction is its ruined fifteenth- and sixteenth-century fortress, set on a basalt rock. It was built for the bishops of Meissen, who in 1559 exchanged it for another belonging to the Prince-Elector of Saxony. Retreating towards Dresden in 1813, the French demolished much of this fortress, which had been extended in 1675 by W. C. Klengel. Its Siebenspitzenturm (or 'Tower with Seven Caps') was built in 1476, the Schlösserturm dates from 1484 and the four-storeyed Johannisturm from 1509. In the latter, Augustus the Strong's former mistress, the Countess of Cosel, was imprisoned from 1716 to 1738. She must have appreciated the superb view of the Elbe massif from here as well as the tower's fine coffered vault, for given the opportunity to leave she refused, and stayed voluntarily until her death in 1765 at the age of eighty-five. The former stables now display cannons and other weapons of war, as does the guardhouse. The fortress still retains its 82 m deep well, its courtroom, its prison (the Johanniskerker) and a torture chamber with some repulsive implements.

Radeberg is also noted for its Schloss Klippenstein, a Renaissance building of 1543–68. The town has a local-history museum, but is renowned most of all for its excellent beer, the Radeberger Pils.

South-west of Dresden you can make a pleasing excursion through Freital and Tharandt to Freiberg. At the first the Renaissance Schloss (which has a classical Festsaal of 1820 and was partly Gothicized in 1846) is now a museum of local history, with mementoes of the mining industry. Tharandt's church, though rebuilt in the late 1620s, preserves a doorway incorporating late-Romanesque columns. The town also boasts an 18 hectare botanical garden, and woods in which stands a double-storeyed Renaissance hunting lodge built in 1558.

The treasure of this little excursion is Freiberg. A few remains of its fortifications can still be traced in Schillerstrasse. They also incorporated the fifteenth-century Donatsturm in

Donatsgasse, and Schloss Freedenstein, which was founded in the thirteenth century and transformed in 1566.

In the rectangular Obermarkt stretches the long, late-Gothic Rathaus, initially built in the 1470s and preserving an ogival entrance on its south side. In front stands a fountain of 1897, with a statue of Otto the Rich. The entrance to the Ratskeller (in a merchant's house of 1546) is early Renaissance, and is matched in style by several houses in the square, while others are late-Gothic or baroque. No. 15 carries a carving of 1515 depicting God the Father carrying the globe.

By way of Weingasse and Herderstrasse you reach Untermarkt and the cathedral of Unser Lieben Frau. Its core is late twelfth and early thirteenth century, though it was completed only in 1512, after being damaged in a fire of 1484. Its finest doorway, modelled on one at Chartres, is the so-called Goldene Pforte (which once was the cathedral's west door though it has been transported to the south side). Sculpted around 1230, its figures include on the left Daniel, the Queen of Sheba, Solomon and St John the Baptist, and on the right St John the Evangelist, King David, Bathsheba and Aaron. Sculpted on the archivolts are an angel and Abraham welcoming into Heaven the souls of the saved; and in the tympanum the Virgin Mary in majesty is attended by St Joseph, the angel Gabriel and the three Magi.

The masterpieces inside the cathedral do not betray the promise of this doorway. Gottfried Silbermann created its organ in 1712. In the nave is a superb pulpit made by Hans Witten around 1510 and, because it resembles a tulip, it is known as the Tulpenkanzel. On this masterpiece Witten depicted the legend of Daniel revealing to a miner a seam of silver, as well as cunningly concealing in his tulip the busts of the four fathers of the church. Another superb pulpit of 1638, possibly by Hans Fritzsche, has a staircase whose atlantes are a couple of sculpted miners. The cross dates from the 1230s. Wise and foolish virgins are carved on octagonal pillars. On the high altar is a Last Supper, painted around 1560. The chapel of St Anne houses a Virgin Mary, supported by angels, created in 1513.

In the second half of the sixteenth century the choir of Freiberg cathedral was transformed into the mausoleum of the Protestant rulers of Saxony-Wettin. In it is the cenotaph made by Hans Wessel of Lübeck and his assistants for Elector Moritz of Saxony who died in 1553. Other, kneeling princes were sculpted by the sixteenth-century Florentine Carlo Cesare. G. M. Nossini transformed the choir in the Italian baroque style, complete with a *trompe-l'oeil* painted and stuccoed Heaven. And in the All Saints Chapel Balthasar Permoser and his pupils had a hand in the monuments of Princess Wilhelmine of the Palatinate and her sister Anna-Sophia, who died respectively in 1706 and 1711.

Miners bearing a font and carved on a pulpit speak of the traditional industry of this country, part of Saxony's metallic mountain. The city's prosperity began with the discovery of silver here in 1186. On the north side of the Dom late-Gothic buildings house the city's museum of mining. The Untermarkt is also graced with Renaissance and baroque buildings.

Finally, the huge, late-Gothic, three-aisled Petrikirche, which dates from the first half of the fifteenth century, has an interior which was totally reordered between 1728 and 1732. Its treasures are its lectern and its organ, built by Gottfried Silbermann in the early 1730s.

Even more entrancing in my view is a trip from Dresden to Meissen. Leaving Dresden by the Marienbrücke, after 6 km driving beside the river you reach Radebeul, which lies at the foot of the Lössnitzberge. Terraced vineyards rise on the right, up beyond to golden Schloss Wackerbarth, which is approached through a topiary garden. The wine is the rare Lössnitz, which you can buy in the former Schloss stables. Radebeul's favourite son is the writer Karl May (1842–1912), whose novels of American-Indian life entranced countless children. In consequence, no. 15 Karl-May-Strasse is a museum of Indian and trapper life, its *chef-d'oeuvre* a depiction of General Custer's last stand at the Little Big Horn on 25 June 1876.

Make a brief diversion north-east to visit Schloss Moritzburg and some more playgrounds of the former rulers of this Land. Augustus the Strong commissioned Pöppelmann and Longuelune to transform the hunting lodge of Moritzburg into a superb palace. Rising from a sturdy stone base, the yellow Schloss has domes rising from its corner turrets. Four small lakes were merged to set the Schloss in an artificial one (which is drained in winter). Putti and vases decorate its terraces, and inside is a museum of baroque furniture, as well as porcelain from as far afield as China and Japan.

Surrounding Schloss Moritzburg is a baroque park of lakes and woodlands stretching for 2,500 hectares. Near the Waldschränke restaurant you discover the pretty little pink and green Fasanenschlösschen. It was built between 1769 and 1782 for the Friedrich Augustus who ruled Saxony from 1763 to 1826. One turret remains oddly unpainted.

Here is where King Johann would retreat to avoid his tiresome subjects, preferring the eighteenth-century chinoiserie interior and his beloved Dante. A bizarre feature today is the stork's nest on top of it. The Schloss looks down its long flight of steps to the harbour, lighthouse and mole of a lake on which Augustus the Strong and his courtiers staged naval battles.

From Radebeul to Meissen the route runs through gentle countryside, with hills and streams, gabled churches and half-timbered houses with steeply tiled roofs and always the Elbe close by. At Coswig, in between Radebeul and Meissen, is a church which is part-Gothic, part-baroque, of 1735, with a painted, coffered ceiling of 1611. Then the powerful profiles of the cathedral and fortress of Meissen appear ahead, the fortress bad-tempered, and only humanized by the Gothic spires of the former. Washed by the River Elbe, this city was founded by Heinrich I in 929 and was the seat of a bishop only thirty-nine years later. In 1125 the Emperor Otto I elevated the city to the status of a margravate.

The ancient heart of Meissen, the Markt, is shaded by the Gothic town hall of 1472, which has three gabled towers and a roof twice the height of the rest. Other Gothic and Renaissance houses add their charm to this Platz, as well as the Markt Apotheke of 1717, still functioning as a pharmacy. It is worth buying a few pills simply to admire its wooden, painted ceiling. On the façade is a model of Icarus falling, with a scroll declaring NON ALTUM NON HUMILE. On the Hirsch-Haus in the Platz is its date, 1646 (with 1901 added as the date of its restoration). Opposite is an arcaded Gothic house which is worth peeping into for its staircase. Outside the Küfertheke (the house of the coopers) is the gilded sign of a grape, for Meissen produces a wine as scarce as that of Radebeul. Naturally, signs bearing crossed swords, the emblem of Meissen porcelain, also abound in the city.

To the south of the Markt stands the Frauenkirche, itself built in the flamboyant Gothic style in 1457. The bells of this church are made of Saxony porcelain. This *Glockenspiel* created by Professor E. P. Börner in 1929, plays merrily for minutes on end at 6.30, 8.30, 11.30, 14.30, 17.30 and 20.30. The church's Tuchmachertor is a Renaissance doorway dating from around 1600; and its chief treasure is a Coronation of the Virgin on the late-Gothic high altar, which was created just over a century earlier. Here too are sheltered. tombs of the fifteenth to eighteenth centuries.

Beside the church is the splendid, half-timbered Vincenz Richter House of 1647, with its little tower and a wine press built in 1706. On the other side of the church, in An der Frauenkirche, is the brewery of 1571, and another gabled house (today the city tourist office). It boasts a Renaissance porch, with a sculpture of Samson slaying a lion and the date MDLXXI.

Walk through the Tuchmachertor of 1600 and then up beside the Vincenz Richter House to reach Freiheit, where a Renaissance corner-tower identifies the 1515 presbytery of the Afrakirche. Once the church of an Augustinian Convent, the Afrakirche is basically Gothic. A brick gable contrasts happily with the stone and plaster of the rest of the building. Inside the church the altar dates from 1660, and depicts scenes from the Passion and Resurrection of Jesus (including a fine doubting Thomas). To the right is Rote Stufen, with canons' houses, some built in the thirteenth, some in the seventeenth century. You can peer through a Renaissance portal of 1616 to see the even finer Lion Portal of 1610.

The steepish path leads on now beside a battlemented defensive wall. This fortified part of Meissen includes its Burgberg and its cathedral, whose square you reach by way of the Mitteltor, a medieval Gothic gateway restored in 1875. Here are more ancient canons' houses (the Domherrenhöfe), all dated and, it seems to me, all completely different. Opposite them the massive Kornhaus of 1470, later used for the manufacture of porcelain, has a substantial double balcony.

As for the Albrechtsburg, it was rebuilt by Arnold of Westphalia for the Margrave Albert in 1471 in a flamboyant Gothic style which has softened the style of a medieval fortress into a palatial residence. Three exquisite vaulted rooms on the first floor are frescoed with a depiction of the history of the fortress from its original foundation in 929. Then an enormous staircase, the Grosse Wendelstein, leads to the third floor, again a museum of the history of the fortress.

The second floor is crammed with fine art. St Bonaventura and St Jerome, painted on wood around 1500; drawings by Dürer and Holbein; a huge fresco of the Meissen hero, the

Duke-Elector Augustin, who lived from 1553 to 1586. Another Gothic room is the splendid audience chamber. Finally other rooms of the fortress are given over to porcelain, for the Albrechtsburg became a porcelain factory from 1710 to 1864. The Böttger room is devoted to the inventor of European porcelain, the emperor's alchemist, Johann Friedrich Böttger. In the very year that he developed the technique of making true porcelain, it began to be manufactured here in this Schloss.

Meissen cathedral, though begun in the Romanesque era, was rebuilt in the early thirteenth century in the Gothic style and finished in 1480 when Arnold of Westphalia completed the third storey of the tower. Today it comprises three ogival vaults, forming three aisles, which are crossed by a transept. Inside its porch are the bronze funeral brasses and tombs of bishops, knights and their ladies. These include Duke Georg the Bearded, with a tomb housing both himself and his wife Duchess Barbara (who predeceased her husband in 1534 by five years). Some of these superb bronzes were designed by Dürer, and all of them made in the workshop of the Vischer family of Nuremberg. Beyond it is the chapel of St John, where are depicted St John the Baptist, the Blessed Virgin and a deacon, a work from Naumburg of the mid thirteenth century.

The treasures proliferate. There is a triptych of 1534 by Lucas Cranach the Elder. In front of the rood-screen is a triptych of 1526 from the workshop of Cranach. The central window of the choir dates in part from 1270, and Dutch masters made and painted the early-sixteenth-century high altar, with its depiction of the apostles and the Adoration of the Magi. Then retrace your steps down the north side of the cathedral, where in the thirteenth century Naumburg artists created the portraits of Emperor Otto I and his empress Adelheid.

Meissen's episcopal palace is a three-storey Gothic building, and from it you should walk back towards the Markt along Burgstrasse (with Renaissance and baroque houses at nos. 8, 9 and 11). Baaderberg runs off to the left into Theaterplatz, south of which, in Rathenauplatz, is the city museum.

Meissen is in Lössnitz wine country, and on either side of the city vineyards climb to the hills. In the city itself you can sample the local wines in the Winkelkrug at no. 13 Schlossberg or in the Probierstube der Sächsischen Winzergenossenschaft at no. 9 Bennoweg.

When the hotel ship *Prinzessin von Preussen* is moored on the Elbe below Meissen it makes a romantic venue for a meal, which ought also to incorporate a glass of at least one of the local wines. And in recommending its excellent cuisine, may I mention in particular Saxon potato soup. Though exquisitely fitted and decorated in the Jugendstil fashion, the *Prinzessin von Preussen* was built recently enough to incorporate on its prow statues of twin ladies (by the artist Serge D. Mangin), symbolizing the reunited halves of Germany. It moors at Meissen from November to March, and for the rest of the year cruises between Dresden and Hamburg.

On the way to the vast porcelain factory of Meissen, visit the church of St Martin, which still preserves a Romanesque chapel and has a painted pulpit of 1516. Then journey towards the Stadtpark near which is the vast factory and exhibition. The handful of porcelain manufacturers working in the Albrechts-burg in 1710 had become more than seven hundred by the mid eighteenth century, with the result that a new factory had to be found. (Today some thousand workers make porcelain in Meissen.) Meanwhile a tradition of fine work had already been established. The first great porcelain artist to create prized pieces here was Gregorius Höroldt, who was born in Vienna in 1696 and died here in 1755. Höroldt specialized in genre scenes of the type made popular in the paintings of

Watteau. Amongst his colours, cobalt blue was the finest, and it was he who devised the motif of crossed swords which became the emblem of Meissen porcelain.

Next, a pupil of the great Permoser, Joachim Kändler (who lived from 1706 to 1775) brought refined techniques of sculpture to the art of porcelain manufacture, and his was the era which saw Meissen potters develop the superb flower motifs which became renowned throughout Europe. A year before Kändler's death Count Marcolini took over the direction of the factory, remaining a dominant influence here till his death in 1814. Marcolini was helped by the biscuit master Johann Gottlieb Matthäi (1753–1832). The work created under the supervision of all these masters is displayed in the museum, and that of Kändler is particularly comprehensive.

Driving north-west from Meissen towards Leipzig along the F6 you come across treat after treat. First, a little way off to the left of the main road is Lommatzsch, a little town with a Gothic parish church (the early-sixteenth-century work of Peter von Pirna) with a pulpit of 1619 by P. Studtke and a high altar of 1714. At Lommatzsch the baroque Rathaus, built by Christoph Reissig in 1738 (and much rebuilt in 1908) today houses the local-history museum.

Further north-west along the F6 lies Oschatz. In the Neumarkt the ensemble of a fountain of 1589, a gabled Rathaus begun half a century earlier and blessed with a seven-storeyed clock-tower, and the twin spires of the fifteenth-century parish church of St Ägidien (St Giles) is irresistible. The town has other Renaissance houses. Yet none of these is the oldest building in Oschatz, this prize is carried off by the Gothic hall church which once belonged to a Franciscan monastery and dates from 1246.

Twelve kilometres later, at Luppa, make a five-minute diversion left to reach Wermsdorf, with its woodlands, lakes and the 316 m high Comberg. Here stands the superb Schloss Hubertusburg, by the baroque master J.-C. Knöffel. The spacious façade of the central pavilion was almost certainly designed by L. Mattielli. This is an historic spot in European history and recalls the triumph of will displayed by Frederick the Great, whose advance with a Prussian army into Saxony in 1756 launched the Seven Years' War. He was almost defeated. Repeatedly the Russians penetrated into Germany. They reached Frankfurt an der Oder and Berlin. Frederick, who contemplated suicide if he were defeated, was fortunate that his implacable enemy the Tsarina of Russia died on 5 January 1762, leaving her throne to one of his admirers. On 15 February 1763, in this Schloss, the Austrian Empress Maria Theresa was forced to sign the Peace of Hubertusburg, which ended the war.

There is more. Here too between 1872 and 1874 were imprisoned the socialists August Bebel and Wilhelm Liebknecht, and memorials of both are now displayed in the regional museum in the Schloss. And at Wermsdorf do not miss exploring the former hunting lodge, a three-winged Renaissance building of 1626 with gables and a staircase tower. A short way further south-west by way of a lake-strewn countryside, is Mutzschen, with its eighteenth-century houses and baroque Schloss of 1702.

Wurzen is a mere 16 km from Luppa, on the east bank of the River Mulde. Its brick cathedral, dedicated to Our Lady, was built between 1114 and 1515, partly in the Romanesque, partly in the Gothic style. One west tower is Romanesque, the other baroque. The local-history museum, at no. 2 Domgasse, is a Renaissance building of 1667 with an arcaded courtyard, and contains souvenirs of the satirical poet Joachim Ringelnatz (1883–1934), who was born here, at no. 14 Crostigal, into a family named Bötticher and baptized with his proper name, Hans. Wurzen's Marktplatz has gabled patrician houses and its late-Gothic Schloss dates from 1519.

Further east at Machern is a sixteenth-century Schloss surrounded by an eighteenth-century 'English' style park. Laid
out between 1782 and the end of the eighteenth century, its
artificial ruins include Ritterburg, a Pyramid and a Temple of
Hygeia. And 3 km to the north the region is watered by the
Lübschützer Lake. Finally, left of the main road at Brandis is a
baroque Schloss, designed by D. Schatz in 1728, with a rococo
hunting room.

Like Dresden, Leipzig began life as a village of Slav fisherfolk. Its name derives from the wooded countryside in which
they lived, for the ancient 'Lipzk' means town of lime trees. In
724 St Boniface brought Christianity to the region, and two
hundred years later the settlement was important enough for
the Emperor Heinrich I to build a defensive fortress here. His
successor Heinrich II gave both the fortress and the town in
fiefdom to the Bishops of Merseburg, who in turn ceded them
to Margrave Otto the Rich in the early twelfth century. Otto
surrounded the city with huge walls and promoted the fairs on
which the fame of Leipzig still prospers.

The city prospered then too. In 1409 her university was
founded. Ninety-eight years later the Emperor Maximilian set
up two more fairs (forbidding any others within a radius of
fifteen leagues), just in time to see Leipzig plunge into the
turmoil of the Protestant Reformation. Here, in 1519, the
young Martin Luther debated with and decisively won the
argument over the incompetent Catholic controversialist Eck.

Argument did not necessarily win the religious debates of
sixteenth-century Europe. Only in 1539 when Heinrich the Pious
declared his realms Protestant did the citizens of Leipzig dutifully
renounce Catholicism. Protestants were learned Christians, and
their patronage now helped to put Leipzig at the forefront of the
German literary world. The publishers of Leipzig were already
on their way to world renown, printing their first book here in
1481. (Today the city publishes 20 million books a year.)

Between 1723 and 1750 the citizens also employed Johann Sebastian Bach as cantor of the church of St Thomas. Musician or no, any visitor to Leipzig will wish to visit it. Once the chapel of a monastery, the present building is a late-Romanesque church constructed between 1212 and 1222. To this was added a fourteenth-century Gothic choir (with some Romanesque elements still peeping through) and a late-Gothic nave, the latter created by the architects Claus Roder and Conrad Pflüger between 1482 and 1496. An octagonal tower of 1502 tops the southern belfry and the lantern was added exactly two hundred years later by J.-G. Fuchs. Hieronymus Lotter was the architect responsible for the mid-sixteenth-century nave galleries.

As for Bach's bronze tomb, it is a modern work of 1950 by Nierade and Tiemann. (His 1909 statue in the graveyard is by Carl Seffner.) The church also boasts a crucifix designed in 1720 by C.-F. Löbelt and tombs whose dates range from the fifteenth to the seventeenth centuries. And in the church square the Bosehaus is the centre of Bach studies and hosts a permanent exhibition in his memory. Leipzig's Bach archive is in the baroque and rococo Gohliser Schlösschen of 1756, in Menckestrasse, north-west of the main railway station. In the Festsaal it is pleasing simply to contemplate, amidst the memorabilia of Johann Sebastian, the ceiling and wall paintings by A. F. Oeser.

The renown Bach brought to the city leads one to forget that this was also the home of the Gewandhaus orchestra, which Felix Mendelssohn-Bartholdy led to fame in 1843. The Leipzig Thomaner boys' choir, still famed and singing, predates Bach's arrival by nearly six hundred years. Mendelssohn founded Germany's first music conservatoire here, and one of its professors was Robert Schumann. During this musical efflorescence, Leipzig was the patrimony of Richard Wagner, born here in 1813. In 1878 his Ring cycle was performed at the Leipzig opera house.

Leipzig cherishes their shades. If you follow Klostergasse north from the church of St Thomas to Barfussgässchen and Kleine Fleischergasse, you find at no. 4 a coffee-house, Zum Kaffeebaum. This coffee-house, partly built in the fourteenth century, with a façade of 1725 by Ch. Döring, is adorned with a Turk drinking the beverage. Here Goethe, who regarded Leipzig as a Paris in miniature, relished the soup known as *Leipziger Allerlei* ('a Leipzig bit of everything'). Here too sat his literary enemy, the dramatist Friedrich August von Kotzebue, as well as Robert Schumann, followed in later years by Liszt and Richard Wagner. And near the Gohliser Schlösschen, at no. 42 Menckestrasse, is a little exhibition in memory of Schiller, for here in 1785, as well as parts of his *Don Carlos*, he wrote the 'Hymn to Joy' with which Beethoven ended his Ninth Symphony.

In the nineteenth century Leipzig became a political forcing house. Here flourished the social democrat August Bebel, who reached the city in 1860 and was soon joined by his friend and ally Wilhelm Liebknecht. Both of them were sentenced to two years' imprisonment in 1872 for refusing as deputies to vote for military credits. Here Rosa Luxemburg and Franz Mehring published blazing social democratic pamphlets and journalism.

The radical tradition continued. Leipzig was the birthplace of Carl Goerdeler, who, as Bürgermeister from 1930, was a leading member of the resistance to Adolf Hitler's Nazis until his execution in 1937. Hitler had used the city to mount the trial of those accused (almost certainly falsely) of setting fire to the German Reichstag in 1933.

During the Second World War the city suffered grievously from the assaults of the Allies, whose aircraft destroyed the city centre on 18 April 1945 and left a quarter of its buildings in ruins by the end of the war.

Much has been restored. In the Markt, a few paces northeast of the Thomaskirche, stands Leipzig's former town hall, a lovely gabled Renaissance building designed by Hieronymus Lotter in 1556 and today the home of the city's historical museum. Lotter was a leading citizen as well as an architect, and was six times elected Bürgermeister of the city. His Rathaus was enlivened after his death with a baroque onion dome (added in 1744) and arcades (added in 1909). This corner of Leipzig is charming. At no. 8 Markt stands Leipzig's oldest Renaissance house, the Barthels Hof, built by prosperous city merchants in 1523 and given a baroque aspect in 1750 at the expense of its owner, a merchant named Gottfried Barthel. Note its ancient corbels, and the upper floors which used to serve as warehouses. Today the Barthels Hof is a restaurant. On the north side of the Markt stands Lotter's 1555 Renaissance Alte Waage. Here too is the Königshaus, of 1610.

Further east in Naschmarkt is Leipzig's former stock exchange, the Alte Börse, built between 1678 and 1687 in the early baroque style by the Dresden architects Johann Georg Starcke and Ch. Richter. Near by is a Goethe memorial, designed by Seffner in 1903. The two young ladies on the plinth are Käthchen Schönkopf and Friedericke Oeser, with whom Goethe studied at Leipzig between 1765 and 1768. The plinth quotes his celebrated comparison of Leipzig and Paris.

Goethe is rightly remembered here. In the Mädlerpassage, opposite the former stock exchange, Auerbachskeller is the legendary tavern where Dr Faust is said to have given himself over to witchcraft. Mephistopheles is depicted seducing him to blasphemy in its wall paintings.

Hainstrasse runs north-west from the market square past the Barthels Hof to reach Brühl, where you should turn right to find, on the corner with Katharinenstrasse, Leipzig's finest baroque residence, the Romanushaus, which was built for and named after Bürgermeister Franz Romanus by Johann Gregor Fuchs, between 1701 and 1704. Elegant gables rise above its colossal pillars. Wide, grassy and tree-lined Katharinenstrasse, with its row of tall houses with delicate mansard roofs and dormer windows, is more like a park than a street. Here are three baroque façades, the best at no. 11, the Freges Haus with its sweet little tower, built by Johann Gregor Fuchs five years after his Romanushaus. The other two baroque façades front no. 19, created by G. Werner in the late 1740s, and no. 21, built by F. Seltendorff in 1749.

Turn into Sachsenplatz and back to Brühl to walk as far as Nikolaistrasse, named after the Nikolaikirche at its southernmost end. This hall church, founded in the Romanesque era, was enlarged in the late-Gothic style around 1520, while the interior was redone in the classical style between 1784 and 1797 by C. Dauthe and A. F. Oeser. Its mighty organ, built in 1859, has 6,314 pipes. Next to it stands the Nikolaischule of 1511, where Leibniz and Wagner were both pupils.

To find Leipzig's town hall of 1905, whose massive belfry (115 m high) preserves some fragments of the medieval fortress-tower which once stood here, you must walk south from the church of St Thomas to Burgplatz. This is a delightful monster of a building, decorated with symbolic carvings by Professor Georg Wrba of Dresden, who also created the Rathaus fountain, with its scenes from German fairy tales.

Even further south is the city gallery of fine arts, another monster building, this one of 1888–95 and in the high-Renaissance style. It once served as the Imperial Court of Justice, and the very sight of it must have terrified offenders. Inside hang some two thousand paintings ranging from the fifteenth to the twentieth centuries. Although many international masters are represented by superb works, I find myself drawn to the paintings of the great, often neglected Germans of the twentieth century: Marcks, Käthe Kollwitz, Franz Lehmbruck.

In the face of such buildings, one grows attracted to monstrosity, so that the elephants in Leipzig's zoo seem like old friends. Even the bizarrely huge monument to the battle of the nations (the *Völkerschlachtdenkmal*) near the exhibition halls seems somehow homely. Though built only between 1898 and 1913, this 91 m high monument commemorates the battle of Leipzig, those triumphant days between 16 and 19 October 1813 when the combined forces of Prussia, Austria, Sweden and Russia expelled the troops of Napoleon from Germany.

South-east of Leipzig are Romanesque churches, game-filled forests and complex ancient castles. The first of the castles appears at Colditz, along with the 1,700 hectare Colditz forest. Built around 1590, part-Gothic, part-Renaissance, Colditz Schloss bulkily dominates the right bank of the River Mulde. Since it nowadays serves as a hospital, only the sick and the staff are allowed through its monumental doorway (by Andreas Walther). The former town hall of Colditz, with its vaulted gables, was built between 1538 and 1631, burnt down by the Swedes in 1637 and restored in the Renaissance style in the 1650s.

Ten kilometres south-west, the parish church of St Nicholas at Geithain has a Romanesque apse, with a superb Romanesque doorway, to which was added, in the sixteenth century, a Gothic nave. In 1595 A. Schilling came from Freiburg to paint its coffered ceiling.

Two kilometres further on, Rochlitz is dominated by its fifteenth- and sixteenth-century Schloss, which has a delicately traceried Gothic chapel of 1482. Parts of this romantically irregular Schloss, which was founded in the twelfth century, date back to the thirteenth. In the town itself stands the Gothic hall church of St Kunigund. Two paintings, probably by Dürer, illustrate the sufferings of St Peter and the Virgin Mary with forty intercessors. Its sculpted wooden reredos, carved in 1513, depicts St Kunigund, who died in 1033, and her husband the Emperor Heinrich II, flanked by St Anne and the Apostle Thomas. Both Kunigund and Heinrich were canonized after their deaths. Committed, as the phrase goes, solely to their heavenly Lord, they had agreed to a celibate marriage, but Kunigund is said to have been accused by Heinrich of dallying with other men. To prove her innocence, she walked over red-hot ploughshares without being hurt. The bodies of Kunigund and Heinrich lie in Bamberg cathedral, but bits of them have been enshrined in the altar here.

Wechselburg, 8 km further south-east, has a superb Romanesque basilica which once belonged to an Augustinian abbey. Built between 1160 and 1180, its interior was transformed in part in the fifteenth and seventeenth centuries. Its porch has Romanesque capitals. Amongst the splendid sculptures inside this church is a pulpit carved with Christ and his four evangelists, and the tomb of the founders (Dedo and Mechthild de Groitzsch, who died in the 1190s). An early-thirteenth-century ensemble of sculptures on the contemporary rood-screen portrays the Triumph of the Cross. Almost lifesize statues depict Abraham on a lion and Melchizedek borne by a dragon. In line with medieval interpretations of Holy Scripture, the prophets Daniel and Isaiah put in their expected appearance, along with King David and King Solomon.

To complete a round tour of these castles and return to Leipzig, I suggest you drive south-west from Wechselburg to Rochsburg, where, amidst gentle trees and hills, a late-twelfth-century fortress – which Arnold of Westphalia rebuilt in the 1470s and his successors restored after a fire of 1547 – rises above the River Mulde. In part today it is a youth hostel, and in part a museum, with memorials of Heinrich Heine as well as rooms decked out in the baroque, rococo, Empire and Biedermeier styles.

On the way back to Leipzig, drive through fertile agricultural land to visit Kohren-Sahlis. Here (a couple of kilometres west of the town) Burg Gnandstein, Saxony's sole unaltered Romanesque Schloss, dwarfs a black and white half-timbered house. Built in the tenth century to protect the trading route between

Leipzig and Prague, the Schloss shelters two interior courtyards, the Romanesque keep rises to 35 m, the powerful walls
hide a late-fifteenth-century chapel, with coffered vaults and
an altar of 1503 by Peter Breuer. In the little town itself is a
ceramic museum, and here also stands the late-Romanesque
basilica of St Gangolf, built around 1190. An 'English' park
graces the suburb of Rüdingsdorf, with an orangery frescoed
in 1838 by Moritz von Schwind and his pupil Leopold Schultz,
depicting the tale of Amor and Psyche.

But it is surely time for refreshment, perhaps in Leipzig's
Auerbachskeller. One of its frescos recalls Goethe's masterpiece
by depicting an indecorous young woman leading Faust out of
the Keller at Mephistopheles' command. In the Auerbachskeller
I sometimes think that is a fate worth losing one's soul for.

3

THE CITIES AND FORESTS OF THURINGIA

I first arrived at Erfurt after dark, and would recommend anyone to try to do the same. Four of us stood entranced in the cobbled Domhügel, which is shaped like half a circle. Here there is a daily market (save on Mondays) and the last of the stallholders were closing down. High above, on a cliff above the straight side of the Platz, the cathedral and the church of St Severin were illuminated, the former with its 26 m high Gothic apse, the latter with three slender spires.

Erfurt, over 1,250 years old, was founded by the English missionary St Boniface in 742. Boniface clearly chose the spot for a bishopric because of its position as a centre of communications, and for centuries the city remained under ecclesiastical domination, governed by the Archbishop-Electors of Mainz (of which Boniface himself had been bishop). In consequence Erfurt became and has remained a city of churches, and on my first arrival I was standing at its religious heart. The city was walled in 1142, and in 1289 became the capital of the Holy Roman Empire (a privilege it lost a year later when the Emperor Rudolph von Habsburg moved his court elsewhere).

Street plans dub the Domhügel the Domplatz, but my usage corresponds to the placards on the walls. Above the Domhügel, seventy or so monumental steps climb to the superb ensemble of the cathedral and St Severin's church. The former is an enthralling mix of styles. Of the Romanesque basilica, which was begun in 1154 and consecrated in 1253, there remain the lower parts of the towers, part of the nave, and the cloisters (which are partly Romanesque, partly Gothic in style). Then, in the early fourteenth century, the hill on which the cathedral stands was artificially extended westwards to allow the building of the massive, flamboyant Gothic choir between 1349 and 1373. Joining this choir can still be found the former Romanesque sanctuary, to which has been added Gothic vaulting. The Gothic architects were given a new opportunity to display their skills when the Romanesque nave collapsed in 1452. By 1465 most of it had been replaced with the present flamboyant Gothic building and its two mighty aisles.

Although Erfurt cathedral was severely damaged during the 1939–45 war, it has been carefully restored and many of its treasures returned, including the Gloriosa, a bell weighing more than eleven tonnes. Its magnificent triangular entrance has two porches, each carrying a dozen sculptures carved around 1320. One group depicts the twelve apostles, the other the wise and foolish virgins. In the choir are fifteen stained-glass windows of 1370 to 1420, depicting in the sinuous late-Gothic style not only scenes from the Old and New Testaments but also from the daily life of the people of Erfurt. The lavishly carved wooden choir-stalls date from the mid fourteenth century, while the high altar is a baroque delight of 1697 with an eighteenth-century painting of the *Adoration of the Magi* by J.-S. Beck. Below the east end of the choir is a two-aisled crypt, built in 1353.

Other treats in Erfurt cathedral include its altars and tombs. St Catherine and St Barbara are here, painted by Lucas Cranach the Elder. In the south transept is a Romanesque altar of 1160 with a portrait of the enthroned Virgin Mary, Christ and ten saints (including two bishops of Erfurt, Adolar and Eoban). In this transept is also what many suppose to be a portrait of the twelfth-century founder of the cathedral, a statue of a bearded man named Wolfram, who carries a candelabrum and is oddly accompanied by carved cats and monkeys. In the north transept is a lovely triptych of around 1460 which depicts the Virgin Mary with a unicorn, a medieval image symbolizing virginity. And the finest tomb in the whole cathedral is that of Prior Henning Goden (in the passage between the choir and the nave), who died in 1521 and is here celebrated by the craftsmen from the great workshop of Hans Vischer of Nuremberg.

After visiting the cathedral treasury, whose works of art range from the middle ages to the baroque era, cross to the church of St Severin, which once belonged to the Augustinian canons of Erfurt. Begun in 1280, to replace a Romanesque church, this hall church with its five aisles was basically finished by the mid fourteenth century, but the huge roof was added in two successive bursts of building, around 1400 and in the early 1470s. St Severin, who was bishop of Erfurt, is sculpted on the south doorway (a carving of 1365) and also lies here in a sarcophagus of 1365 on which is sculpted not only the saint himself but also his wife and daughter. How was a medieval bishop married? The carvings on the sarcophagus reveal how. Severin, living placidly in Ravenna, had no intention of becoming a bishop, until a dove, representing the Holy Spirit, inconveniently landed on his head and he was forced by this sign to become a prince of the church. Look out also for the font, sculpted in 1467, and for an alabaster relief of St Michael of 1467.

North-west of these two magnificent buildings stands the Peterstor, a baroque gateway of 1673 which was part of the city's fortifications. Here are the remains of the former citadel (begun in 1664, finished in 1869) and the former Benedictine monastery church of St Peter, which was built in the mid twelfth century and smashed to pieces by French artillery in 1813.

Erfurt is a city of winding, often narrow, cobbled streets with overhanging, sometimes half-timbered, houses, painted pink, green, yellow, orange and white. One of these streets, the pedestrianized Marktstrasse, dignified by a fine late-seventeenth-century house (no. 21) runs from Domhügel eastwards towards the late-Gothic, double-aisled church of All Saints' (the Aller-heiligenkirche), built in the early fourteenth century. Its tower, rising to 53 m, dates from 1487. This ancient part of Erfurt is known as the Steinerne Chronik (its finest house, I think, is at no. 11 Allerheiligenstrasse, a Gothic treat of 1459 with an oriel window).

Shortly after All Saints' church, Marktstrasse reaches Fisch-markt, in which stands a statue of Roland set up in 1591. The finest Renaissance houses of Fischmarkt are both gabled. At the pinnacle of the richly ornamented Haus zum Breiten Herd, which was built in 1584, a flamboyant knight brandishes a standard. The Haus zum Roten Ochsen, likewise gabled, has a merry frieze above its ornate Renaissance porch, though its gentle pale yellow façade is milder than the strident red of its neighbour.

These delights are almost overpowered by the Gothic town hall, built in the early 1870s, which was frescoed inside in the 1880s and 1890s by Peter Jansen of Düsseldorf and Eduard Kämpffer of Munich. The themes are classically romantic: the tales of Tannhäuser, the Count of Gleichen, Faust, Alexander the Great, Boniface, St Elisabeth of Hungary (Landgravine of Thuringia in the early thirteenth century), Henry the Lion, the emperors Frederick Barbarossa and Rudolph von Habsburg; the tumultuous years of the Reformation, the victorious entry into Erfurt of Johann-Philipp von Schönborn in 1664, a eulogy of the Prussians and the supposedly glorious resistance of the citizens to Napoleon in 1806.

Walk on to reach the river and the shopkeepers' bridge (the Krämerbrücke). This is Erfurt's Ponte Vecchio. It first spanned the water in 1133, was rebuilt in stone in the mid fourteenth century and supports thirty-four houses. It also curves bizarrely, and is even more picturesque when you look up at it from the river's bank. At the other end in Weinige Markt you can see the square white tower of the church of St Giles (the Ägidienkirche), built in the mid fourteenth century. Since the Ägidienkirche guards the Krämer bridge spiritually, it is what the Germans dub a *Brückenkopfkirche*.

To the left along Schottenstrasse stands the church of St James. Founded by Irish monks (and thus known, in the curious German fashion, as the Schottenkirche), this twelfth-century Romanesque basilica boasts a Gothic choir of 1480 and a baroque western façade added between 1711 and 1729.

On this side of the river in this city of churches there are four others which deserve seeking out. South of the Grosses Hospital stands the Kaufmannskirche, the Church of the Merchants, almost certainly on the site of the first church founded here by St Boniface, though itself mostly built in the early fourteenth century. Further south, the Ursulines built their collegiate church in the thirteenth century. It still displays a superb Gothic Pietà of 1325.

The church of St Lorenz is a few paces south-west from here. Built in the thirteenth and fourteenth centuries, it houses a reredos (made in Lübeck) of 1448, and family tree of the Blessed Virgin of 1521 by Peter von Mainz. Opposite this church is the former Jesuit college, the present building dating from 1737, save for its doorway of 1612.

Finally, still further to the south-west, rises the Barfüsserkirche, an early-fourteenth-century, three-aisled Gothic basilica built for the Franciscans, its choir dedicated in 1316. Much damaged in 1945, it none the less displays a fine collection of religious treasures: early-thirteenth-century stained glass in the choir, depicting the life and Passion of Jesus as well as scenes from the life of St Francis of Assisi; a flamboyant

Gothic high altar of 1446, its sculptors Hans von Schmalkalden and Jakob von Leipzig, its painter Michael von Wiespach; and a triptych of the Crucifixion donated by the Dyers' Guild (some of whose members are portrayed here) in 1460.

In the middle ages Erfurt became noted for its learning. Its university, founded in 1392, was, after that of Cologne, the oldest of the former German empire. The King of Prussia closed it down in 1816. One of Erfurt's medieval masters was the mystic Johannes Eckhart, who was born at nearby Gotha around 1260. After joining the Erfurt Dominicans as a novice, Meister Eckhart gained his master's degree in Paris. On his return to Erfurt in 1303 he became provincial of the order, as well as inspiring a popular mystical movement throughout Germany. Soon he was involved in mediating between the King of France and Pope Boniface VIII. In 1320 Eckhart became a professor at the University of Cologne. But his star now began to wane. Meister Eckhart's tracts were written not in Latin but in German and, perhaps because of this, orthodox theologians grew to distrust him. In consequence, in 1326 he was accused of heresy and tried before the Archbishop of Cologne. Three years later he was summoned to Avignon, before Pope John XXII, who condemned seventeen of his propositions as heretical.

The former Dominican abbey church in which he worshipped still rises proudly, in Predigerstrasse, opposite the Gothic Paulus tower of 1465. The street is called after the colloquial name of the church, the Predigerkirche. This is a tall three-aisled basilica built and lavishly decorated in the fourteenth century. Its rood screen dates from 1410. Another of its masterpieces is a mid-fourteenth-century painting of the Crucifixion in which several contemporary patricians of Erfurt appear. From the same era dates a sculpted Madonna and Child. The fine double-winged reredos by Linhart Koenbergk was carved out of wood and painted in 1492, while the most celebrated tomb here – that of Gottschalk Legat – was chiselled in 1425 and signed simply 'i'.

Godliness, good learning and religious controversy did not disappear from Erfurt after Meister Eckhart's condemnation. In 1501 the young Martin Luther enrolled at its university. Luther was to join the Erfurt Augustinians four years later. The Augustinians were rich enough to own three of the city's major churches. The finest is St Severin, which we have already seen. A second, now known as the Reglerkirche, still stands just north of the main railway station. Its doorway and one of its towers are Romanesque, and inside is a winged reredos which Luther must have known, painted by a Rhineland master around 1450 and depicting Jesus crowned with thorns and beaten, as well as Pentecost and the Ascension.

The church that Luther knew best, however, was the Augustinerkirche, within the northern fortifications of the city (close by two towers, the Nikolaiturm of 1360, the late-Gothic Johannisturm, and the Renaissance commandery, or Komturhof, of 1570). This three-aisled basilica dates from the late thirteenth and early fourteenth centuries. Early-sixteenth-century stained-glass windows depict the life of St Augustine, whose teachings on salvation enormously influenced Luther himself. To the south are the Gothic cloister and abbey buildings.

Luther came here in 1505, and his cell is now a place of Protestant pilgrimage. Here he became a monk in 1506, then a priest, and for a time he taught patristic texts at Erfurt, before moving on to Wittenberg in 1511. Luther's attacks on the clerical corruption of his epoch, which triggered the Reformation, were matched at Erfurt by those of his contemporaries Ulrich von Hutten and Eobanus Hessus. The university was by now a centre of humanism, and when Luther himself was put under an imperial ban, his followers here were also dubbed heretics. Nevertheless, radicals still fought against their lawful rulers, and during the Peasants' Revolt of 1525 the insurgents held the city for several months.

Radical religion flourished here even before Luther's time. Erfurt possesses a rare copy of the Bible translated into Thuringian which, done in 1428, predates Luther's translation by a hundred years. It is today displayed in the Amploniana, which was founded in 1412 and houses a library of medieval manuscripts virtually unmatched in the country, some 4,000 texts, amongst them a prized example of a Carolingian English–Latin dictionary.

This city is extremely well served by its museums. The Angermuseum, housed in the Packhof of 1705, not only displays prehistoric finds from the region but also has an exhibition devoted to the history of the region, medieval sculptures and paintings, and nineteenth- and twentieth-century works of art (including Karl Spitzweg's entertaining paintings and the works of Lyonel Feininger, Liebermann, Slevogt and Corinth). Here too is an exhibition of fourteenth- and fifteenth-century German sculpture. Another pleasing exhibition, devoted to natural history, is housed in the lovely, late-Renaissance Haus zum Stockfisch; and in the Grosses Hospital, founded in 1358, is the city's folklore museum.

By the end of the fifteenth century the city's fortunes had begun to decline. Part of her prosperity depended on the dye from a plant cultivated in profusion here (*Isatis tinctoria*, or woad), but by now its use was gradually being supplanted by indigo brought from India and central America. The seventeenth century saw more disasters, in particular the capture of the city by Gustavus Adolphus's troops during the Thirty Years' War, and prosperity returned only in the 1660s, when Erfurt came under the suzerainty of the new and liberal-minded Archbishop-Elector of Mainz, Johann-Philipp von Schönborn. Happily, the value of woad having declined, a new horticultural inspiration developed in Erfurt under the aegis of Christian Reichart, who in the 1750s produced a series of volumes detailing new methods of cultivating plants, fruit and vegetables, and Erfurt has remained renowned since then for its seeds.

Well worth while is a visit (best by car, along the road towards Gotha) to the international horticultural exhibition (Internationale Gartenbauausstellung), which was set out in the 1960s on the hillside where the fortress of Cyriaksburg once rose. Here are thirteen exhibition halls, a museum of horticulture outlining its development from the Renaissance to the present day, restaurants and a temporary exhibition tower.

Erfurt, which became part of Prussia in 1802, played a leading part in the often cataclysmic political events of the nineteenth and twentieth centuries. In 1806 Napoleon Bonaparte's troops occupied the city, which remained under the emperor's rule till 1814. Here, in 1806, took place his celebrated meeting with Tsar Alexander I, together with the Kings of Bavaria, Saxony, Westphalia and Württemberg. Napoleon had an eye for a fine building, and at Erfurt he set up his headquarters in the Statthalterei on the corner of Meister Eckhart Strasse and Marstall Strasse. Once the home of the governor of Mainz, this is a splendid building of 1720, built in the Austrian baroque style by Maximilian von Welsch.

At Erfurt, in 1892, was held the congress of the revolutionary social democratic party, presided over by Bebel and Liebknecht. (At nos. 15 and 16 Futterstrasse is a house of 1831 with a classical façade, today a museum devoted to this congress.) The city remained part of Prussia till the end of the Second World War. And in 1970 it was the venue for a decisive meeting, the first ever between the head of the Federal Republic and the head of the former GDR, when Willi Stoph welcomed the West German chancellor Willy Brandt to the city.

Clearly much of this secular history is celebrated here. A small (though much appreciated) aspect of the past can be savoured while you eat in the 1538 hostelry Zur Hohen Lilie, in the cathedral square, for here Gustavus Adolphus of Sweden once stayed during the Thirty Years' War.

But Erfurt still seems to me predominantly a city of splendid churches. Whichever way you walk from Domhügel you reach some of them. South-west in Brühlerstrasse across Mainzerhof Platz rises the early-fourteenth-century tower of the church of St Martin, which began as an early Gothic building but was later partly rebuilt, first in the Gothic fashion of 1480 and then in the baroque style of 1755. Cross Domplatz (noting at no. 31 a Renaissance house of 1537) and turn left along Andreasstrasse to find the Gothic church of St Andreas (in part rebuilt in 1868) with a bas-relief of 1455 depicting the mocking of Christ.

You can of course readily escape this mass of religious art, perhaps by visiting the Thuringian zoo, which was set up on the hill known as the Roter Berg in 1958 and shelters some 900 animals, including rare cockatoos and monkeys, or else the city aquarium (again on the north side of Erfurt, in Nettelbeck-ufer), which has more than a thousand tropical and indigenous ornamental fish. Hikers make for the Steigerwald, to the south of the city past its sports stadium, where there are some twenty marked walks through the woods.

Erfurt is the finest place to begin a tour of the western part of the Thuringian forest, a tour rendered all the more spectacu-lar by the Rennsteig, an ancient road running for 168 km along the crest of the Thuringian forest and the Schiefergebirge mountains. The letter R, painted on tree trunks, along with notices announcing the 'Hohenweg des Thüringer Waldes', mark this path, which stretches eastwards from Hörschel on the River Werra to Blankenstein on the River Saale. A succes-sion of grasslands and forests, with rare alpine plants including wild orchids has prompted the Germans to declare the whole region a protected natural park.

In winter the snows covering the Rennsteig are welcomed by long-distance skiers, and the region naturally includes numerous winter-sports centres. Amongst these Oberhof is the most important in eastern Germany. Another is Lauscha, set between steep slopes on a stream of the same name. Here, in 1597, Hans Greiner from Swabia and Christoph Müller from Bohemia set up the first glassworks in the region, and today the town is the centre of the Thuringian glass-blowing industry, whose main product is Christmas tree decorations. Lauscha's Museum of the Glassmakers' Art is at no. 10 Oberlandstrasse.

In past times the Rennsteig served as a natural border between the Franks and the Thuringians, and hikers come across border stones planted by the rulers of these peoples. An annual May event is the 45 km run, entered by several thousands, from Neuhaus am Rennweg to Schmiedefeld am Rennsteig. The 916 m high crest of the Great Inselberg also rises above the Thuringian forest in this region, and is approached by countless paths.

To explore these and other delights, take the F4 south from Erfurt towards Arnstadt. At Ichterhausen you discover a Romanesque basilica, partially rebuilt in the eighteenth century, which once belonged to a Cistercian convent. Three kilometres north from here Schloss Molsdorf, nowadays a cultural centre, was built as a moated fortress in the fourteenth century and transformed into a baroque and rococo palace by Gottfried Heinrich Krohne and his colleagues in the mid eighteenth century. The Schloss is still moated; its restful park was laid out in 1826; and today, where the princes of Gotha disported themselves, you can visit its museum and eat in its restaurant.

Five kilometres from Ichterhausen is Arnstadt, a city founded in 704 and for many years the principal residence of the Counts of Schwarzburg, their fame eclipsed by that of Johann Sebastian Bach, who in 1703, at the age of eighteen, became organist at the church which is now called in his memory the

Bachkirche. Bach had initially been approached simply to perform some virtuoso concerts demonstrating the organ which the splendid Thuringian organ-builder Johann Friedrich Wender had just finished for the church. So superb was his performance that he was instantly offered the post of organist, at an annual salary of 84 florins and 6 Gröschen. It was from here that he made his celebrated journey, on foot, to Lübeck and back – some 800 km all told – to meet and learn from the celebrated organist of the Marienkirche there, Dietrich Buxtehude.

Bach was well-connected at Arnstadt. One of his ancestors, Gaspard Bach, had been in charge of the watchtower here in the 1620s. His great-uncle Heinrich and his uncle Johann-Christoph were organists here. And here Johann Sebastian married his cousin, the daughter of Johann-Michael Bach. The Bach Museum is at no. 2a Bahnhofstrasse; and even more evocative in my view is the local cemetery, in which are buried twenty-four members of the Bach family.

The Bachkirche had been rebuilt in the baroque style in 1683 after a fire had burned down the previous Gothic one. A statue of the composer, sculpted by Bernd Göbel in 1985, stands in front of it. The church shades the Marktplatz, whose town hall was built in the Dutch Renaissance style by Christoph Junghans in the early 1580s. This Rathaus boasts a couple of voluted gables. Its niches house statues of the Blessed Virgin Mary, Jesus and a bishop earlier in date than the present building, sculpted around 1375. Two other churches grace the town. The Oberkirche was built for the Franciscans in the Gothic era and vaulted in 1725. Its furnishings include the early-seventeenth-century font, altar and pulpit by Burkhard Röhl, and a votive painting of 1554 by Frans Floris.

As for the Liebfrauenkirche, this exceptionally fine, double-towered hall church, displaying the transition from Romanesque to Gothic, dates from 1180 to 1330, with a choir finished around 1300. Inside is a 1498, late-Gothic and winged reredos of the Coronation of the Virgin, as well as tombs by the Prague Parler family (for Günther XXV von Schwarzburg and his wife Elisabeth, who died in 1368 and 1381) in the Schwarzenburg mausoleum. The Parlers were also probably responsible for the tomb of Theoderich von Witzleben, who died in 1376.

The rococo salons of the Neues Schloss at Arnstadt, a baroque building of 1728–32, contain an attractive exhibition of dolls displaying life at every level of society in early-eighteenth-century Thuringia, sixteenth-century Brussels tapestries, rococo sculpture, and above all porcelain from Saxony, China and Thuringia itself. Its *chef d'oeuvre* is the puppet town 'Mon Plaisir', which incorporates more than 400 baroque mannikins housed in twenty-six houses with eighty-four rooms. It was made by craftsmen and ladies-in-waiting working for Augusta Dorothea von Schwarzburg-Arnstadt, who passionately wished to preserve the memory of the daily lives of her subjects.

A diversion of 10 km to the north-west reaches three stunning ruined fortresses, known as the Drei Gleichen ('The Three Equals'), built to guard the trade routes of the region. On its 365 m conical hill, Schloss Gleichen, built in the eleventh century and rebuilt in the fourteenth, has been a ruin since the early seventeenth. In its keep is an exhibition detailing the history of the Drei Gleichen. The most romantic of the tales connected with Schloss Gleichen recounts that in 1228 the crusader Count Ernst III was captured by the Turks who sold him as a slave to a sultan. Fortunately, the sultan's exquisite daughter Melechsala fell in love with the Thuringian and helped him to escape. Count Ernst was already married, but the Pope granted him permission to take Melechsala as his second wife provided he loved her merely as a sister – which, possibly, he did.

The Wachsenburg, on its 420 m hill (from which you can

see as far as the Wartburg at Eisenach), is even older, parts of its fallen self twelfth-century Romanesque, while the rest is Gothic and seventeenth century. Its well of 1651 is 93 m deep. Today this restored ruin has been transformed into a hotel and restaurant. This is the only one of the Drei Gleichen that you can drive to; the rest can be approached solely on foot. Southwest of this Schloss are the ruins of the oldest of the three, the Mühlburg, rising on a 360 m hill; it was begun in 704, though most of the buildings date from the thirteenth century.

The F4 runs south along the Ilm valley from Arnstadt through Plaue, parts of whose Gothic fortress and keep still stand guard, to reach, after 20 km, Ilmenau, a town affectionately remembered by Goethe (hence the Goethe museum in the Amtshaus, where he lived from 1776 as a civil servant promoting the town's industries on behalf of Saxony-Weimar). Its Renaissance parish church was in part rebuilt by the baroque master G.-H. Krohne, who was responsible for the impressive pulpit. Two hours away to the south is Kickelhahn, whose panoramic view Goethe eulogized in his letters to Charlotte von Stein. Here is the Goethehäuschen, which he made memorable in his poem 'Über allen Gipfeln/ist Ruh'.

> Over every peak is repose.
> You feel that in the trees
> Is scarcely the stir of a breeze.
> In the forest quiet birds are nesting.
> Wait, for you too soon
> Will be resting as they are.

Goethe also loved a hunting lodge here, staying there for the last time in 1831. Fittingly, it is now a museum dedicated to the theme 'Goethe and Thuringia'.

For more memories of Goethe, continue along the F4 from Ilmenau to the winter-sports resort of Stützerbach. Between the two towns hikers can follow an 18 km route known as 'Auf Goethes Spuren' ('On Goethe's Traces') signposted with the letter 'G'. At Stützerbach Goethe would stay in the baroque house at no. 18 Sebastian-Kneipp-Strasse, transformed into a Goethe and glass museum (for part of his duties included supervising the local glassworks). Three kilometres further on turn right and follow the Rennsteig route as far as the F247, where you turn right for the winter-sports centre of Oberhof, whose massive Interhotel was built by Yugoslav architects in 1969.

If instead of turning right you turn left on reaching the F247 you shortly reach Zella-Mehlis. Fortresses proliferate in this region: that to the west at Schwarza is moated and parts date as far back as the thirteenth century; so does the former fortress of the Knights of St John further on at Kühndorf. Suhl, 6 km south of Zella-Mehlis, boasts among its half-timbered houses one by the riverside which once belonged to the Knights of Malta, as well as two fine churches: the Gothic parish church with a rococo pulpit; and the baroque Kreuzkirche, with its sumptuously decorated altar and its baroque organ and pulpit. The suburb of Suhl-Heinrichs has a church dedicated to St Ulrich with late-fifteenth-century frescos. Here the Rathaus of 1657 rises from a lower storey built in 1551. And the town is surrounded by five mountain peaks, including Thuringia's highest, the Grosser Beerberg.

A statue of an armourer honing a sword tops the fountain in the Marktplatz at Suhl. The mining and processing of iron brought prosperity to this region of eastern Germany. Today Suhl thrives on making, not swords, but mopeds, precision instruments and food processors. Its craftsmen used to make beautifully ornamented firearms, and many are displayed in the town's oldest building, the exquisite Malzhaus.

Drive on west through the hamlet of Dietzenhausen with its half-timbered houses to Rohr, where the parish church dates from the Carolingian era and, though much-restored in the sixteenth and seventeenth centuries, retains its ninth-century Carolingian crypt, possibly the oldest surviving building in Thuringia. Five kilometres further west is the city of Meiningen on the River Werra, the capital of the Dukes of Saxony-Meiningen from 1680 to 1918. Their most useful scion was Duke Georg II, who, married to a celebrated actress of the day, devoted himself between 1874 and 1890 to reviving Thuringian theatre here, building up a company which toured the capitals of Europe. The present handsome theatre at Meiningen, resembling a Greek temple, which stands in the 'English-style' Goethepark (with its artistic 'ruins' and its monuments to Brahms and Reger), was built after his death in 1908. This garden, its lakes, streams and cascades, was designed by Christian Zoecher in the 1780s.

Although the neo-Gothic parish church of Meiningen dates from 1889, it shelters a Madonna and Child of 1430. As for the city museums, they are housed in the splendid stuccoed rooms of the winged, baroque Schloss Elisabethenburg, which was built by Samuel Rust in the decade after 1682. Since Johann-Ludwig Bach (Johann Sebastian's cousin) taught music to the Princes of Meiningen from 1701 to 1731, since Richard Wagner was a crony of Duke Georg II, since Hans von Bülow premiered several of Brahms's works here, and since Max Reger directed the Meiningen orchestra between 1911 and 1914, the Staatliches Museum in the Schloss is a mecca for music-lovers. It also encompasses Georg II's study and his theatrical sketches (as well as storing more than 11,000 theatre programmes). Here too is the Max Reger archive. In the face of such riches, one might be pardoned for neglecting the works by Carlo Cignani, J.-H. Tischbein, the Spaniard José de Ribera and Lucas Cranach the Younger.

A curiosity, 4 km north along the F19, is the eleventh-century Schloss at Walldorf, which was transformed into a

Renaissance church, preserving the Romanesque keep as its west tower. Wasungen, 7 km further on, is a village with sixteenth- and seventeenth-century half-timbered houses. Here the Renaissance parish church of 1596 has a late-Gothic tower.

Shortly afterwards, at Niederschmalkalden, turn right to reach the ironmongery centre of eastern Germany, Schmalkalden, famed above all for the Protestant Schmalkaldic League which was set up here on 31 December 1536, and helped to ensure the survival of the Reformation. This alliance was forged in the early-fifteenth-century Gothic town hall, uniting German Protestants in self-defence against the Holy Roman Emperor Charles V. For these negotiations Luther stayed in a green and white half-timbered house in what is now called Lutherplatz. The building dates from 1520, though its decoration is late seventeenth century. Luther was suffering from the stone as well as from the dampness of the sheets in some of the inns he slept in on the way to Schmalkalden; but he declared that here he ate the best trout in the world.

The Lutherhaus is but one of many half-timbered buildings in Schmalkalden. The town hall, rebuilt in 1903, rises in the Altmarkt, a fresco in the vestibule depicting Schmalkalden in the sixteenth century. Apart from several lovely Renaissance houses, Schmalkalden's chief treasure is the parish church of St Georg, Romanesque in origin but with some ravishing Gothic vaulting and an altar of the Holy Family carved around 1520. The towers remain sturdily Romanesque; the Gothic choir backs on to the Altmarkt, where fruit and vegetable stalls are set up under colourful umbrellas.

One of the finest half-timbered Renaissance houses in Schmalkalden, the 1553 Hessenhof (at no. 5 Neumarkt), has preserved from an earlier self a cycle of Romanesque frescos dating from the mid thirteenth century. They depict episodes from *Iwein*, a poem written by Hartmann von Aue. These are the oldest frescos illustrating a secular theme in Germany.

Other frescos, some by the Dutchman W. Vernukken, adorn the stuccoed rooms of the Renaissance Schloss Wilhelmsburg, which was built in the late sixteenth century for Landgrave Wilhelm IV von Hesse-Cassel and finished for his son Moritz in 1627. Schloss Wilhelmsburg, which rises above the steep roofs of the town to the east, is an entirely beguiling ensemble of noble rooms, stables, a pottery, a bakery, a chapel, a brewery and a towered redoubt. It lies in terraced gardens cooled by fountains. Today the ornate doorway of this splendid gabled building opens into stuccoed rooms which house the local-history museum.

Leave Schmalkalden in the north-easterly direction and turn left at Seligenthal to drive through the winter-sports centre of Trusetal and reach the thermal resort of Bad Liebenstein, a spa whose modern baths attract sixteen thousand visitors annually, who can also admire its ruined Gothic fortress, which stands on the 464 m high Schlossberg. Another spa, Bad Salzungen, is a mere 11 km further west, its waters enriched with the greatest percentage of salt (27 per cent) of any in Germany. Here are a couple of Gothic churches and some seventeenth-century houses, though a fire in the next century took away most of their companions.

This tour reaches Eisenach, 16 km to the north, by way of Wilhemstal, with a baroque Schloss of 1719 which G.-H. Krohne enlarged in 1740 and later generations transformed in the neoclassical mode. At Eisenach, where an early-thirteenth-century bridge spans the Werra, Martin Luther's mother, Margarethe Lindemann, was born. And on 21 March 1685, Maria Elisabetha Lämmerhirt, wife of Ambrosius Bach, gave birth here to their son Johann Sebastian. Long before their time the Landgraves of Thuringia had fortified the Wartburg and patronized the great minnesingers of medieval Germany: Walther von der Vogelweide, Albrecht von Halberstadt, Harbord von Fritzlar, Heinrich von Veldeke and Wolfram von Eschenbach, who wrote most of his *Parzifal* here.

This was the city in which Elisabeth of Hungary spent her youth, from 1211 when she was only four years old and already betrothed to her future husband, Ludwig IV of Thuringia. Whenever this devout woman entered church, she would remove her bejewelled crown, since she could not bear to be so adorned when contemplating Jesus with his crown of thorns. Whenever her husband was away she exchanged the apparel of the court for coarse, undyed cloth. During the famine of 1225 she gave away her whole crop of corn. Conscious that the infirm were unable to climb up to her Schloss, she built a hospital for them at the foot of the rock; here she was often seen cooking for them and making their beds. Small wonder that Elisabeth was canonized in 1235, a mere four years after her death.

The road from Meiningen enters Eisenach from the south and joins Wartburgallee, where you turn sharp left to visit the Wartburg itself. A complex Schloss, well restored in the nineteenth century and the 1950s, it is built around two courtyards, the first surrounded by fifteenth- and sixteenth-century half-timbered buildings, the second incorporating the finest part of the Wartburg, the Palas. Built for Landgrave Ludwig III between 1190 and 1220, and given a further storey in the mid thirteenth century, the Palas has a Romanesque knights' hall (the Rittersaal), a pillared dining hall (the Speisesaal), and Elisabeth's bower (the Kemenate), which is decorated with mosaics of 1906. The origins of the entrance hall date back to the twelfth century. A fine staircase, lovely ceilings and sixteenth-century tapestries add to the ambience. The keep dates from 1859 and the 'women's hall' from 1860.

Virtually every part of this Schloss incorporates architecture and furniture much older than its later restoration. Of particular note is the chapel of 1320, and the Elisabeth gallery on the first floor, which Moritz von Schwind and his colleagues frescoed in the mid nineteenth century with scenes from the life of St Elisabeth. In another room dedicated to the Hungarian saint, art nouveau mosaics also illustrate her life.

The troubadours' hall, where medieval minstrels took part in the *Sängerkrieg*, a celebrated minstrels' contest of 1207, inspired Wagner's *Tannhäuser*. Above all, the Wartburg is crammed with souvenirs of Martin Luther, for here between 4 May 1521 and 6 March 1522, under the name of Junker Jörg, he hid from his Catholic enemies while working on his translation of the New Testament. In the Luther room hangs his portrait and that of his wife Katherine, both by Lucas Cranach the Elder. Here is displayed his Bible of 1541, annotated in his own hand and that of his disciple Melanchthon, as well as his table and bookcase.

Drive back along Wartburgallee and then along Marienstrasse to reach the Bach-Haus at no. 21 Frauenplan, where (possibly) Johann Sebastian was born on 21 March 1685. His father was master of music at the court of Eisenach, and died when his son was a mere ten years old. The young boy moved from here to Ohrdruf, where he was taken in by his uncle Johann-Christoph.

The ground floor of his home at Eisenach has a collection of historic musical instruments, and the first floor is set out as an authentic home of the late seventeenth century, with its living-room, kitchen and bedroom (though none of the furniture on show actually belonged to the Bach family). Here are portraits of every known musical Bach, as well as a room devoted to his most celebrated interpreter, the Alsatian Albert Schweitzer. In the garden is the tomb of Wilhelm-Friedrich-Ernst Bach, master of music at the Prussian court, Johann Sebastian's last known descendant, who died on Christmas Day, 1865.

From here Luther-Strasse curves to Luther Platz and Frau Cotta's house (Gothic, with later half-timbering) where the future Reformer lodged as a schoolboy from 1498 to 1501. Young Luther is said to have charmed Ursula Cotta and her husband Konrad with his singing. A fascinating exhibition details, through manuscripts and contemporary paintings, the religious situation of the time. Here are translations of his Bible, and an edition of his notorious ninety-five theses of 31 October 1517. Three charming pictures, which once hung in the Wartburg, depict the young Luther singing for Frau Cotta, his arrival at the Wartburg in 1521 and his meeting with Swiss students the following year. Upstairs is a far more specialized exhibition: documents collected since 1925 by Pastor August Angermann relating to men and women who have promulgated Protestantism.

In the Markt, just beyond Lutherplatz, rises the flamboyant Gothic church of St Georg, last resting-place of many of the Landgraves of Thuringia, while to the right, in the narrow Karlstrasse, stands the town hall. Begun in the Gothic style in 1508, continued in the Renaissance style in 1564, the Rathaus of Eisenach had to be rebuilt after a fire of 1636 and again after the air raids of 1945; its tower leans slightly. A further delight of this street is the pharmacy opposite, which was begun in 1560.

Walk on beyond St Georg to Eisenach's Schloss, a baroque and rococo treat built for the Dukes of Saxe-Weimar in the 1740s by Gottfried H. Krohne and now the home of the Thuringian museum. Porcelain and glassware vie with ducal portraits, mythological frescos and nineteenth-century heroic paintings by such local luminaries as Friederich Preller the Elder. Evidence that pottery has long flourished here is displayed from the bronze and iron ages. An upper floor is devoted to folklore, local costumes, ironwork and the like.

Four other churches at Eisenach are well worth a visit. Georgenstrasse leads north-west from the Markt to the hospital church of St Anne, basically a flamboyant Gothic building. Walk south from here to the cemetery, whose baroque Kreuzkirche was built by J. Mützel in 1695 and whose mortuary is a neoclassical building by C.-W. Coudray. Then, on the way back to the Marktplatz, pass by the Predigerkirche, a Gothic building of the late thirteenth century, restored in 1902 and full of splendid wooden sculptures of the middle ages. Margrave Heinrich Raspe stands here, sculpted around 1300; here is a Madonna and Child of 1410, and a Pietà of 1420. Equally superb are two altars, that of St Anne carved in 1498, that of the Virgin of Probstella carved some ten years later. A massive, very-early-sixteenth-century Pietà dwarfs its companions.

The fourth and finest of these churches, the Nikolaikirche, stands east of the Schloss. A Romanesque basilica built between 1172 and 1190 and later given a Gothic interior, its capitals remain deliciously Romanesque. But what adds allure to this church is the juxtaposition of its hexagonal tower and Eisenach's venerable Nikolaitor. Once part of the late-eleventh-century fortifications of the city, the Nikolaitor is the oldest town gate in Thuringia.

Those who relish old motor vehicles will walk south from here to find the Eisenach automobile museum in Wartburgallee. Musicians and poets will contine to no. 2 Reuter Weg, a museum dedicated to Fritz Reuter and Richard Wagner. Fritz Reuter, who was born in Stavenhagen in 1810, dedicated his considerable talent to the virtually incomprehensible *Plattdeutsch* dialect of that region (to such effect that Stavenhagen is officially known as Reuterstadt-Stavenhagen).

Eleven years before his death, he made his final home in Eisenach, and the house contains his own furniture. Reuter's home is also a Wagner museum. Wagner reached Eisenach for the first time in 1842. The vast collection housed in the museum was brought here only in 1895, bought in Vienna by an Eisenach savant named Joseph Kürschner, who had made Wagner his life's work. Here are displayed some 200 letters and manuscripts of the composer, as well as another 5,000 volumes devoted to him, and, finally, his death-mask.

Lying between Eisenach and Erfurt, Gotha is renowned for its sausages, as well as for the massive baroque Schloss Friedenstein which overlooks Müntzerplatz. In front of it is a statue of the man who paid for it, Duke Ernst the Pious. His Schloss, with its monumental staircase, was built between 1643 and 1655 and is packed with baroque, rococo, Empire and Biedermeier treasures. Its art gallery is similarly impressive, the acknowledged masterpieces on display being statuettes of Adam and Eve carved by Conrad Meit in 1515 and an *Adoration of the Magi* by Lucas Cranach the Elder. (Cranach lived for a time at no. 17 Hauptmarkt, on the corner of Lucas-Cranach-Strasse.) Gotha's Schloss also boasts a chapel and a baroque theatre, built between 1683 and 1745 and thus the oldest in eastern Germany. In Neumarkt rises the Margarethen-kirche, a triple-naved hall church begun in 1494 and given its baroque aspect in the seventeenth century. Numerous fine patrician houses enliven the town, in particular the Renaissance Altes Waidhaus in Gretengasse, another reminder of the former importance of woad to the prosperity of these towns, and the Renaissance town hall which was built in 1577. Gotha also has a zoo, in which roam wolves and bears.

Drive 19 km north from Gotha to reach Bad Langensalza, a sulphuric spa, of whose thirteenth- and fourteenth-century fortifications no fewer than seventeen towers are still standing. In the Marktplatz rises the parish church of St Bonifatius, a Gothic hall church of 1395 to 1427 whose tower was finished in 1590 in the Renaissance style. Its finest feature is the Last Judgement, sculpted on the tympanum of the west door in 1370. Inside are fifteenth-century paintings and a baroque pulpit of 1720. Bad Langensalza has a three-storey baroque hotel of 1752 (with a late-Gothic tower) which overlooks a fountain of 1582. And the irregular half-timbered houses add much to the charm of the Altstadt.

From here a brief excursion 6 km south-east leads to

Gräfentonna, whose parish church of St Peter and St Paul has a baroque altar bearing late-Gothic reliefs of the Last Supper, the Crucifixion, the Deposition and the Entombment of Jesus carved by Hans Nussbaum. Its Ketenburg is a Renaissance Schloss set around a Gothic tower.

An excursion in the other direction, north-west, reaches Mühlhausen, the headquarters of the Reformer Thomas Müntzer, who was radical enough to despise Martin Luther as much as he despised the papacy. In 1525 Müntzer led the peasants in a revolt against their masters, lost and was executed. In consequence its local-history museum is filled with Müntzer memorabilia. Müntzer preached his revolutionary theology from the pulpit of the Marienkirche, whose spire rises to 98 m.

The church gleams white over the red roofs of the town. Inside the spacious building, which dates from the mid fourteenth century and rises on delicate slender pillars, are statues of the Emperor Karl IV, his wife and what are said to be courtesans. Its choir is lit by stained glass made at the turn of the fourteenth and fifteenth centuries. Müntzer lived in a house in An der Marienkirche which was rebuilt in 1689 (with a portal embellished with coats of arms) after a fire. Coincidentally, this was the house in which the architect Friedrich August Stüler was born in 1800.

The town archives are displayed in the Rathaus, which was built in the early fourteenth century and enlarged in the nineteenth. Mühlhausen has also preserved some impressive fortifications, with towers and gates, and other fine Gothic churches. The Franciscan Barfüsser monastery church in the Kornmarkt is now a museum of the Peasants' Revolt. In the same square the Renaissance Apotheke dates from 1625. The church of St Blaise, in Bach Platz, was built for the Teutonic Knights in 1227. The others include the thirteenth- and fourteenth-century Jakobi-Kirche, while at no. 8 Jakobistrasse is a half-timbered house of 1571 with a baroque entrance added in 1768, and at no. 22 in the same street is a second half-timbered house, this one built in 1629. In Langensalzaer Strasse to the south-east of the town a baroque tower, built by J. G. Kötze in 1735, rises from the Gothic church of St Martin, while another baroque tower tops the Gothic church of St Kilian to the east of the town. At the other side of the town the Petri-Kirche dates from the fourteenth century.

Naumburg is 27 km east of Bad Langensalza, and the route to that city runs along the F176, beside the River Unstrut. This is spa and Schloss country. At Bad Tennstedt the citizens and a baroque church of 1659–82 are protected by the remains of fifteenth-century walls. So in part is Sömmerda, 10 km further on, its remaining fortifications dating from the fourteenth and sixteenth centuries. These sixteenth-century walls still preserve six towers and incorporate the medieval Erfurt Gate of 1395. Here the parish church of St Bonifatius, built in the 1560s, retains a tower of 1462, a late-Gothic winged altar and two fifteenth-century paintings (one of the Crucifixion, the other the Resurrection). Sömmerda's late-Gothic Rathaus dates from 1539. Weissensee, 8 km north-west, is also surrounded by ramparts, further protected by a late-Romanesque fortress, and boasts a church with a flamboyant Gothic reredos.

Kölleda, 10 km north-east of Sömmerda, has a couple of Gothic churches, the earliest, St Johannis, built around 1300, the other, St Wigbert, built in the fifteenth century and later given a baroque face. Nearby Rastenberg is still defended by two fortified towers, one fifteenth century, the other sixteenth.

Passing through the spa of Bad Bibra the route next reaches Laucha, set beside the Unstrut. Its Gothic Untertor dates from the fifteenth century. Here is a bell museum, the bells made between the fifteenth and the nineteenth centuries and displayed in a reconstructed eighteenth-century bell foundry. Not far away, dominating the river, is the Renaissance Schloss

Burgscheidungen, built from the late sixteenth century until 1635 and then in part rebuilt as a baroque palace (with a terraced, Italian-style park) in the 1720s, while the Marien-kirche, with its 56 m high tower, dates from 1496.

The wine town of Freyburg, a mere 10 km from Naumburg, is also washed by the Unstrut. Freyburg's grapes, ripened on the gentle slopes outside the town, produce a wine celebrated at an annual feast in the last week of September. The chequer-board layout of the town dates from the thirteenth century, as does its Romanesque Schloss with a chapel of 1220 whose lovely capitals illustrate medieval bestiaries and floral designs and whose well is 120 m deep. Part of it is a museum devoted to the minnesinger Heinrich von Veldeke. This chapel is di-vided into two parts, so that the nobility, in the upper part, could remain aloof from the common folk. Freyburg's parish church of St Mary began as a Romanesque buiding, with two western towers and the choir verging on the Gothic. In 1499 the nave was rebuilt in the Gothic style. Inside are a late-twelfth-century *Coronation of the Virgin* and a painting of the Holy Family done in the sixteenth century. Freyburg is cel-ebrated as the home of Friedrich Ludwig Jahn, the father of modern gymnastics, who lived here from 1825 till his death in 1852. His home (at no. 1 Schlossstrasse) is now the Jahn museum.

Finally the F180 reaches Naumburg, whose bishopric was founded in 1028; the city still retains fragments of its medieval fortifications. Although the western choir of Naum-burg cathedral (dedicated to St Peter and St Paul) was built in 1250, scarcely ten years later than the Romanesque nave and east end, it already displays the influence of Gothic architects. The two impressive eastern towers are crowned with baroque onion domes, themselves topped by cupolas, while the two western towers have Gothic spires. Inside, the cathedral grows progressively more Gothic as you walk east; the choir is an early Gothic jewel. Some of the stained glass is contemporary with this choir, while the rest dates from the nineteenth century.

What above all draws pilgrims to Naumburg cathedral is its ensemble of magnificent thirteenth-century sculptures, those on the two screens and, above all, the statues of the twelve founders of the cathedral. Carved in the 1250s and clearly influenced by the Gothic master sculptors of Amiens, these represent Dietrich von Brehna, Gepa, Gerburg and Konrad (the two last apparently carved some thirty years after the others), Hermann and Reglindus, Dietmar, Sizzo von Käfernburg, Wilhelm von Camburg, Timo von Kistritz and – supreme among these masterpieces – Ekkehardt and Uta. The realism of these statues remains astonishing.

The same Naumburg workshop must have created a second set of statues, these depicting the Passion of Jesus, on the western rood-screen (which, dating from 1225, is the oldest in Germany). Once again the realism is fabulous. The Last Supper, the traitor Judas receiving his thirty pieces of silver, Christ captive, St Peter denying his lord, two guards, Jesus before Pontius Pilate, Christ's flagellation and (on the doorway of the rood-screen) a superb carving of Jesus carrying the cross depicts him between the Virgin Mary and St John. In the midst of this wealth, spare a glance at the carved capitals.

Naumburg has a good sprinkling of fountains, one in Domplatz, another in the market square, though this one, dating from the sixteenth century, is dwarfed by the flamboyant Gothic town hall with its six gables (and a sculpted doorway of 1610). I warmed to the modern fountain in Holzmarkt, which is overlooked by a house with an impressive oriel window. In this town too are more Renaissance and baroque houses and the Gothic church of St Wenzel. Built around 1520, St Wenzel is wider than it is long, its interior remodelled in 1724. It shelters two paintings by Lucas Cranach the Elder (an

Adoration of the Magi of 1515 and *Jesus amongst the Children* of 1540). Zacharias Hildebrand built its organ in 1743, and its baroque high altar was created in 1680.

Drive on from Naumburg for 3 km to discover another splendid church at Schulpforta. In the mid twelfth century Cistercian monks built their abbey church of St Maria here, and in the mid thirteenth century it was transformed by French architects into a Gothic basilica, with a tall and narrow west façade delightfully sculpted. In 1543 the monks departed and Moritz of Saxony transformed the cloister into a school. In later years its pupils included Klopstock, Fichte, the great historian Leopold von Ranke and Friedrich Nietzsche.

Our route now runs through the Saale valley, where grasslands are interspersed with woodlands and where castles, some ruined, some in excellent repair, dot the hills. Scarcely 5 km further on from Naumburg, at the spa of Bad Kösen, stands middle Germany's oldest secular building, the Romanisches Haus of 1038, which now serves as a local-history museum. Fourteen kilometres away along the F87 rises a magical medieval ruin, Schloss Eckartsberga, and then the road runs on to two more evocative Romanesque castles: Rudelsburg, with four extensive wings, and Burg Saaleck, whose Romanesque keep dates from the mid twelfth century.

At Rudelsburg lived the poet Franz Kugler, who in 1826 wrote the doggerel ditty which begins:

> *An der Saale hellem Strand*
> *Stehen Burgen stolz und kühn.*
>
> (On the bright banks of the Saale,
> Stand the castles, bright and bold.)

Of the medieval fortress at Camburg, our next stop, all that remains is the 37 m high round keep. Camburg's Gothic and baroque parish church is crowned by a high, pyramidical tower. The local-history museum is housed in a house built in 1742. Here the only remaining covered medieval bridge in the Saale region crosses the River Mühllache.

From Camburg a road to the right speedily reaches the wine village of Dornburg, which is guarded by three castles: the Altes Schloss, half Romanesque but mostly thirteenth-century Gothic with a south wing added in the sixteenth century; the Rokokoschloss, built in the mid eighteenth century by G. H. Krohne for Duke Ernst-Augustus of Weimar (and restored under Goethe's direction in the early nineteenth century); and the Goetheschloss, a Renaissance castle with gables and a monumental staircase added in 1608. This last derives its name from the fact that the poet and dramatist stayed here, writing amongst other works his *Iphigenie in Tauris* and several major poems.

Jena, with its rich souvenirs of Goethe and Schiller, lies on the Saale to the south. Luther's ally Melanchthon came to think that its university, founded in 1558, was a more secure base for the Reformation than that of Weimar. Other scholars flourished in the shade of its walls, in particular the mathematician Erhard Weigel (who introduced the Gregorian calendar into the Holy Roman Empire) and the nineteenth-century optician Carl Zeiss whose lenses and microscopes became world famous.

Under the benign rule of Prince Carl Augustus of Saxe-Weimar, the Schlegel brothers and Ludwig Tieck were drawn to the city, as also was Goethe, who came here to study anatomy. The brilliant brothers Alexander and Wilhelm von Humboldt lent their prestige to the city, as did Johann Gottlieb Fichte (who taught philosophy here from 1794 to 1799) and Friedrich Hegel, who as *Privatdozent* (unsalaried lecturer) at the university, collaborated with Friedrich Wilhelm Joseph Schelling in the first decade of the nineteenth century in editing their seminal *Kritische Journal der Philosophie*. And until his death in 1919 the naturalist and champion of Darwin Ernst Haeckel was a Jena professor.

But this was pre-eminently the city of Schiller. In his *Jenzingberg* Schiller enthused over the slopes on which the city is set. Honorary professor of history here from 1788 till 1799, he produced masterpiece after masterpiece till his death (at Weimar) in 1805. Fittingly, then, the university is dedicated to Schiller. His home between 1797 and 1802 is furnished in the fashion of his time.

Jena also boasts a Goethe Museum (at no. 26 Goethe-Allee), in the house where he completed his *Wilhelm Meisters Lehrjahre* in 1796 and his *Hermann und Dorothea* two years later, while also directing the new layout of his garden. And Carl Zeiss is commemorated not only by the Planetarium Zeiss in the Botanical Garden but also by the Optical Museum in the nearby Griessbach Garden. As for Ernst Haeckel, his museum is at no. 7 Berggasse.

Unfortunately, although they spared Schiller's house and parts of the Michaeliskirche, the bombardments of 1945 destroyed much of the ancient part of the city. Most of the ramparts were destroyed, leaving only the medieval powder magazine (the Pulverturm) and the early-fourteenth-century St John's Gate (Johannistor). Unsightly blocks of flats surround the city. Zeiss is today commemorated by a massive modern tower and the Zeiss factories include a skyscraper.

The human face of Jena reappears in the parish church of St Michaelis, initially a Romanesque building of the mid thirteenth century, where Cistercian nuns worshipped. Well restored after the Second World War, its later Gothic form (the result originally of work done between 1390 and 1506) and its belfry of 1566 are imposing, while the Bride's Portal is a filigree masterpiece. Inside is a statue of the archangel Michael (the 'Angelus Jenensis') carved at Bamberg in the first half of the thirteenth century, and a pulpit of 1607 bearing the arms of the Electors of Saxony.

South of the church is the Marktplatz, with its late-fourteenth-century Gothic town hall, in part reordered in the baroque style in 1775. The Jaquemart on its clock dates from the late fifteenth century, and its cellars serve excellent beer. In the square is a statue of Elector Johann-Friedrich the Good, carved by F. Drake in 1858. Johann-Friedrich founded Jena's university; none the less the students and everyone else have irreverently shortened his name to dub the statue Hanfried. Bombs spared the nearby Göhre, an early-sixteenth-century Gothic mansion on the corner of the narrow, covered Mühlgässchen. The poet Fritz Reuter spent a year in this street in the 1830s, his home still proudly pointed out.

I wish I did not think that the hilly and green environs of Jena are more entrancing than the city itself, but I do. In the suburb of Lodeburg are the late-twelfth-century ruins of Schloss Lodeburg, with twin Romanesque windows and a decent café. The city lies on the edge of the Thuringian forest; and some of the towns in the Saale valley further south-west are particularly enticing.

At Kahla, some 15 km away, is a parish church with a Gothic choir built in 1413 over a vaulted crypt. Kahla preserves some of its fortifications, which hardly seem necessary since it is guarded by the thirteenth-century fortress of Leuchtenberg, which peers benevolently down from its hilltop, was restored in the nineteenth century and now is a museum of hunting, armour and porcelain. (Kahla boasts the largest porcelain factory in Europe.) Even more powerful is the fortress at Orlamünde, 5 km further on. Built like a cube, its walls 3 m thick, the fortress is known as the Kemenate. It has splendid chimneys for the fires which once warmed its stern rooms.

Two spots further along the River Saale should not be missed. Rudolstadt has a Gothic and baroque Rathaus from which you climb 220 steps to reach the eighteenth-century baroque Schloss Heidecksburg (the work of J.-Ch. Knöffel and

G.-H. Krohne among others), with its collection of rococo furniture and arms, and a little picture gallery. The late-Gothic Stadtkirche dates in its present form from 1634, though it has stood here much longer and its furnishings are now mostly baroque. In the Altstadt is the three-winged, baroque Schloss Ludwigsburg. And at what is now no. 1 Schillerstrasse lived Friedrich Schiller. Here on 6 December 1787, he met his future wife Charlotte von Lengefeld.

Saalfeld is another lovely town, with its four medieval gates and the wall which still preserves medieval bastions and towers. Its church of St Johannis was begun in 1380 and finished in 1456. A Last Judgement is sculpted on its tympanum, and inside are more fine carvings, in particular a superb St John the Baptist carved in wood around 1500. The winged Gothic altar dates from the last quarter of the fifteenth century. As for the town's castles, beside the ruins of the fortress of Hoher Schwarm at Saalfeld these rises the late-Gothic Schloss Kitzerstein, while a third Schloss is baroque. The early-sixteenth-century Rathaus has a polygonal staircase tower, while in the same square stands an Apotheke of 1180. Another splendid building is the restaurant Das Loch in Blankenburger Strasse, half-timbered and with a frescoed outside wall. And just outside Saalfeld you can visit a disused slate mine which closed down in 1846. Here in 1910 were discovered the colourful stalactites and stalagmites which have earned it the name Fairy Grottoes.

Weimar likewise, lying 27 km north-west of Jena along the F7, lets nobody down. The environs of Weimar comprehend three lovely castles, set amidst forests and parks. Peacocks strut on the grass around Schloss Belvedere, to the south-east, a summer palace built in the early 1730s for the Dukes of Weimar by G.-H. Krohne, which derives both its name and its baroque pattern from Hildebrandt's palace in Vienna. Its 'English' park was originally laid out to plans of Goethe himself, though the grounds were modified some forty years later by the horticulturalist and landscape gardener Prince Pückler-Muskau. Its orangery has a carillon of thirty-five bells; a red tower of 1828 offers a fine panoramic view; and the Schloss is now a museum of rococo art.

Four kilometres north-east of Weimar stands Schloss Tiefurt, a late-sixteenth-century building, modified in 1776 and the summer residence after 1781 of the cultivated dowager-duchess Anna-Amalia. Again, the Schloss is surrounded by an 'English' garden, while its rooms display rococo, classical and Biedermeier furnishings and decorations. At Ossmannstadt, some 6 km away, is a baroque house which once belonged to the poet Christoph Martin Wieland. He and his wife Sophie Brentano lie buried in its garden.

The baroque and classical Schloss Ettersburg, north of Weimar, has another 'English' park, this one also modified by Prince Hermann Pückler-Muskau, who was influenced by our own Humphry Repton. On the slopes of the Ettersburg, Schiller composed the last part of his *Don Carlos* and Goethe wrote his '*Wanderers Nachtlied*'.

But this part of eastern Germany takes on a much more sombre aspect, for in July 1937 the Nazis, having destroyed the post-war democratic republic set up in Weimar in 1919, began building the concentration camp of Buchenwald in these woods. Of the 238,000 persons interned here in the next eight years, 56,545 were murdered. They are remembered in a statue depicting eleven of them by Fritz Cremer, which stands in front of a huge belfry on the way to the former camp. It is on the site of three circular mass graves, where some 10,000 victims were buried just before the end of the Second World War.

Buchenwald concentration camp (which is closed on Mondays) is now a memorial to the dead, and the displays in the former barracks are the grimmest possible reminder of human inhumanity. Here are isolation cells, with photographs of some of those tortured to death in them. An exhibition outlining the history of the Third Reich details its connections with this spot. Other photographs show some who escaped with their lives. Sketches made by prisoners themselves and music written by others are also on display. The barracks back on to roll-call square, where the whole camp would be assembled for hours, whatever the weather. The camp crematorium is still here, as well as a stake from which prisoners were hung and a cart loaded with bricks which others were made to drag. Jewish prisoners and prisoners of war had their own blocks. In block 46 the SS performed medical experiments on prisoners, sometimes injecting them with fatal illnesses. The gateway to this hideous spot near where Goethe earlier found peace is inscribed '*Jedem das Seine*', 'to each his own'. Once the Soviet rulers of eastern Germany had left, the Germans took little time to point out that when the Second World War was over the Russians imprisoned some 32,000 people here, not all of them Nazi criminals, and that by 1950 13,000 of them had died of hunger and disease.

Weimar itself was celebrated long before Goethe reached the city. Its situation on the banks of the Ilm is clement and entrancing – as prehistoric men and women evidently knew, for near by, in the suburb of Ehringsdorf, was discovered the skull of a woman who died in her mid-twenties some 100,000 years ago in the palaeolithic age. Stone age men and women left behind pottery and ceramics which have been excavated in our own time.

In historical times the region was inhabited by Germanic tribes. In the mid fifth century AD Amalaberga, niece of the Ostrogothic king Theodoric, ruled the region along with her husband Hermannfried. From this era the town derives its name, for in Old High German 'Weimar' signified 'sacred pool'. A document of 1254 refers, for the first time, to '*civita nostra Wimar*', as a dependency of the Counts of Orlamünde, who had built a fortress here. Two hundred years later Duke William III elevated this part of Thuringia into a duchy, with Weimar as its capital. After exactly forty years, in 1485, its status diminished. Weimar became the property of the Elector Ernst, who made it only his second capital.

The Reformation gave it a new boost. Luther preached here, and soon Protestantism was dominant, Catholicism proscribed and monks and nuns driven out. The greatest artist of the Reformation, Lucas Cranach the Elder, spent the last year of his life here. Shortly before Cranach's death in 1553, the Emperor Charles V defeated the Protestant Elector Johann-Friedrich of Saxony at the battle of Mühlberg in 1547, the elector (whose temporary imprisonment was shared by Lucas Cranach) was forced to cede many of his Thuringian possessions and took up residence at Weimar. Thenceforth Weimar remained the capital of Saxony-Weimar until 1918.

In the mid seventeenth century a society devoted to the promotion, development and restoration of German language and literature was founded here, attracting to Weimar noted poets and scholars. (Because its coat of arms included a palm, the society – whose ponderous title was the Fruchtbringende Gesellschaft zur Förderung, Pflege und Reinigung der deutschen Sprache und Literatur – became known simply as the 'Palmenorden', 'the Order of the Palm'.) Another brilliant coup was the engagement of Johann Sebastian Bach as court organist and leader of the court orchestra from 1708 to 1717. Not long before he arrived, Johann Conrad Weishaupt had rebuilt the organ in the chapel of the ducal palace, and on it Bach composed the first of his mature cantatas. Alas, chapel, organ and palace disappeared in a fire of 1774.

Goethe's arrival on 7 November 1775, invited by Duke Carl Augustus at the age of twenty-six, brought Weimar its greatest renown. In truth the inspiration behind the invitation was not

Carl Augustus but his mother, the widowed Grand-Duchess Anna-Amalia, who was a princess of Brunswick and niece of Frederick II of Prussia. Married at sixteen, she bore two sons and was widowed at eighteen. Anna-Amalia had engaged Christoph Martin Wieland, Germany's leading classicist and first translator of Shakespeare, as tutor to her children, and at Weimar he wrote his finest work, the heroic poem *Oberon*. Wieland and Goethe became close friends. Soon Johann Gottfried Herder and then Schiller followed in their footsteps to Weimar.

Schiller bought a house of 1777 at Weimar in 1802, only three years before his death. The street in which it stands has been renamed Schillerstrasse, and the house converted into a Schiller museum. Weimar's theatre had been rebuilt in 1779, and here were first performed Schiller's *Wallenstein*, *Maria Stuart* and *Wilhelm Tell*. This theatre was burned down in 1826; the present handsome classical building, with its swags and graceful iron balcony, was opened in 1948. In front of it in the Theaterplatz, Schiller and Goethe stand united in a statue of 1857 by the Dresden sculptor Ernst Rietschel. One imagines the older man whispering his celebrated words to Schiller, 'You gave me a second youth and once more made me a poet.'

Adjoining the Theaterplatz is the Wittumspalais, the baroque 'palace of widowhood', built for one of Anna-Amalia's ministers in 1767 and her home from 1774 to 1807. Her portraits and those of her husband, family and entourage, look down on the rooms where she would entertain the most brilliant savants of Europe. Here is the very table round which they would gather; here Goethe presided over regular Friday salons. And a section of the palace has since 1963 been devoted to the life and work of Christoph Martin Wieland, who died just outside Weimar in 1813.

One man who failed to get on with Goethe at Weimar was the poet and philosopher Johann Gottfried Herder. A Protestant pastor, Herder had been appointed as church super-intendent-general at Weimar on Goethe's recommendation. Goethe did his best to remain friendly, and eventually the two men did manage to collaborate. But even when Herder was persuaded to follow his ally's example and make a trip to explore the antiquities of Italy, he remained sour. 'Basically I regard all these as puddles from a dead sea,' he wrote, 'however much Goethe exaggerates their sweetness.' So the two men fell out again. Herder died here in 1803, deeply miserable.

Yet he had produced a seminal work on Hebrew poetry and made a splendid collection of German folksongs. His statue of 1850, by Ludwig Schaler, stands outside the church of St Peter and St Paul where he preached (which everyone in Weimar dubs the Herderkirche), a triple-aisled hall church with a polygonal apse, built between 1498 and 1500 and given a baroque interior between 1735 and 1745. The contrast between the Gothic exterior and the interior, with its lovely rococo furnishings, is startling. Between May and September the church is the venue of Sunday evening concerts.

Herder lies buried under the organ loft, his tomb carved with three words chosen by himself, LICHT LIEBE LEBEN ('Light, Love, Life') circling the letters Alpha and Omega. His tomb attracts far more visitors than those monuments to the family that employed him, though these are fine, particularly those of Ernst I and his descendants, and above all that of Johann Wilhelm, sculpted by Sebastian Gromann in 1576 and set against the north wall of the choir. Close by, at no. 10 Jakobstrasse, the Kirms-Krakow-Haus, part sixteenth century, part classical, and with a baroque façade and a charming courtyard, has been transformed into a Herder museum.

Another tomb in this church depicts the bearded Lucas Cranach the Elder, his hat in his hand as befits a man in church. Sculpted by Nikolaus Gromann, it comes from Cranach's grave in the cemetery church of St Jakob. Finer than anything else in the Herderkirche is a winged altar which Cranach was working on at his death and which his son Lucas Cranach the Younger finished. On the left wing of the triptych are depicted the Duke Johann-Friedrich and the Duchess Sybil; on the right their three sons, who commissioned it as a memorial of their parents.

The central panel is devoted to the Crucifixion and, as ever, Cranach has packed his painting with symbolism. Jesus appears twice, both crucified and to the left of the cross. In a superb red cloak, he is depicted destroying sin and death. Death is a skeleton; sin is a dragon covered in pustules, his claws vainly trying to hold back the spear which Jesus is plunging into his throat. At the foot of the cross is a lamb, a reference to Jesus' title as the Lamb of God who takes away the sins of the world.

Since it was John the Baptist who gave him this title, he too appears to the right of the cross, pointing to the crucified Christ. Beside the Baptist Cranach the Younger has painted a posthumous portrait of his white-bearded father. And next to his father stands Martin Luther, with an open Bible. In the background are more scenes typifying salvation: Adam pursued by the devil and running towards the cross; the children of Israel escaping from Egypt; Moses holding up a serpent's cross. The reverse side of the wings depict the baptism of Jesus and his Ascension.

Before leaving the Herderkirche, look up at an idealized portrait on the wall opposite the baptistry of Goethe's patron-ess Anna-Amalia. She died in 1807 and now lies in front of the altar, her husband's tomb on her left. Close by the church is a gabled Renaissance building of 1566, a knight perched on top. Carl Augustus gave it as a present to his mistress, the actress Karoline Jagemann, whom he then elevated as Countess von Heigendorf.

After Goethe's illustrious era, Weimar attracted other geni-uses, in particular the musician Franz Liszt, the early-twentieth century-painter Henry van de Velde and thirdly the architect Walter Gropius, who founded the Bauhaus here in 1919 in what is now the Architectural High School (in Geschwister-Scholl-Strasse), a building designed by Henry van de Velde between 1904 and 1911. The Bauhaus soon moved to Dessau and has left few mementoes in Weimar, but Liszt is still commemorated here in the Liszt-Hochschule, south of the Markt and housed in the baroque former Fürstenhaus of 1774.

His museum is further south, in Marienstrasse on the way to the Belvedere Schloss. In this house he habitually took up summer residence from 1869 until shortly before his death twenty-seven years later. It contains a bust sculpted only eleven days before his death by A. Lehnert, as well as his death-mask and casts of his hands. Here too are portraits of his ancestors and family, as well as of the great love of his life, Princess Caroline Sayn-Wittgenstein. His study contains furniture he actually used; and the Liszt museum also displays letters to the composer from illustrious musical contemporaries, including Berlioz, Schumann, Wagner, Smetana and Mendelssohn.

As the Herderkirche, the Wittumspalais, Schiller's house and the Liszt museum reveal, much of Weimar's rich history glitters through the present architecture and art of the city. To explore more of thus superb heritage, walk south from Herderplatz to the market square, with its Neptune fountain created by Martin Klauer in 1774. Amongst its splendid buildings, no. 3 is a beautiful Renaissance building, designed by Nikolaus Gromann in 1549, in which Cranach the Elder lived. It did not in fact belong to Cranach, but to his son-in-law the Chancellor Christian Brück, who allotted the third storey to Cranach. The Rathaus at the opposite side of the Platz is a jolly building whose façade of 1581 was perfectly restored in 1945. It was given a set of bells made of Dresden china in 1987.

The ancient inn on the Marktplatz named Zum Elefanten

was first mentioned in 1561 and served its first guests in 1696. For lovers of Goethe and Thomas Mann the name of this inn is resonant. Mann's novel *Lotte in Weimar* is devoted to Goethe and Charlotte Buff, who met Goethe in Wetzlar in 1772. He fell passionately in love with her, but she was already engaged to J. G. C. Kestner, whom she married in 1773. Goethe's sensationally successful novel, *Die Leiden des jungen Werthers*, published in 1774, is partly based on this episode. Goethe and Charlotte did not meet again until 1816, over forty years later, when she visited Weimar to see what she called 'the might-have-been'.

Thomas Mann's novel touchingly exploring this tale begins in the Marktplatz. 'In October 1816, early in the month, when the weather might still be called summery, a strange thing happened to Herr Mager, head waiter at Zum Elefanten in Weimar,' he wrote. Three women, Charlotte and her daughters, descend from the Gotha coach. As the novel progresses, they meet a different Goethe from the one Charlotte loved. And the novel ends at the same inn. Goethe says a last goodbye to Lotte, and as his long-familiar accents die away she replies, 'Peace to your old age.' An astonished Mager runs across the pavement to the coach and takes Charlotte's arm, exclaiming, 'How can I refrain from helping Werther's Lotte out of Goethe's carriage – an experience that someone should certainly record.'

On either side of the hotel stand two others: the Schwarzer Bär with its Renaissance arcardes, and the Parkhotel, which received Napoleon Bonaparte, Franz Liszt and Richard Wagner. To its left is a house whose plaque declares that it was the home of J. S. Bach between 1708 and 1717. Here were born six of his sons, including the composers Wilhelm Friedemann, in 1710, and Carl Philipp Emmanuel, in 1714.

I cannot say why, but the Ratskeller of Weimar is not in the town hall itself but in the gaily gabled Stadthaus, a building next to Cranach's former home. The Ratskeller doesn't close till midnight, and its substantial food is exceedingly reasonable. Thuringians eat well, and are particularly fond of *Rostbrätl*, spare-rib steak served with onions.

Daily, save Sundays, a flower, fruit and vegetable market is set up in the Marktplatz. Beyond it an equestrian statue of Carl Augustus (the work of Adolf Donndorf in 1875) looks up towards the Rotes Schloss, a Renaissance treat of the early 1570s, red as its name implies, with an imposing main entrance. In front of its neoclassical north façade is a fountain dedicated to St Idelfonso, patron saint of Madrid and copied from an original in that city.

Weimar's Schloss, guarded by its ancient tower (the Bastille), stands in Burgplatz, a few paces north-east of the Markt. Here the town's rulers lived till 1918. Successive fires destroyed first their medieval fortress, which was replaced by a Renaissance palace designed by Nikolaus Gromann and then Gromann's palace, which was supplanted by an Italian baroque building by Giovanni Bualino; finally Bualino's palace burned down, so that what we see today (with some additions) is a classical three-aisled palace built under the direction of Goethe himself. The fine-art collection, ranging from the sixteenth to the twentieth century (including twentieth-century works by Lieber-mann and Max Beckmann) makes a visit a delight. Superb frescos, wall-paintings and furniture add to one's pleasure.

South of this Schloss stand successively the Renaissance Grünes Schloss and the baroque Gelbes Schloss. The first, the Green Palace, was built in the 1560s for a member of the ruling family. Grand-Duchess Anna-Amalia had it transformed two hundred years later into a rococo library, and that is what it remains to this day, now sheltering over 750,000 volumes of classical German literature, the national library of Thuringia and the library of the German Shakespeare Society. The Gelbes Schloss, the Yellow Palace, dates from 1702; and near by, between Ackerwand and Seifengasse, stands a pink house which was once the home of Charlotte von Stein, lady-in-waiting to the Grand-Duchess Anna-Amalia. Ten years married, seven years older than Goethe and the mother of seven children, she struck up a passionate relationship with the poet between 1779 and 1781. Goethe once said, *Was man in der Jugend wünscht, hat man im Alter die Fülle*' ('What a person longs for in his youth he reaps in full in older age'). In affairs of the heart his own habit was to reap whenever he felt like it. 'She could never have been beautiful,' Schiller wrote of Charlotte, 'but her face has a gentle gravity and a most exceptional frankness.' Soon Goethe was returning her ardour, their relationship rendered all the more convenient because he was living at no. 16 Seifengasse near her home and because her husband (who was in charge of the ducal stables) was often away.

Straddling the Ilm is the Goethe Park, a French-style park when Goethe found it, but soon laid out to his own specifications between 1778 and 1796 in the 'English' style. (The landscape-gardener Prince Pückler-Muskau partly transformed the park in the mid nineteenth century.) At the southernmost end of the park is the so-called Römisches Haus, a summer pavilion which Goethe designed for Carl Augustus, who gave him his head with the declaration, 'Our tastes are always identical.'

The park has an orangery and a Teesalon, as well as two ruins, one real (the Tempelherrenhaus), one artificial (the Künstliche Ruine). A statue of the sphinx in the grotto dates from 1786, and its Shakespeare memorial from 1904. Just across the river stands the Goethe Garden House, a seventeenth-century house where he lived in his early Weimar years. Now a museum, it contains fascinating drawings by Goethe himself.

Goethe did not stay here long. The Weimar Goethehaus, on

the corner of Frauenplan and Seifengasse, is today the Goethe national museum. Here the master lived from 1782 to 1832, and its classical furnishings were overseen by him. He watched closely over the construction of the staircase and spied on those laying out his garden. The mineralogical collection displayed here was selected and classified by him. Here is his study, with his rough pine working desk. Pinewood also served for his bed, and beside it is the sofa on which he died, on 22 March 1832. Two unmissable works of art are Angelica Kauffmann's painting of Goethe in Rome in 1787, and Goethe's own drawing of Christiane Vulpius asleep, in 1789.

He married Christiane in the baroque Jakobskirche in 1806, and she lies buried in its cemetery. (He inscribed on her grave, 'The only mitigation of my life is to weep for her loss.') Goethe's mortal remains now lie in a crypt designed by himself and Carl Augustus (but built only in 1825) in the same cemetery. Schiller's bones were the first to be brought here, in 1828, followed by those of the duke, and finally Goethe's own, in 1832.

4

SAXONY-ANHALT
AND A TOUR OF THE HARZ MOUNTAINS

When in 1502 the Elector Frederick the Wise of Wittenberg gained the Pope's approval to found a new university in his capital city, he clearly had no intention of splitting western Christendom in two. As far as religion was concerned, Frederick simply wished to appoint to the chair of theology a priest named Martin Luther, who had already made a brilliant reputation for himself in expounding Holy Scripture at the university of Erfurt. Fifteen years later, Luther pinned on the doorway of the Schloss church ninety-five theses, attacking the papal practice of granting indulgences – the remission of years suffered in Purgatory for sins committed on earth, in return for money. As he hammered them on to the doors, his blows were demolishing the structures by which Catholicism had maintained its sway in western Christendom ever since the split with the eastern orthodox church in the fifth century.

Luther's assaults did not cease. On 15 June 1520, Frederick's protégé would be burning volumes of canon law and a papal bull in the centre of Wittenberg, convinced that they were contrary to the teachings of Jesus and St Paul. Luther was summoned before the Diet of Worms in 1521, and then took refuge in the Wartburg, where he translated the New Testament into German. He then returned to Wittenberg and spent most of the rest of his life there. Wittenberg thus became and has remained pre-eminently the city and birthplace of the Protestant Reformation.

Wittenberg centres on its Marktplatz. Here in front of the town hall are statues of Luther and Melanchthon, designed respectively by J. G. Schadow in 1821 and by Friedrich Drake in 1860 and sheltered by Gothic *baldacchinos*. Luther holds a Bible. The plaque on the front of the plinth proclaims 'Believe in the Gospel', with the reference St Mark x, 15 (where Jesus declares 'I tell you solemnly, anyone who does not welcome the kingdom of God like a little child will never enter it'). On one side another inscription records the first verse of Luther's stirring hymn, 'A safe stronghold is our God', and the inscription on the other side declares that whereas the values of God last for ever, human values are doomed (*Ists Gottes Wert, so wirds bestehen, Ists Menschen Wert, wirds untergehen*).

One side of Melanchthon's plinth quotes verse 46 of Psalm 119, 'I shall proclaim your decrees before kings without fear of shame.' The other side carries a less provocative text, as befits the more irenical of the two reformers, namely a quotation from Ephesians iv, 3: 'Be diligent to preserve the unity of the Spirit through the bond of peace.'

Luther and Melanchthon stand in front of a superb Rathaus, which was begun in 1522. It is part Gothic, part Renaissance; its elaborate Renaissance doorway by Georg Schröter of Torgau is inscribed with the date 1573 and topped with a statue of Justice. Several gabled Renaissance houses also enhance the Marktplatz, as does a Renaissance fountain of 1617. Next to it, on Tuesday, Wednesday and Friday, is an open-air fruit and vegetable market, with useful stalls also selling cooked fish and snacks.

On the left behind the Rathaus, plaques on a handsome classical house tell you that Napoleon Bonaparte stayed there on 22 October 1806, and Maxim Gorki in 1903. A plaque on a pink sixteenth-century house on the south side of Marktplatz declares that Lucas Cranach the Younger was born here on 4 October 1515. Overlooking the houses on the side of the Platz to the right of the Rathaus are the twin octagonal towers of the Marienkirche, which were finished in 1558. You reach its delightfully irregular Kirchplatz through a little alleyway.

Here is a bust of one of Luther's allies, Johannes Bugenhagen. Bugenhagen had been a Premonstratensian priest and rector of the city school in Treptow, but he embraced the Reformation and married in 1522, three years before Luther did. Since he then had to give up his Catholic post, Luther found him a new one as a pastor in Wittenberg and asked him to be his confessor. The two worked together translating the Bible. In 1528 he was in Brunswick, reorganizing the church there. In 1537 King Christian III of Denmark asked him to come and reorganize the Danish church and Copenhagen University on a Protestant basis. On 12 August in that year this learned man, whose humble bust graces the garden of the Kirchplatz here, crowned Christian III and his queen.

The choir of Wittenberg's Marienkirche dates from 1300, while the rest was not finished until 1470. This is where Martin Luther preached the Reformation, though the pulpit we see today, enriched with a sounding-board and a gilded Holy Spirit, is not the one he preached from. Luther and his teachings are visually commemorated in a splendid reredos of 1547 by his friend Lucas Cranach the Elder. The lower panel depicts the reformer preaching. Between him and the congregation is a crucified Jesus, for Cranach was convinced that Luther taught not some new-fangled gospel but the only true one of Christ crucified. The cloth around Jesus's loins swirls deliriously. Melanchthon appears on the altar wings, as well as the baptism of Jesus.

The rest of this altarpiece, on which Cranach's reds gleam particularly brilliantly, depicts the three sacraments which Luther believed were central to Christianity. On the left wing is portrayed baptism, on the right confession. Here too is a portrait of Melanchthon. But the central panel is the most extraordinary. The scene is the Last Supper of Jesus and his disciples. The disciples and their Lord are seated at a round stone table. Cranach has included some traditional elements in the scene: the beloved disciple St John reclines on Jesus' breast; the traitor Judas has a bag of money; other disciples are anxiously asking who will betray their Lord.

But there is one radical change. Whereas Jesus had twelve disciples, here are thirteen. Martin Luther is present, as the last great apostle. Cranach has painted him with his beard and moustache, disguised as the Junker Jörg who took refuge from his religious enemies in the Wartburg we have already seen at Eisenach. Through the window we can see that same Wartburg, painted by Cranach. Moreover, the reformer is turning away from the rest to receive from a servant a chalice bearing the wine of the Last Supper, for Luther insisted against contemporary Catholics that all Christians and not just the priest should partake of the wine when they commemorated the Last Supper at Holy Communion.

Small wonder that Spanish soldiers furiously slashed this altarpiece as a sign of their opposition to the Reformation (though today it is perfectly restored). This was in fact the first church in Western Christendom in which Holy Communion was administered to the laity in both kinds, in 1522. It was also the building in which the Augustinian monk Luther married the Cistercian nun Katharina von Bora in 1525.

The Marienkirche at Wittenberg houses other treasures, including a bronze font of 1457 by Hermann Vischer, and other paintings by both Cranachs. Here too is an alabaster relief of 1610 in the Renaissance style, the work of Sebastian Walter of Dresden. It derives from the tomb of Lucas Cranach the Younger.

As you stroll along Collegienstrasse which runs east from

139

the Marktplatz, hoping to discover the original buildings of Frederick the Wise's university, all you can see is one of its doorways. The rest has gone. Near by is a Renaissance house built in 1535 which became the home of Melanchthon. Luther's less tempestuous ally died here, and today it serves as his museum. Luther's own home is close by a less truncated part of the university, for the Collegium Augusteum, first built in the second half of the sixteenth century, today retains the baroque form it assumed in the eighteenth. In its courtyard lived Luther, in a house of 1502 built for the Augustinian canons of Wittenberg. It scarcely resembles the home he knew, since F. A. Stüler transformed the building into a museum of the Lutheran Reformation in the nineteenth century, but the porch of 1540, sculpted with the arms of the Reformer, remains authentic.

Luther's study is virtually as he used it. Here is the pulpit in which he preached, brought from the Marienkirche. Since Luther's translation of the Bible, which represented a major attempt to bring the Scriptures to the common people, was the foundation of modern German, inspired his followers in other lands to make translations of their own and enraged his theological enemies, it seems fitting that the museum houses many such editions of Holy Writ. Alongside these are portraits of Luther, beginning with those of 1520 and becoming increasingly imaginary throughout the succeeding centuries. Cranach also painted portraits of Luther's parents, which hang here.

Pilgrims, whether Protestant or Catholic, make their way finally to the Schloss church where his earthly remains still lie. It rises along Schlossstrasse, west of the Marktplatz. No. 1 Schlossstrasse is now known as the Cranach-Höfe, for in its courtyard Lucas Cranach the Elder lived for nearly forty years. As well as painting, Cranach was mayor of Wittenberg and also ran an apothecary. Here, according to tradition, he welcomed and painted Katharina von Bora. Behind the Höfe, parkland runs down to the River Elbe. And since the air here has in the past been a trifle polluted by Wittenberg's factories, I have found it wise to pause in the nearby restaurant for a glass either of Edelherb Pils from Kulmbach's Reichel brewery or of Krombacher Pils – or a glass of each.

Ahead along Schlossstrasse rises the huge tower of the Schloss church, 88 m high, with the first line of Luther's most famous hymn, '*Ein'feste Burg ist unser Gott*', worked in mosaic around it. At the far end of Schlossstrasse a notice identifies the house used here by the radical reformer Thomas Müntzer. On the doors of the church Luther hammered his ninety-five theses. These doors were destroyed by French gun-fire in 1760, to be replaced in 1855 by the present bronze ones on which are inscribed all ninety-five theses.

Conrad Pflüger designed this church in the 1490s, and although it was entirely restored and in part altered between 1883 and 1892 it remains a beautiful building, lierne vaulted, with Gothic crests on its galleries and a boss of the Holy Spirit over the high altar.

On 18 February 1546, Luther died at Eisleben. On 22 February he was buried in the Schloss church. Johannes Bugenhager preached the funeral sermon, and Melanchthon gave a Latin address on behalf of the university. Luther's pewter coffin lies beneath a bronze tablet near the pulpit, its Latin inscription declaring that he lived for sixty-three years, two months and ten days. Near by on the wall of the church is a copy of a bronze memorial to Luther, which was made in Erfurt and found its way not to here but to the church of St Michael, Jena. His podgy face is instantly recognizable, and he wears comical boots.

On the left, opposite Luther's tomb, the corpse of his colleague and ally Philip Melanchthon, who died at Wittenberg on 19 April 1560, lies in his tomb. The Latin inscription reads, 'Here lies the body of the devout man Philip Melanchthon, who died in this city on 9 April in the year of Christ 1560, having lived for sixty-three years, two months and two days.'

Their protector Frederick the Wise, who died in 1527, has a bronze tomb made by Peter Vischer of Nuremberg and designed by Lucas Cranach the Elder. Frederick holds a sword and looks exceedingly stern. Opposite him is the bronze memorial to the equally stern Prince-Elector John the Steadfast, this one created by Hans Vischer of Nuremberg in 1534.

Massive, brooding, rising in front of a sweet garden, the Schloss of Frederick the Wise, built between 1490 and 1525, has been greatly altered since his death. Today it shelters the historical and ethnological museums of Wittenberg.

Gloomy Dessauerstrasse, running west from the Schloss church, soon transforms itself into the attractive Coswigerland-strasse. After 13 km it reaches Coswig and the start of a delightful series of exquisite villages, each with a superb Schloss. That at Coswig is the largest (though not the finest), built in the Renaissance style in the 1670s and given a more powerful aspect in the nineteenth century. Coswig's gabled Rathaus is also Renaissance with an impressive spire, most of it dating from 1569, though its core is a late-Gothic building of around 1500. Lots of the houses here are noble classical buildings, with a sprinkling of half-timbered ones. The church of St Nicholas is also worth a leisurely glance. Still basically a thirteenth-century Gothic building with a Romanesque west tower built around 1250, its interior was enlivened in the baroque era, from which times date its altar, font, organ and pulpit. Classical and Gothic tombs stand against its outside wall.

Leave Coswig by the route signposted 'Elbfähre', for to reach Schloss Wörlitz you must cross a tributary of the Elbe by a little car ferry. As the ferry winds across the water, it affords the best view of Coswig's Schloss. Schloss Wörlitz is 6 km away, along a narrow, often tree-lined road which runs beside the water. It would be idyllic, save for the cobbles which rattle your bones. (The cycle track beside the road is much smoother.)

Schloss Wörlitz was built by Friedrich-Wilhelm von Erdmannsdorff between 1765 and 1763 as a summer residence for Leopold Friedrich Franz von Anhalt-Sachsen. A passionate admirer of all things British, the prince enthusiastically espoused the new methods of agriculture and landscape gardening being developed there, and English elements continually recur at Wörlitz. Its iron bridge is patterned on that which spans the River Severn at Coalbrookdale. Villa Hamilton, built in the first half of the 1790s, is named after the English diplomat and antiquary Sir William Hamilton whose wife was Nelson's mistress. The English seat of 1765 derives from a model at Stourhead. Even the Chinese bridge is patterned on one Erdmannsdorff had seen at Kew.

F. -W. von Erdmannsdorff had also studied Palladian houses in England. He modelled the sober façades of the Schloss itself on Claremont in Surrey, and this is the first building in the English country-house style in the whole of Germany. Under its portico is a clock with the signs of the zodiac, and its inscription reads 'FRANCISCVS. PR. AEDIF. INSTRVXIT. LVDOVICAE. CONIVGI. DIGNISS. D.' The palace is crammed with fine art, including works by Canaletto and Rubens, and the so-called Wörlitz Amazon, a Roman copy of a fifth-century Greek original.

The contrast between this building and the nearby Gothic church of 1810, with its slender tower, reveals the exuberantly eclectic aspect of the buildings of the park which surrounds Schloss Wörlitz. A spiky Gothic house begun in 1773 is the oldest example of this style in the grounds of the Schloss. Here beautiful also meant useful, another notion imported from England. This park was meant to be farmed, with cattle grazing in its pastures.

But much in this park is merely fanciful and not useful at all. Erdmannsdorff's Wachhaus zum Pferde (Horse Guard House) of 1769 is a half-timbered building with a façade designed to represent an antique tomb. The façade is sculpted with a naked youth leading a horse. Erdsmannsdorff also built a Venus Temple in 1794, incorporating a plaster cast of the Venus de' Medici. Here is a synagogue, again the work of Erdmannsdorff. The garden stables are Gothic, built in the mid-1770s.

Everything lives harmoniously together, simply because of the all-embracing landscape. The initial designs of the park were by Johann Friedrich Eyserbeck. The prince's chief gardener was Johann Leopold Ludwig Schoch (who after his death in 1793 was rightly given a grave on a grassy hill at Schloss Wörlitz). Here in 1778 Goethe first learned the art of English landscaping which he put to such splendid effect at Weimar. (He described the park here as a 'quiet dream-picture'.) Schoch and his gardening colleagues made brilliant use of the waters around the Schloss, particularly the Wörlitzer lake, the Grosses Walloch and the Kleines Walloch, which they joined together with narrow canals. A 'Rousseau Island', laid out by Erdmannsdorff in 1782, bespeaks another Romantic influence on the park of Schloss Wörlitz. Italy puts in its appearance in a Pantheon and in a farmhouse copied in 1792 from one in Piedmont.

A pause in Wörlitz village, for a glass of Wörlitzer beer (brewed in the local brewery) is surely in order after all this. Then travel 8 km south to Oranienbaum. Here you cross a bridge and spy suddenly on the right the yellow and white Schloss, a gorgeous building with two wings embracing its lawns and drive, created by Cornelis Ryckwaert in the 1690s for Princess Henrietta Katharina. She was of the Dutch House of Orange, hence the name of this little town. The Schloss is surrounded by its park, with a pagoda and a tea house, and the town has a baroque parish church built between 1704 and 1712.

Turn right here and drive through the woodlands to Dessau. First recorded in history in 1213, as 'Dissowe', Dessau, set at the confluence of the Rivers Elbe and Mulde, became a market town, embraced the Reformation in 1530 and in 1603 was chosen as the principal seat of the little principality of Anhalt-Dessau. This was the birthplace in 1729 of the Jewish humanist and philosopher Moses Mendelssohn, who throughout his life (he died in 1789) strove for the emancipation of the Jews in Germany and gained the admiration of both Goethe and Lessing. Although most of Dessau was destroyed in a bombing raid of 7 March 1945, and although today the city is given over to industrialism, enough has been restored to give an inkling of what we have lost. The baroque church of St George (on Askanische Strasse), which was built in the second decade of the eighteenth century and given its cruciform shape in 1821, has been well restored externally, though it now has a modern interior.

Schlossplatz must once have been a splendid ensemble, but today all that remains of the once proud princely Schloss is the Renaissance Johannbau. The square centres on a statue of a trapper in a three-cornered hat, one of the entertaining characters from the Indian stories of Karl May. Near by the Rathaus remains impressive, its massive tower piquantly askew. This monster building dates from 1899 to 1901 and was restored in 1988. A year later work began on restoring the ruined brick Gothic Marienkirche behind it, at the top of whose tower is the date 1554.

The loveliest building in Dessau stands in the Georgengarten on the north side of the city, with its exotic trees and antique portico of seven columns (the *Sieben Säulen*). The two-storeyed, austerely classical Schloss Georgium was designed by Erdmannsdorff. Here hang works by seventeenth- and eighteenth-century Dutch masters, in particular Pieter Bruegel, Rubens and Frans Hals. As for German painters, the gallery harbours some choice works by Lucas Cranach the Elder and Hans Baldung Grien.

In this same part of Dessau, just south of the Georgengarten, is the Bauhaus, which was designed by Walter Gropius in 1925, damaged in 1945 and reconstructed in 1977. Near by stand Gropius's *Meisterhäuser* (teachers' houses) of 1926. Gropius also inspired the 316 modernistic villas of the Bauhaus settlement in Dessau-Törten to the south of the city centre.

Gropius had set up the Staatliches Bauhaus at Weimar in 1919, combining the Saxon academy of arts and the Saxon school of arts and crafts in a new school of design. He called it the Bauhaus, which means 'house of building' by turning on its head the word *Hausbau*, which means 'building a house'. His aim was to teach his pupils not simply art but also the practical techniques of pottery, weaving, the firing of stained glass, metalwork and the like. His courses were run by such gifted colleagues as László Moholy-Nagy, Josef Albers and Johannes Itten. Soon painters such as Paul Klee and Wassily Kandinsky were on the staff, with Gerhard Marcks teaching pottery classes.

The Bauhaus moved to Dessau in 1925 and two years later a fully-fledged architectural school was established here, under the control of the Swiss architect Hannes Meyer, who directed the whole Bauhaus project when Gropius resigned in 1928. By now their distinctive philosophy was clear. Under Gropius's impulse, the Bauhaus aimed to adapt functional craftsmanship to the demands of mass-production; the buildings they designed were among the first to use industrial elements such as glass curtain walling.

Undergirding these views was a political philosophy reflected in Meyer's left-wing opinions, but these were increasingly anathema to the Dessau authorities and in 1930 he was forced to resign. Ludwig Mies van der Rohe took over; but the revolutionary, functionalist style of the Bauhaus was soon to be totally proscribed in Nazi Germany. In a vain hope of survival in its native land, the Bauhaus moved to Berlin in 1932. The following year it was closed down, and its leading members fled Germany to promulgate their ideas in the United States of America and founded the Chicago Institute of Design.

Schloss Georgium at Dessau houses an extensive collection of Bauhaus memorabilia. Personally I find their teapots superb and buildings hideous, the Bauhaus itself being particularly so, its metal and glass-fronted façade hanging from a reinforced concrete skeleton. I have tried to eat in its architecturally miserable restaurant but never managed to stay long enough to taste the food. Fortunately there is an excellent, inexpensive and traditional restaurant near by, the Gaststätte Kieferneck in Fischerweg.

In the suburb of Waldersee, in an eighteenth-century park with a Chinese bridge and an orangery, Erdmannsdorff built the little classical Schloss Luisium for Leopold Friedrich Franz in 1775. Dessau's citizens swim in the natural Adria pool, visit its theatre (which seats 1,250) and take boat trips along the Elbe as far as Wittenberg or the Saale. In another suburb, Dessau-Mildensee, the Gothic village church, once part of a Benedictine priory, was rebuilt in the nineteenth century. It has the honour of housing a reredos by Lucas Cranach which once adorned the chapel of Dessau's Schloss.

But what most makes up for the lost splendour of Dessau is G. W. von Knobelsdorff's late-baroque Schloss Mosigkau, some 7 km south-west of the city. Stone half-columns in the Corinthian style set off its yellow walls. The far side, which is the main entrance to its gallery, is yet more impressive, with a grassy courtyard, surrounded by wrought-iron rails and gates, with urns on columns, and a long alleyway. In the rose-filled gardens nymphs hide in arbours, and the little lake, an oriental tea house and a maze are captivating. The Café Knobelsdorff opens from Wednesdays to Sundays between 10.00 and 17.00. Inside the Schloss is displayed a collection of rococo furniture and porcelain, as well as paintings by Jordaens, Rubens and Van Dyck.

Between 1717 and 1723 at Köthen, 20 km south-west of Dessau along the 36A, J. S. Bach spent the happiest time of his life. This was the principal seat of the Princes of Anhalt-Köthen from 1603 to 1847. Prince Leopold, who succeeded to the title at the age of ten, in 1707, was a passionate and skilled musician, studying at Berlin and abroad. By the time he returned to Köthen in 1713 the prince had learned to play the violin, the harpsichord and the bass viol with considerable skill. He now decided to create what he called a Collegium Musicum, and in 1717 he made Bach his orchestral director, commissioning unsurpassed chamber music from the composer. Here Bach composed his Brandenburg concertos; here he married his second wife, Anna Magdalena Wilcke, who was daughter of the court trumpeter at Weissenfels. Naturally enough, Bach souvenirs dominate the town: they are to be found in the local-history museum, at no. 4 Museumsstrasse, and in the former chapel of the Renaissance Schloss, which dates from 1597 to 1604 and was built by P. Niuron. Bach's bust, sculpted by Heinrich Pohlmann in 1885, stands in Wallstrasse, outside what is alleged to have been his home (though no one can be sure of this).

Apart from these delights, Köthen also offers the visitor its late-Gothic church of St Jakob, the oldest in the town, finished in 1514. In the middle window of the choir is sixteenth-century Gothic stained glass. The Agnuskirche is a baroque building of 1699, which houses paintings from Cranach's workshop. Köthen's neoclassical and Catholic Marienkirche was paid for by the last Prince of Anhalt-Köthen, who had converted from the Protestantism of his forebears.

Drive on to Bernburg, dominated by a massive Schloss set on a cliff above the River Saale. Although a fortress has stood at this strategic spot since the eleventh century, Schloss Bernburg today is a Renaissance building with sumptuously carved wings. The first architect responsible for the present Schloss was Andreas Günther of Halle, who began building the Langhaus in 1538. Next, another Halle architect, Nickel Hoffmann, took over, completing the transformation of the Schloss into a Renaissance palace enlivened with oriel windows. Its reliefs of 1569 are by the sculptor Peter von Echternach. Bernburg's Romanesque, Gothic and baroque houses are still in part protected by a defensive wall built in the fifteenth century and considerably embellished later. Its churches include the early-Gothic Nikolaikirche, the late-Gothic Marienkirche and the baroque St Ägidien.

In a flat and extremely fertile plain north of Bernburg, Magdeburg straddles the River Elbe. When Hester Lynch Piozzi (better known as Samuel Johnson's friend Mrs Thrale) arrived here in 1786 she noted, 'Never was I so weary in my life as when we entered Magdeburg, where, instead of going out to see sights as usual, I desired nothing so much as a hot supper and a soft bed, which the inns of Germany never fail to afford us in even elegant perfection.' That remains true at Magdeburg, especially if you relish such delicacies as eel soup (*Aalsuppe*), a saddle of hare in a red wine sauce (*Hasenrücken mit Rotweinsosse*) and marinated beef pot roast (*Sauerbraten*).

Here in 967 Otto I founded an abbey and an episcopal seat. But its site remained the principal reason for the subsequent prosperity of the city, a crossroads and a border between the eastern Holy Roman Empire and its western vassals. This ancient Catholic city adopted the Lutheran faith in 1524, becoming a member of the Schmalkaldic League. Its citizens were to suffer dearly for their convictions when, on 20 May

1631, during the Thirty Years' War, the Catholic General Tilly successfully besieged Magdeburg. His troops slaughtered two thirds of its 30,000 inhabitants, flinging their corpses into the river. Only the cathedral, a few churches and a hundred or so houses escaped destruction.

After the Peace of Westphalia Magdeburg was born again as a baroque city. Flourishing in part as a refuge for persecuted Protestants after King Louis XIV of France turned against them in 1685, Magdeburg suffered her next most savage destruction in the Second World War, when 90 per cent of her ancient buildings were destroyed in an overnight air raid on 16 and 17 January 1945, which lasted less than forty minutes.

Modern Magdeburg is thus neither the Gothic city of the middle ages nor the baroque city of the late seventeenth and eighteenth centuries. Yet it well merits a visit, and often, driving from Helmstedt to Berlin in the days when Germany was divided, I regretted that I was forbidden to turn off the prescribed route to savour this fine spot. Parts of the Ottonian cathedral still incredibly survive in the Dom of St Mauritius and St Katharina, as do remains of the late-Romanesque building in the choir. Much of the rest, damaged by a dozen separate bombs in 1945, has been exquisitely restored. What we see today is Germany's first pure Gothic building, in its original form partly constructed by French architects during the episcopate of Archbishop Albrecht I, which lasted from 1207 to 1232. Albrecht had studied in Paris, and clearly responded avidly to the early Gothic architecture of that city. His French architects evidently worked with Germans to build the ambulatory and the radiating chapels of the choir. Next they worked on the crossing, building also the easternmost pillars of the nave and the lower storeys of the east towers.

Cistercian architects from Burgundy next worked on the cathedral in the half decade after Albrecht's death, working in particular on the east wing of the cloister. Then a new inspiration appears in the cathedral, due to an architect (or group of architects) that no one has yet identified. The masons of the cathedral now doubled the width of the nave and raised the cathedral vaults yet higher, at the same time laying the foundation for the west tower. The next generation of builders crowned this with flamboyant Gothic work – in the completion of the nave, the second storeys of the west towers, more buildings in the cloister, and above all the 'Gate of Paradise', depicting the five wise and the five foolish virgins.

Today the grey stones of Magdeburg cathedral support twin towers with spiky spires and octagonal tops. The interior is spacious and airy. Whenever I reach this overpowering building, I make first for its ambulatory. Its capitals are extremely rich, sculpted with stylized plants and such Biblical figures as Adam and Eve in the garden of Eden. On one is depicted an elephant with a howdah.

If you enter the ambulatory from the left side of the high altar, look to the right at two damaged statues, sculpted between 1209 and 1220 and depicting the Annunciation, the angel smiling and curly haired, the Blessed Virgin complaisant. Look out too for the damaged sandstone statue of St Maurice, recognizable by his armour and carved around 1150. Here too is a bronze, Romanesque funeral plaque of Archbishop Wichmann von Seeburg, who died in 1132, and another of Archbishop Friedrich von Wettin, who died twenty years later.

The stone rood-screen of Magdeburg cathedral is superb (and especially its carving of Jesus' Passion). The statues of the Apostles in the choir were sculpted in the thirteenth century for a west doorway that was never completed. Splendid Gothic choir stalls depict scenes from the Old and New Testaments. Equally luxurious is the marble Renaissance pulpit of 1597, the work of Christoph Caput. Beside it, in a six-sided chapel which looks rather like a stone bell-tent, are sheltered precious statues of Otto I and his wife Editha, carved in the mid thirteenth century.

This house of God contains many elaborate funeral memorials, but two – one ancient, the other modern – ought on no account to be missed. The former, at the west end of the cathedral, is a complex, very-late-fifteenth-century work by the stupendously gifted Vischer family of Nuremberg, probably by Peter Vischer the Elder. It commemorates Archbishop Ernst of Saxony. The second, to the left of the choir, is a war memorial, sculpted in wood by Ernst Barlach in memory of the German dead of the First World War. As a Jew, Barlach in any case incurred the hostility of the Nazis; as a brilliant modernist artist he further incurred their wrath; and here, in 1929, he enraged them by expressing in this memorial all his regrets at the pity of that war. His carving exudes immense gloom; the soldiers are sad soldiers, not the heroic caricatures Hitler gloried in; and a woman's face is completely concealed in sorrow. The disciples of Hitler indignantly removed this sculpture from the cathedral, but it was returned in 1956.

To the left of Barlach's memorial, open the doors to find yourself in the Gate of Paradise (the Paradiesvorhalle), carved with five happy virgins who were ready to welcome their Lord and five exceedingly sad ones who had no oil in their lamps when he arrived. These statues, like those of the Apostles which adorn the choir, were sculpted in the thirteenth century for the portal that was never created.

The cathedral cloister is similarly crammed with delights, its south side created in the twelfth century, late-Romanesque in style, its east side built in 1236 in the early-Gothic style, its north and west sides flamboyant Gothic. The cathedral refectory abuts on this cloister, built in the mid fourteenth century. So does the Redekin chapel of 1405 (whose paintings also display the beguiling traits of flamboyant Gothic), and the mid-fifteenth-century Marienkapelle, which today shelters twelfth-century plaques from other parts of the cathedral and a reredos of 1360.

Magdeburg cathedral stands in a spacious square with attractive baroque palaces on all but one side, all restored after 1945. On the east side rises Giovanni Simonetti's Königliches Palais of 1707, as well as the Domdechanei of 1728, which stands next to another baroque building of 1732 (no. 5). The three-storeyed baroque palace on the north side was built by the Dutch architect Cornelius Walrave in the 1720s. And due west, in the centre of the town, rises the half-Gothic, half-Romanesque former monastery church of St Sebastian, which has some elaborate Gothic capitals in its nave.

As you leave Madgeburg cathedral, note the remains of the city's walls, built in part in the fifteenth century, in part in the sixteenth, with two remaining gates (the Turm and the Wehrturm). Then find the church and abbey of Unser Lieben Frau, a few paces north of Domplatz across Gouverments Berg. Consecrated in 1160, this Romanesque church was given Gothic vaulting in 1160. Differently coloured sandstone accentuates its lines, and its crypt matches the main church in boasting three aisles. The modern bronze doors now proclaim that the church has become the Georg Philipp Telemann concert hall, dedicated to the brilliant musician and composer who was born in a Magdeburg parsonage in 1681. As for the conventual buildings, these too are Romanesque, dating from 1135 to 1150, and house a library of some 25,000 volumes (most of them from the nineteenth and twentieth centuries) and a museum of the history of civilization.

Then, overlooking the walls and the river, stretches a string of fine churches, beginning with the little Magdalenekapelle with its vaulted Gothic nave. Next comes the Petrikirche, which was built for fisherfolk. It has a twelfth-century Romanesque tower and a Gothic nave whose exquisitely traceried windows were finished around 1400. Napoleon Bonaparte was insensitive enough to utilize the building as a storehouse. Allied bombers destroyed it in 1945, and it was rebuilt between 1970 and 1988.

The last church in the string is dedicated to St Augustine, but is known here as the Wallonerkirche. It derives its first name from the Augustinian monks who founded their abbey here in 1285. By 1311 enough of their church had been built for them to start worshipping in the tall choir. As an Augustinian monk, Martin Luther was almost bound to preach here, and did so in 1516. The following year the Augustinians who lived here were the earliest Magdeburg converts to his views.

The Wallonerkirche was happily spared much damage when the Catholic General Tilly captured Protestant Magdeburg on 20 May 1631 and allowed his soldiers to run riot. It was in this same century that the Wallonerkirche gained its present name, for after the Revocation of the Edict of Nantes by Louis XIV of France in 1685, Protestants in his territories were subject to a persecution which drove many to seek refuge elsewhere. Amongst them Protestant Walloons (that is, French-speaking citizens from Belgium and other territories belonging to the Sun King) sought protection here. Destroyed on 16 January 1945, the church has been painstakingly restored. Its tower was finished in 1980, and today the Wallonerkirche houses a late-Gothic altar of 1480 which once belonged to the Ulrichskirche of Halle (which is now a concert hall). It depicts the coronation of the Virgin Mary, who is attended by St Ulrich and St Ludger. Here too is a font of 1430, made by Ludolfus of Brunswick, and a pulpit of 1488. In this church Lutherans today worship in the nave, while Calvinists, spiritual descendants of the Walloons, worship in the south chapel.

A few other buildings in Magdeburg escaped the conflagration of 1945, in particular the baroque town hall of 1698, whose Ratskeller is Romanesque. The equestrian statue under a canopy in front of it, the Knight of Magdeburg, is a bronze copy of the Romanesque one carved around 1240 which now is sheltered in the city's historical museum. Marktplatz has a modern fountain of the jester Till Eulenspiegel. Over the roof of the Rathaus you can see the towers of a ruined hall church, St Johannis, Gothic and built between 1380 and 1490. It has been left in ruins in remembrance of those who died in the bombardments of 1945.

Eastern Germany is a region of fine public gardens, and there are two which should not be missed at Magdeburg. A series of hothouses (the Städtische Gewächshäuser of 1896) in the Pioneerpark (south of the Dom and west of the Elbe) nurtures numerous exotic plants. The park itself was designed by Peter Joseph Lenné in 1824. Between the Elbe and its tributary the Alte Elbe is the cultural park of Rotehorn, laid out in 1927 with its lakeside restaurant, its sports hall, its viewing tower and its little tourist train (the Liliput-Eisenbahn). Magdeburg Zoo, with some 1,100 animals of 190 kinds, is north of the city, on the way to the Barleber Lake, with its bathing stations and boats.

Three attractive towns fan out to the north of Magdeburg. On the way north-west to Haldensleben you pass through Gross Ammensleben; the former abbey church rises from Romanesque pillars and has a couple of saints sculpted around 1300. Haldensleben boasts half-timbered seventeenth- and eighteenth-century houses as well as gateways from the fifteenth-century ramparts. Its long russet and white Rathaus was built in 1703 and given its present classical face in 1823. In front of it is an equestrian statue of Roland, a copy of one sculpted in 1528. Such statues have great symbolic value, proclaiming the city's independence. Haldensleben's Marienkirche was once Gothic, but was rebuilt in the 1660s and 1670s, after a fire.

North-east of Magdeburg is Burg, whose winding streets are dominated by the two quite dissimilar spires of the church of Unser Lieben Frauen. The church has a sandstone choir built in the 1360s, while its nave was finished in 1450 and the eastern gable added in 1567. The sandstone pulpit was made by Michael Spiess of Magdeburg, who added his signature and coat of arms.

Magdeburg is a perfect starting-point for a tour of one of the finest, and most mysterious parts of the Harz mountains. In Old High German '*Hart*' means forest, as does its present-day equivalent. The F81 leaves Magdeburg to the south-west in the direction of Egeln, where the parish church, built between 1701 and 1703, is baroque, as is the Catholic church, which was built thirty years later. The Altstadt also boasts a pretty gabled town hall.

Turn west here and 10 km later, with hills gently rising on the left, you reach the hamlet of Kroppenstadt, still partly walled, with a Gothic town hall and Renaissance and baroque houses. Opposite is a cross, set up in 1651. The Gothic parish church of St Martin has a late-Gothic tabernacle, but its baroque doorway alerts you to the baroque pulpit and furnishings. At the substantial village of Gröningen, 5 km further on, the church of St Veit is an early-twelfth-century Romanesque basilica. Enough remains of the Schloss which Christoph Tendler of Torgau built in 1594 for Bishop Heinrich Julius of Halberstadt to make one regret the disappearance of the rest.

Our next city, Halberstadt, boasts a cathedral dedicated to St Stephen, with a treasury virtually unrivalled in Germany. Charlemagne founded a bishopric here in 804. Halberstadt lost over two hundred and twenty half-timbered houses in the Second World War but fortunately retained this cathedral, whose architecture displays with delightful clarity three separate phases of German Gothic art. Primitive Gothic (here dating from 1240 to 1276) appears in the westernmost span of the nave and at the base of the towers; mature Gothic (here built between 1354 and 1402) is displayed in the choir and ambulatory; flamboyant Gothic glows in the rest of the nave, which was finished in 1491. The towers date from the late nineteenth century and perfectly complement the rest with their own slightly different Gothic. Inside, the gallery and the rood screen, built between 1500 and 1510, bespeak flamboyant Gothic. Fourteen early-fifteenth-century statues of saints and apostles deck the pillars of the choir. Here too is a late-Romanesque crucifixion group of around 1220, a green marble Romanesque font of 1195 and an Annunciation of around 1360.

It seems absurd, in the face of this splendour, to insist that the cathedral treasury is almost as precious as the cathedral itself. The treasures are displayed in the refectory and chapter house, part of the extensive thirteenth-century cloisters. The manuscript collection begins with the late Carolingian era and continues into the late middle ages. Here are to be found Romanesque tapestries, a mid-twelfth-century one depicting the saga of Abraham, a late-twelfth-century one devoted to scenes from the life of the Virgin. The collection of vestments and reliquaries begins with priceless objects from the twelfth century, amongst them a Byzantine platter for holding conse-crated bread, a rare treasure brought from the crusades by Conrad von Krosigk in 1205.

Standing in the long, tree-shaded Domplatz you can see beyond the cathedral the towers, one higher than the other, of the church of St Martin. This three-aisled Gothic building has a portal of 1300 depicting the four rivers of Paradise, a bronze font with reliefs of the life of Jesus and a splendid seventeenth-century pulpit. The church of St Martin stands in the Markt-platz, where Halberstadt's independence is proclaimed by a statue of Roland dating from 1380.

The cathedral priory is a Renaissance gem of 1592–1610, behind which rises the Gothic hall church of St Andreas, whose reredos dates from 1440. Near by, at no. 36 Domplatz, in the Spiegelsche Kurie, a canon's house of 1782, is housed Halberstadt's museum of history and prehistory, with Renais-sance and baroque furniture and Dutch and Romantic paintings.

Those who warm to stuffed birds and birds' eggs can examine over 16,000 of the former and 5,000 of the later in the Heineanum at no. 37 Domplatz, which houses the mid-nineteenth-century collection of the ornithologist Ferdinand Heine.

The Renaissance arcades of the escutcheoned Standesamt run around a corner on the west side, where a grim, carved face under the eaves peers down. The west end of the Domplatz is shaded by the clover-leaf apse of a former Augustinian church, the Romanesque basilica of Our Lady (the Liebfrauenkirche) which was built between 1140 and 1170 (and completely restored after the Second World War). Its two stern west towers, connected with Romanesque arches, are matched by two octagonal Romanesque towers with pointed spires at the east end. Saved from destruction in 1945 is a late-Romanesque sculpture of the Madonna, Jesus and his apostles, carved around 1190 and now displayed in the choir.

Romanesque architecture merges into Gothic in the Moritzkirche of Halberstadt, whose choir-stalls date from the fifteenth century. Near by are some fine half-timbered houses, particularly in the Johannes fountain square, in Taubenstrasse, Gröperstrasse and Bei den Spritzen. Halberstadt's oldest house, built in 1416, is no. 2 Moritzplan, while its finest is probably the richly carved house of 1551 at no. 15 Lichtengraben.

Beyond Halberstadt the Harz mountains reveal their gentle foothills. But before exploring them, three enticing places south-east of the city ought to be visited. The first, little Quedlinburg, set on sandstone, is dominated by its Schloss, pierced by narrow tortuous streets and blessed with fifteenth-, sixteenth- and seventeenth-century half-timbered houses.

Quedlinburg is ancient. Otto I founded a convent here whose abbesses for centuries chose to live in the Schloss (since most of them were imperial princesses who had little regard for the ecclesiastical authorities and even at times voted in the imperial diets). Here in 1724 was born the poet Friedrich

Gottlieb Klopstock, whose birthplace at the foot of the Schloss-berg (no. 12 Finkenherd) is now the Klopstock museum – though the memorabilia of others share his home, including those of the first woman doctor in Germany, Dorothea Christiana Erxleben (1715–62) and the innovative gymnast J.-C.-F. Guths Muths (1759–1859). Climbing up the Burgberg you are offered a magnificent view of the city, the Harz mountains and their hinterland. On either side are two magnificent buildings: the abbey church of St Servatius and the Schloss. The former, founded in the ninth century, was rebuilt between 1070 and 1129 after a fire. A Gothic apse was added in 1321, yet this abbey church remains a virtually unspoilt example of the three-aisled masterpieces raised by the Romanesque architects who were drawn to this part of Germany. Some of them came from northern Italy (probably from the abbey of San Abbiondo in Como, where the carvings are uncannily similar), to sculpt the capitals and the frieze of the nave, as well as the chapel of St Nicholas beside the crypt. The massive crypt itself, which you enter by way of a Gothic doorway of 1320, boasts the same pattern as the upper church, with three aisles, while here the capitals of the pillars were carved when the first church was built in 968.

Heinrich I and his wife Mathilde lie in dilapidated sar-cophagi, under vaults with the remains of late-twelfth-century frescos. Here too are the Byzantine-style tombs of early abbesses. Beneath them is a crypt in which lie noblemen and women, in particular Maria, Countess von Königsmarck, mistress of Augustus the Strong and sometime abbess of Qued-linburg.

She and the other abbesses used to worship in the gallery at the west side of the church, while living in the neighbouring Schloss, which now displays eighteenth-century furniture and preserves a throne room built in 1735 and the abbess's room, built in the Flemish style in 1756.

The Altstadt of Quedlinburg is equally entrancing. Hohe Strasse is lined with half-timbered houses, the oldest probably no. 8, which was built in 1576. To the right is the baroque church of St Blaise (the Blasiikirche), crammed with galleries of 1715, with an altar designed by J. W. Kunze in 1723 and a west tower which is all that remains of the Romanesque predecessor of this building. Near by, in Wordgasse, is an early-fifteenth-century house rising on wooden pillars. As for the Marktplatz, its prize possession is a statue of Roland placed here in 1427. The steeply roofed Renaissance town hall has a marvellously ornamented porch of 1615, approached by a wide flight of steps, and a little hexagonal Gothic corner-tower. To the south-east of the Marktplatz the late-baroque Grünhagen house has a splendid staircase.

Quedlinburg's former tribunal, the Amtsgericht, is another delight, built in the baroque style in the early eighteenth century. Bockstrasse boasts the Renaissance Freihaus of 1574, while in Breite Strasse rises the half-timbered Gildehaus zur Rose of 1612. Following this street you reach the towers and bastions which survive from the old fortifications of the town, as well as St Ägidienkirche (St Giles), a Gothic church whose reredos dates from 1420.

The Wipertikirche is the last treasure to be explored here. This former convent church is a Romanesque basilica, founded in the ninth century; but the building we see today was restored after the Second World War. Its charms include a Romanesque doorway, and – for architectural historians especially – the circular crypt, which may well date back to the late ninth century. This crypt, undoubtedly the oldest of its kind in Saxony, boasts an ambulatory, with capitals carved in the Ottonian era.

Now the route runs south from Quedlinburg to find at Gernrode the oldest completely preserved Ottonian church in Germany. The church of St Cyriakus once belonged to a

Benedictine convent founded in 959 by Margrave Gero the Cruel at the time of the Holy Roman Emperor Otto I (who was crowned king of the Germans in 936 and emperor in 962). Gero's cruelty appealed greatly to Otto, since it proved handy in subduing the Slavs. When Gero's eldest son died in 959, his widow Hathui became the first abbess of the monastery. Gero then gave his foundation a rich endowment and even obtained one of St Cyriakus's arms for it.

This explains a curious alignment of the monastery church, for the angle of the choir and nave are askew. Initially Gero intended to dedicate the church to the Virgin Mary, so the church was planned to face the rising sun on 15 August, the feast of her Assumption. The arrival of the arm of St Cyriakus changed everything, and when it was time to build the nave it was oriented to face the rising sun on his feast day, 8 August.

First consecrated in 965, the church of St Cyriakus was extended and reconsecrated in 980 in the presence of Otto I and his wife the Byzantine princess Theophano. There are many Byzantine elements in its architecture, including the device of alternating pillars and columns. Although in the first half of the twelfth century two towers, the western choir and the crypt were added, basically the church presents a stunningly pure example of tenth-century Romanesque Ottonian architecture: a three-aisled basilica, with galleries and an eastern choir and transept, its columns and pillars and its carved capitals (with human heads peeping through the vegetation) all dating from the same epoch.

These are not the only splendid survivals in St Cyriakus. In front of the twelfth-century western crypt is a late-twelfth-century font, sculpted with depictions of angels, St John the Evangelist, the Virgin Mary and Christ himself. Margrave Gero's own funeral monument is here, a late Gothic tomb of 1519. The Holy Sepulcre on the south side of the church dates from around 1100. Outside, on the north wall, are bas-reliefs of Jesus and the Blessed Virgin Mary. On the outside west wall are fantastic and symbolic reliefs, carved probably around 1100. You can make out the Lamb of God, John the Baptist and Moses, and St Mary Magdalen at prayer before the tomb of Jesus.

The 36A runs east from Gernrode as far as Aschersleben, whose defensive walls are even earlier than those of Bernburg, for they date from 1266, when the settlement received its charter as a city. It is hard to judge which is finer: the Pfarrkirche St Stephan, a Gothic hall church with a Renaissance gallery of 1596 and a late-fifteenth-century Flemish painting of St Stephen and St Catherine, or the ensemble of Renaissance houses by the market square. The late-Gothic Rathaus of 1518 has a charming seventeenth-century tower. Zu den drei Klee-blättern (which means 'At the House of the Three Cloverleaves') is a building of 1788 which once housed the local freemasons and now houses a regional museum devoted to mining, the history of potassium and the like.

The quickest way from Halberstadt to the Harz mountains runs south-west along the F81. At Blankenburg are two Schlösser: the Oberes Schloss, a baroque building of 1705 to 1718, and the Unteres Schloss, which was built between 1725 and 1777 and is now the local-history museum. It incorporates the peaceful cloisters of a former monastery, where stone Gothic arches support a half-timbered upper storey. The centre of Blankenburg is charming, with little parks and winding streets. Its Rathaus in the Marktplatz is Renaissance, and behind it rises the early Gothic parish church of St Bartholomew.

Wernigerode lies a few kilometres to the north-west. Still in part fortified, its delightful half-timbered houses date from the fifteenth to the nineteenth century, ranging from Gothic through the Renaissance and baroque styles to the classical. The town hall tops them all, double-storeyed and multi-winged, dating chiefly from the 1490s and the early 1530s. It carries twin pointed towers and its main doorway is approached by a double staircase. Between this Rathaus and the early-fifteenth-century Gotisches Haus, a passage leads to the Harzmuseum, where amongst the exhibits depicting the geology of the Harz mountains is a splendid outline of the various techniques of building the half-timbered houses of the town.

Further along the street you reach Oberpfarrkirchhof, with the Gothic Oberpfarrkirche of St Silvester, which shelters tombs of the fourteenth to the seventeenth centuries and a late-fifteenth-century reredos depicting scenes from the life of the Virgin Mary. Around this square the half-timbered houses of many dates are quite stunning, their oriel windows, allegorical sculptures, double storeys, little personal touches charming, so that one might almost forget to look out for the Pfarrkirche St Johannis, which is Gothic apart from its Romanesque west tower and has a triptych of 1425 depicting the Virgin Mary protected by angels as well as scenes from the Passion of her son. Another church well worth a visit is the little Theobald-kirche, Gothic, with a painted gallery and a baroque group of 1696 depicting the Triumph of the Cross. Finally, the Schloss, its present form dating from 1883, overlooks the town from its wooded height and houses a so-called Feudal Museum which in fact comprises the history of the region from feudal times to the twentieth century. The courtyard hosts concerts.

Leave Wernigerode by way of the 36 m high Gothic Westentor and drive south into the Harz mountains by the F244 to Elbingerode, where you take the F24 eastwards to Rübeland, with its two subterranean caves. Both can be visited, with guides: the Baumannshöhle and the yet more spectacular Hermannshöhle, where blind fish swim in an underground lake. The Baumannshöhle even houses a theatre, known as the Goethesaal. Then climb to the Rappbodetalsperre dam and lake. Here you can hire little boats, to sail on an artificial lake 450 m long and 106 m deep which contains 110 m³ of water.

Now the serpentine route follows the Bode valley, much sung by Heinrich Heine. Heine, still a law student, had undertaken a strenuous walking tour of the Harz mountains, and in 1826 he published the first of four travel books whose success enabled him to devote the rest of his life entirely to writing. *Die Harzreise* made his name; in prose and poetry he romantically evoked the lives and customs of the peasants who lived in these hilly woods:

> *Auf dem Berge steht die Hütte,*
> *Wo der alte Bergmann wohnt;*
> *Dorten rauscht die grüne Tanne,*
> *Und erglänzt der goldne Mond.*

> *In der Hütte steht ein Lehnstuhl,*
> *Ausgeschnitzelt wunderlich,*
> *Der darauf sitzt, der ist glücklich,*
> *Und der Glückliche bin ich!*

> (On the mountain stands the hut,
> Where the old miner lives;
> There rustles the green fir tree,
> And shines the golden moon.

> In the hut stands an armchair,
> Beautifully carved.
> The one who sits on it is happy,
> And I am that happy one!)

Small wonder these mountains, which are some 30 km wide and 90 km long, and are clad with evergreen and deciduous trees, attract countless holiday-makers. Hikers have been provided with marked paths, including some to the region's highest peak, the 1142 m high Brocken. Bison and bears, elks and wolves, lynx and deer and the rare, curly-horned moufflon roam its forests. For those who like to explore at ease, the Harzquerbahn, a narrow-gauge steam railway, runs from

Wernigerode to Nordhausen, on the southern side of the Harz mountains. The Harz obviously attracts more visitors in summer, but I think it is even more exquisite when the lakes are frozen and snow lingers amongst the trees and covers the meadows.

Delightful little villages dot the Bode valley: Altenbrak, a winter-sports centre in the forest; Treseburg, another winter-sports centre whose houses entrancingly overlook the river. Thale, which sits on the mountainside at the beginning of the Bode gorge, is a major tourist resort. From near here a chair-lift carries you up to the 403 m high cliffs known as the Rosstrappe and even higher to the Hexentanzplatz (the 'Place where the Witches Dance'), which stands 454 m above sea level and 250 m above the Bode valley. The Hexentanzplatz so much excited Goethe that he set a crucial scene of his *Faust* here.

The F81 is the main route through the Harz mountains, reaching Nordhausen at its southern foothills. As you arrive a signpost points across a little stream to the left towards the notorious concentration camp Dora. Here for twelve hours a day prisoners from Buchenwald were forced to work underground manufacturing V bombs. Since they thus learned vital secrets of Hitler's new weapon, these men were inevitably condemned to death, and some 18,000 of them were murdered.

Nordhausen itself arose around a monastery founded by Mathilde, wife of Heinrich I, and became a city in 931. Though much was destroyed by Allied bombers in 1944, a good deal of the fortifications, dating from the twelfth to the fifteenth centuries, was spared. The cathedral, first built in Mathilde's time, is today a Gothic hall church, most of it built in the mid fourteenth century, though its reticulated vaulting was created in the early sixteenth. Inside stand six crowned statues which were sculpted around 1300. Amongst the carvings on the stalls, which were chiselled a century or so later, are imaginary portraits of the foundress and her husband. The baroque altar dates from 1726, while the crypt is all that remains of an earlier twelfth-century building.

The statue of Roland outside Nordhausen's Renaissance Rathaus dates from 1717 (though an earlier Roland statue was put here in 1414). He stands under his canopy in his long red coat, well buttoned up against the cold and carrying a shield with an eagle. The city boasts another Gothic church. Dedicated to St Blaise, it possesses a Romanesque west façade with a couple of octagonal towers.

From here the road winds through rolling countryside, crosses the River Heime and rises to Sondershausen, where you can visit a Schloss which the princes of Schwarzburg-Sondershausen built in the sixteenth century and carried on building till the nineteenth. The stuccoed court pharmacy was built in 1650, while the huge Riesensaal, which occupies the whole of the second storey, has a coffered ceiling and frescos, both added around 1700. By contrast, the white salon is stuccoed in the rococo style. In the Schloss courtyard is a Hercules fountain of 1771, while in the Schloss park stands an octagonal pavilion of 1709, which is now a concert hall. The town has a baroque parish church built in 1691.

Seventeen kilometres east of Sondershausen, Bad Frankenhausen lies at the foot of the Kyffhäuser peaks and the Schlachtberg. On the former is a massive, slightly comical monument of 1865 depicting Barbarossa. The latter was the scene in 1525 of the decisive battle of the Peasants' War, when the forces of Thomas Müntzer were defeated and he himself captured (and executed a few days later). Bad Frankenhausen, a spa with saline baths, has a little Romanesque castle, the Hausmannsturm, and a baroque church. Its baroque Schloss houses a museum devoted to the Peasants' War. Just outside the spa, the Altstadtkirche is twelfth-century Romanesque.

Drive on to Artern and turn north to reach Sangerhausen

and the foothills of the Harz again. At Sangerhausen the basilica of St Ulrich is Romanesque, with a baroque tower and a font made around 1300. Overlooking the Marktplatz, with its half-timbered houses and classical well, is the late-Gothic church of St James. Inside is a late-fifteenth-century retable of the Passion and the early baroque tomb of the Tryller family. The town has a Renaissance Schloss of 1622 and a local-history museum devoted to copper mining, as well as a rosarium in its park with six thousand wild and cultivated roses.

Eisleben, 12 km to the north-east, is officially called Lutherstadt-Eisleben because Martin Luther was born here in 1483 and died here in 1546. His father, Hans, came to Eisleben from Eisenach to work in the mines, quitting Eisleben for Mansfeld a year later. The house in which the great reformer was born is at no. 16 Lutherstrasse, and is today filled with mementoes of him, as is the house at no. 7 Andreasplatz, where he died.

Eisleben is a hilly spot, and on a steep slope beside the market place (with its Gothic town hall) stands the Andreaskirche, for the most part also Gothic, though with a few remains of the Romanesque. Its reredos of 1500 is sculpted with a coronation of the Blessed Virgin; its tombs, of the Counts of Mansfeld, date from the sixteenth century.

High up in the new town, founded for his miners by Count Albrecht VII in 1513, the Annenkirche (church of St Anne, the patron saint of miners) is yet more remarkable, on account of its twenty-six sandstone reliefs of Old Testament scenes carved by Hans Thon Uttendorp in 1585. Other fine Gothic churches are the Nikolaikirche, with its powerful square tower and a flamboyant reredos depicting three bishops, and St Peter and St Paul, with a reredos of 1501 depicting the miners' patron saint accompanied by the Virgin Mary and St Elisabeth. Luther was baptized here. When I was last in Eisleben a statue of Lenin of 1927 graced the main square. Is it still there?

Halle is 34 km from Eisleben. On the way there you pass through the lakeside town of Seeburg, whose fortress, much rebuilt over successive centuries, dates from the Romanesque era. It glowers over the boats on the Süsser lake. The suburb of Halle-Neustadt appears next, built in 1964 to accommodate some seventy thousand industrial workers and their families.

The city of Halle itself is washed by the entrancing River Saale. In 961 Emperor Otto I bequeathed the spot to the abbey of St Moritz at Magdeburg. The citizens prospered on salt; indeed, the name of the city means 'salt'. (Halle's Saline Museum is at no. 52 Mansfelderstrasse, close by which is a salty swimming-pool.) With trading links as far afield as Holland, Danzig and Prague, the city was soon wealthy enough to join the Hanseatic League in the thirteenth century, and Halle received its charter as a city in 1361.

Two centuries later Archbishop Ernst von Magdeburg built here the Moritzburg which still dominates the city. Its gabled and arcaded courtyard incorporates a six-sided tower. Begun in 1489 and finished in 1509, the Schloss today houses the state gallery of Halle (the Staatliche Galerie Moritzburg). It should on no account be neglected. Its gallery of ceramics is fine enough, but what entrances me most is its modern collection: first the drawings of Hans Thoma (1839–1924), and above all the wildly beautiful expressionist sculptures of Ernst Barlach. That said, the gallery has magnificent works by Georg Kolbe, Franz Marc (of the Blaue Reiter group), Lyonel Feininger and Fritz Cremer, as well rare works by Hans von Marées, a German romantic who lived from 1837 to 1887.

German expressionism has never received enough acclaim outside its own country. To explore it at the Staatliche Galerie Moritzburg at Halle is enthralling. Max Slevogt and Lovis Corinth introduce a superb sequence of paintings by the Die Brücke group: Ernst Heckel (represented by a delicious painting of a visit to a hairdresser), Otto Müller, Ludwig Kirchner,

Karl Schmidt-Rottluff and, supremely, Paula Modersohn-Becker, who was born in Dresden in 1876, studied in Paris and died in 1907.

I do not think it perverse to recommend this gallery before anything else in Halle, yet the city is as magnificent. In Domplatz stands the splendid Protestant cathedral, a Gothic hall church with a nave and two aisles. We owe its sumptuous decoration to Cardinal Albrecht von Brandenburg. Can one imagine his chagrin in 1541 when Halle opted for the Protestant faith and he was forced to leave his beloved city and cathedral? The building is filled with treasures. An early Renaissance pulpit is sculpted with the apostles and fathers of the church. A Franconian master sculpted the intricate choir-stalls in the same epoch. And in the early 1520s an unknown master created some superlative statues for the entrance to the choir. They represent Christ, his apostles, and three saints, Andrew, Maurice and Mary Magdalen.

Italian architects influenced the exquisite door to the sacristy, as they did the Neue Residenz which abuts on to the cathedral, its Tuscan columns dating from 1529. Follow Domstrasse to find at no. 5 the geological museum of the Geisel valley.

In 1685 Halle was the birthplace of Georg Friedrich Händel, and celebrates its musical heritage with an annual festival. Händel's home (no. 5 Grosse Nikolaistrasse) is now a museum, and the composer's statue (of 1859) rises at the centre of Halle's market square.

Here too rises the 85 m high, late-Gothic Roter Turm (Red Tower), which was built between 1418 and 1506, a statue of Roland erected in 1719, the Blaue Turm (Blue Tower) and the parish church of Our Lady (the Marktkirche), in which Luther preached and Händel learned to play the organ. This church was originally two smaller ones, joined together by the local architect Caspar Kraft between 1528 and 1536, and then enlarged with galleries and towers by the Renaissance architect Nickel Hoffmann in the second half of the sixteenth century. Inside is a reredos which portrays the Madonna and Child and, at her feet, Cardinal Albrecht von Brandenburg, who commissioned it in 1529. The font of 1430 is by Ludolfus von Braunschweig; and the church possesses a library started in 1561 of some 28,000 volumes.

To take the other churches of Halle in chronological order, you should visit the twelfth-century Romanesque St Laurentius (added to in the Gothic era and the eighteenth century); St Ulrich, which was begun in 1339, not vaulted until 1510 and consecrated in 1531 (its reredos dating from 1488 and depicting the coronation of the Virgin, the patron saint of the church and St Leger); and the baroque St George, built in the shape of the Greek cross in 1710.

Other treats at Halle include the cemetery, designed by N. Hoffmann in the second half of the sixteenth century. Martin Luther is commemorated in the Luther University, whose buildings are in the early-nineteenth-century classical style and whose botanical garden includes over 4,000 open-air plants.

Halle is the starting-point for a tour of those parts of the Saale valley which we have not yet explored. Merseburg, 14 km away, rises exquisitely beside the tree-lined river. The city flourished because of a palace built here in 919 by the Emperor Heinrich I, which was followed by a bishopric and cathedral in 1015. Here, between 1656 and 1738, lived the Dukes of Saxony-Merseburg. Today the city prospers on the chemical and rubber industries. Traces of an earlier Romanesque cathedral, dating from around 1040, can be discerned in the crypt of the present Dom. In the early thirteenth century the rest was rebuilt in the early-Gothic style. Between 1500 and 1517 the nave was again rebuilt, this time in a gorgeous flamboyant Gothic fashion, its three aisles of equal height, nervous vaulting rising from slender octagonal pillars. Inside are superb works of art: the tomb slab of Rudolph von Schwaben (slain at the battle of Hohenmölsen in 1080) in the choir; a mid-twelfth-century font; another tomb slab, of Bishop Friedrich II von Hoyen, who died in 1382; a thirteenth-century processional cross; an early-sixteenth-century sculpted wooden pulpit; a painting of a battle against the Turks, dated 1525; the sarcophagus of Bishop Sigismund von Lindenau, who died in 1544, a Renaissance masterpiece by Hans Vischer of Nuremberg.

The early-Gothic cathedral cloister gives access to an eleventh-century Romanesque chapel which houses a mid-thirteenth-century knight's tomb. And in the cathedral treasury is a valuable Vulgate Bible, illuminated around 1200, as well as the tenth-century Old High German text of the 'Incantations of Merseburg' (the *Merseburger Zaubersprüche*).

Beside the cathedral stands the Schloss (today the regional museum), its present form begun in 1483 and finished in 1665, thus incorporating Gothic, Renaissance and early baroque architecture. Its most delicate feature is the doorway and oriel which Melchior Brenner of Dresden created in the early sixteenth century. Before leaving Merseburg, enjoy the market square, whose former town hall was begun in 1475 and finished in the high-Renaissance era of the 1560s, while the Marktkirche St Maximi is a flamboyant Gothic hall church of the second half of the sixteenth century. In the Neumarkt stands the Romanesque church of St Thomas.

An excursion 10 km north-east of Merseburg reaches the village of Bad Lauchstädt, noted for its baroque park (laid out from 1776 to 1780, with cure installations) and its Goethe theatre. Goethe himself supervised the construction of this neoclassical building, which was designed by H. Gentz in 1802. The spa buildings were begun in 1735 and finished by Schinkel in 1823, thus traversing the baroque, rococo and classical eras of German architecture.

The F91 runs from Merseburg for 18 km to Weissenfels, where the composer Heinrich Schütz once lived. His home in Nicolai-strasse is now a Schütz museum. The Marktplatz is surrounded by baroque buildings and the baroque Schloss of Neu-Augustus-burg. Built between 1660 and 1690, this massive Schloss has a richly stuccoed chapel by G. Caroveri. The Marienkirche is late-Gothic in style. And at no. 22 Grosse Burgstrasse lived and died the poet Friedrich Leopold von Hardenberg (1772–1801), who wrote under the pseudonym Novalis.

Seventeen kilometres further on is Naumburg, which we have already seen. After his own Harz journey Heine continued through it, intent on meeting Goethe in Weimar. Heine had already become a radical democrat, a political stance which sent him into voluntary exile in Paris. His political notions even surface in some of the dreamy poems in Harzreise, where he transforms the peasants of the forests into monarchs:

> *König ist der Hirtenknabe,*
> *Grüner Hügel ist sein Thron;*
> *Über seinem Haupt die Sonne*
> *Ist die grosse, goldne Kron.*
>
> *Ihm zu Füssen liegen Schafe,*
> *Weiche Schmeichler, rotbekreuzt;*
> *Kavaliere sind die Kälber,*
> *Und sie wandeln stolzgespreizt.*
>
> *Hofschauspieler sind die Böcklein;*
> *Und die Vögel und die Küh,*
> *Mit den Flöten, mit den Glöcklein,*
> *Sind die Kammermusizi.*
>
> (The shepherd boy is king,
> His throne the green hill;
> Above his head the sun
> Is his great golden crown.

At his feet lie sheep,
Soft flatterers, wearing red crosses;
His cavaliers are the calves,
And they proudly strut.

His court actors are the little goats;
And the birds and the cows,
With their flutes, with their little bells,
Are his chamber musicians.)

Goethe by no means shared such sentiments, and when they met the two poets did not get on well. 'I was utterly appalled by Goethe's appearance,' Heine later wrote. 'His face is yellow, like a mummy's. His toothless mouth twitches anxiously. His whole figure is an image of human decrepitude – possibly the result of his latest illness.' Then Heine's tone softens before Goethe's undoubted genius. 'Only his eye is clear and shining,' he conceded, adding, 'that eye is the sole thing in Weimar worth seeing.'

5

THE MARK OF BRANDENBURG

The Mark of Brandenburg (or, as the phrase is sometimes translated, the Brandenburg Marches), at the heart of which lies Berlin, has long been associated above all with Prussia, but its warlike history goes back much further than Frederick the Great. Its first margrave, Albrecht the Bear, who was Count of Ballenstädt, had faithfully served the Holy Roman Emperor in Italy and in 1134 was rewarded with the gift of extensive domains between the rivers Elbe and Oder. For centuries German and Slavic tribes had fought each other over this region, but within four years Albrecht had conquered the northern and western regions of the Mark.

In 1157 he made not Berlin but Brandenburg his capital, for Berlin did not exist then. Brandenburg had been given to him by the last Slav ruler of the region, King Pribislav-Heinrich, who had converted to Christianity. Albrecht took the title Margrave of Brandenburg. Albrecht's dynasty, the Ascanians, prospered. By the end of the thirteenth century the margraves had founded some hundred new towns in their realm, including Berlin, Köpenick, Frankfurt-an-der-Oder, Neuruppin, Stolpe and Jüterbog. The Ascanians also encouraged Cistercian monks to spread Christianity here, and such monastic foundations as Lehnin, Zinna and Chorin also prospered, leaving superb ensembles of religious architecture. But the Ascanian line died out in 1320, and the Mark was once more ravaged by feuding barons and by quarrels between townsfolk and their would-be rulers.

Only in 1411, when the Holy Roman Emperor made the Hohenzollern Count Friedrich IV of Nuremberg hereditary governor (Statthalter) of the Mark did peace return, a peace the Hohenzollerns enforced ruthlessly. At the Council of Constance in 1417 Friedrich was made Elector Friedrich I of Brandenburg. Their position was strengthened by his third son, Albrecht, who inherited Ansbach in 1440. When his brother abdicated as elector in 1470, this wily Hohenzollern became Elector Albrecht III. Known as Achilles, in 1473 he published his *Dispositio Achillea* which established the law of primogeniture in his territories, thereby ensuring that after his death, in 1486, the electorate of Brandenburg would remain undivided.

Another member of this ambitious family, also named Albrecht, was elected Grand Master of the Teutonic Knights in 1511, became a Protestant and on Martin Luther's advice declared himself Duke of Prussia. Prussia remained the sole independent part of the territory of the electorate till 1618, when Elector Johann Sigismund managed to acquire the duchy. These two territories now fused, basically as the Brandenburg we know today, one of the five Länder of eastern Germany.

Under the Great Elector Friedrich-Wilhelm, who ruled Brandenburg from 1640 to 1688, the territory slowly recovered from the devastation of the Thirty Years' War. In spite of his peace treaty with Sweden, the Swedes were persuaded by the Catholic King Louis XIV of France to invade Brandenburg, but the Great Elector's forces managed to repel them. And when Louis expelled Protestants from his realms by the Edict of Nantes in 1685, Friedrich-Wilhelm welcomed them into Brandenburg by the Edict of Potsdam. French, Dutch, Bohemian, Jewish and Silesian refugees not only found shelter here but brought invaluable skills to the Great Elector's realm.

The next decisive change in the fortunes of Brandenburg occurred in 1701. In that year Friedrich III, who had become elector in 1688, declared himself King Friedrich I of Prussia. This was the benevolent monarch who established the University of Halle and founded the academies of sciences, painting and sculpture in Berlin. His son watched over the family fortune like a miser, and he left his successor, Frederick the Great, an army of 80,000 soldiers and a vast treasury. A lover of the arts as well as a military genius, Frederick the Great raised the strength of the Prussian army to 220,000 men, and his military adventures more than doubled the size of his kingdom.

This is the region which apart from Germany's capital Berlin, I explore in this chapter, though of course where it is convenient I plan to cross over its borders into other Länder. Start a first tour of the Mark at Potsdam, on the south-west side of Berlin about 30 km from the city centre. A historically redolent way into the centre of Potsdam is by the Glienicke bridge, for during the Cold War this was where spies were exchanged, and no one from the west was allowed to cross it. From the centre of Berlin you reach the bridge by taking the S-Bahn to Wannsee and then the bus to Schloss Klein-Glienicke, which is set in a 90 hectare park laid out by Peter Joseph Lenné. This was his first Prussian garden, its winding paths and romantic views designed in 1816. Later developments involved extending the park towards Potsdam and giving it an Italian aspect. To this end Prince Carl of Prussia brought statues and ornaments from Italy. Antique fragments dot the garden. The Schloss of 1826 is the work of Karl Friedrich Schinkel and his pupils Ludwig Persius and Ferdinand von Arnim. Schinkel also designed a temple, a casino, a bridge and a rotunda, all fashioned on Italian buildings.

Boat trips run from the other side of the bridge to the island of Sakrow. Just beyond the ferry station you can take a tram along tree-lined Berlinerstrasse into Potsdam. I will never forget doing so just after the city had been reunited. My trip was a revelation. The opulent houses flanking the road were desperately run-down. From one dilapidated window hung a stick with a white flag: 'Surrender'.

Then the tram turned a corner and beyond the drab blocks of flats appeared the green copper dome of the Nikolaikirche. Schinkel designed this classical church in 1830. Its dome, patterned on London's St Paul's cathedral, was added by Schinkel's pupil Persius in 1849. Its Corinthian interior is splendid, intricately carved balconies fronting its three galleries. Frescos by the Nazarene painter Peter Cornelius adorn the walls.

In front of the church is an obelisk designed by Georg Wenceslaus von Knobelsdorff. Beside it stands the former Rathaus of Potsdam, a baroque building by Johann Boumann, built in the mid eighteenth century and inspired by Italian models. Corinthian columns adorn its façade, an Atlas surmounts its cupola, groaning under the weight of the globe. The Knobelsdorff house next door, named after its architect, sports two caryatids supporting its wavy balcony, while the windows are topped by three comically grimacing busts.

Across a grassy square towards the centre of Potsdam rise 134 houses built in the Dutch style on the orders of Friedrich-Wilhelm I, the Soldier King of Prussia, to make his Dutch immigrants feel at home. But for Friedrich-Wilhelm, Potsdam would have been a ghost town. The Thirty Years' War and an epidemic had reduced its population from nearly 1,800 to 711. The town was deeply in debt. Friedrich-Wilhelm paid the debts and made Potsdam his second home. His good fortune included the fact that the architect of these homes, Johann Boumann, also happened to be Dutch. Boumann, however, could turn his hand to other matters, and he also built the Französische Kirche in 1752 for the French colony at Potsdam.

To the right of the Dutch quarter rises the Catholic church of St Peter and S. Paul, an oddity here since it was built of brick, in the Byzantine style, in 1870. Its 80 m high tower is modelled on that of St Zeno in Verona. The apse is patterned on the Hagia Sophia of Istanbul. Its altar houses an authentic western painting of 1739 and not a pastiche: *Jesus on the Mount of Olives*, by Antoine Pesne. The apse mosaic is a remarkable sight in Potsdam, since it dates from 1180 and once belonged to the church of San Cipriano on the island of Murano near Venice.

Outside is held a daily fruit and vegetable market, which shuts down at two o'clock in the afternoon. Another 'foreign' church, this one for Russians, stands in the Alexandrovska quarter of Potsdam. It was built in 1829, along with some still-standing Russian-style wooden houses, to house some singers and their families who had formed a choir when the Russian army helped to drive Napoleon's troops out of the town.

Potsdam has a third such architectural curiosity, the Nauener Tor. Built in 1755 on the north side of the old town, this monumental mock Gothic gateway by the architect J. G. Büring is the first appearance in continental Europe of the style which was gaining a hold on the England of Horace Walpole.

On the south side of the town are buildings more relevant to Potsdam's original military purpose: the stables, built by Knobelsdorff in 1746 and signalled by horses sculpted by F. C. Glume, and the massive baroque military orphanage (the Militär-Waisenhaus). Frederick the Great, conscious of the sacrifice he demanded of his men, wished this to be the finest building in the town, and his architect Gontard obeyed to the letter. A little further north stands the former guard house, designed in the Tuscan style by A. L. Krüger in 1797.

Pedestrianized Brandenburger Strasse is Potsdam's main shopping street. Many of the houses in this part of old Potsdam have dormer windows, for the Soldier King decreed that each householder should give lodging to two, three or even four soldiers. His favourite grenadiers, a company of exceptionally tall soldiers known as the Lange Kerls, were particularly favoured here. Each night corporals would patrol the streets, saluted from the windows by other ranks to demonstrate that they were safely at home and out of mischief.

Brandenburger Strasse widens at its far end, opening into the Platz in which stands the impressive Brandenburger Tor, raised here in 1770. In part a copy of a Roman triumphal arch, its architect, Karl von Gontard, has managed to infuse the antique pattern with baroque exuberance. Its sculpted decorations include Hercules and Mars guarding a shield.

From the right-hand side of the square, take the Allee nach Sanssouci. Lined with chestnuts, it leads to the celebrated Schloss Sanssouci. On the right an arch leads to the Friedens-kirche, begun by Ludwig Persius in 1845 on the orders of Friedrich-Wilhelm IV and patterned on San Clemente, Rome, complete with golden mosaics. It has a cloister half surrounded by water.

The road cunningly bends so that your first view of Sans-souci is a sudden one, stepped hedges, statuary, columns, clipped hedges, yew trees, flowers and vines rising above the lake and the fountains to the Schloss itself. Sanssouci's garden, with its parterres, fountains and obelisks, is a rococo wonder. So is the Schloss. Knobelsdorff built this masterpiece for Freder-ick the Great between 1745 and 1748. Its garden façade is enlivened by twenty-six caryatids and atlantes sculpted by F. C. Glume. The women simper, but I pity the men groaning under the inscription SANS SOUCI. One of them seems to have a pain in his stomach, and clutches it with a free hand. Colonnades behind the Schloss curve, to break for a view on the hill of the Ruinenberg, a fake Greek ruin where there is a reservoir to feed the fountains below.

Entry to the Schloss is by the courtyard of honour (with its

semicircular colonnade), which Knobelsdorff probably modelled on the Palais Bourbon in Paris, which he had seen in
1740. The interior is a rococo riot of stucco, swirls, elaborate
mirrors and precious woods. The concert room exudes asymme-
try. The music room is painted in white and a delicate blue,
and stuccoed with shells. Rococo paintings by Watteau's pupils
match the architecture and décor. Gilded stucco and marble
Corinthian columns enrich the central dining-room. Frederick
the Great's study seems out of place, until one learns that its
present classical aspect was decreed by his successor.

Sanssouci's park is divided into two. Part is a so-called
northern garden, designed by Lenné; part is the so-called
Sicilian garden with plants that would die if they were not
protected in winter. To shelter them Ludwig Persius designed
a 330 m long orangery, but Friedrich Augustus Stüler thought
to transform it later into a pastiche of an Italian Renaissance
palace. Knobelsdorff designed the baroque Neptune grotto,
which turned out to be one of his last works, for he died
shortly afterwards in 1753. Beside it rises J. C. Büring's rococo
picture gallery. Beneath its concave, shallow ceiling hang
masterpieces by Van Dyck, Rubens and Tintoretto.

From the great fountain at Sanssouci a long, straight avenue
leads to the Neues Palais. Its social function was to flatter
Frederick the Great after his success in the Seven Years' War
of 1763–9. Crowned with a dome, the Neues Palais is 213 m
long, the building boasts 322 windows, more than 400 putti
and 230 pilasters. In front stand the temples of friendship and
antiquity, created by the architect of the Palais itself, Karl von
Gontard, in 1786. His Palais incorporates a rococo theatre
designed by Johann Christoph Hoppenhaupt.

Statues of Frederick the Great abound, of course. Beside the
main park a garden landscaped by Lenné encompasses Schloss
Charlottenhof, which Schinkel and Persius modelled on an
Italian villa in the 1820s on behalf of King Friedrich Wilhelm

Above: Fritz Cremer's memorial to those who suffered and died in Buchenwald concentration camp.

Below: The River Ilm flows under Weimar's ancient bridge.

Above: The Rathaus of Weimar, begun in 1581 and superbly restored after the Second World War.

Below: Schloss Weimar; its powerful tower was given a baroque dome in 1732.

Above: Bust of the writer Louis Fürnberg (1909–57) in the Burgplatz, Weimar.

Below: An equestrian statue of Duke Carl Augustus (1757–1828) whose mother Anna-Amalia was Goethe's Weimar patron.

Above: Schloss Mosigkau, near Dessau, is the work of the rococo architect Georg Wenceslaus von Knobelsdorff.

Below: Wörlitz Palace, between Wittenberg and Dessau, designed by Friedrich-Wilhelm von Ermannsdorff – the first classical palace in Germany.

Above: Halberstadt, with the church of St Andreas and beyond it the city's symbol, the irregular spires of the Martinikirche.

Below: A typical half-timbered house at Halberstadt.

Left: The hymnologist Paul Gerhardt (1607–76) is commemorated by a statue outside the Gothic Nikolaikirche at Lübben.

Below: Schloss Charlottenburg, Berlin.

The old town gates, Potsdam.

Above: The Brandenburg Gate, Berlin, its quadriga now again boasting the once-banned Iron Cross.

Below: The Kaiser Wilhelm Memorial Church, Berlin.

III. Another pastiche of an Italian villa is Persius's Fasanerie. The two architects were also responsible for the so-called Roman baths. The Chinese Tea House, designed by J. C. Büring in the 1750s, is exquisite, and houses Chinese and European porcelain. A gilded Chinaman shelters under an umbrella on top of this fantasy, while other statues depict the Chinese making music and drinking tea.

There are yet more treats at Potsdam. On the northern side of the town Frederick the Great's nephew and successor Friedrich Wilhelm II had a garden park laid out. Known as the Neuer Garten, it was redesigned in the nineteenth century by Lenné. The park surrounds the Marmor Palace which Karl von Gontard and C. G. Langhans built in the late 1780s. In spite of its name, most of the building is in red brick, with only the doorways, windows and frieze made of marble. None the less this is an elegant building, today housing Potsdam's army museum.

On the north side of its 74 hectare park stands Schloss Cecilienhof, which resembles the kind of half-timbered country house one finds in Cheshire. Kaiser Wilhelm II had it built just before the First World War for the Crown Prince. Here in 1945 the leaders of the victorious allies (Roosevelt, Stalin and Churchill, who soon lost an election at home and was replaced by Clement Attlee) met to dismember postwar Germany.

Seven kilometres away, on the north shore of the Havel, rises Schloss Babelsberg, which Schinkel planned in 1834 as a neo-Gothic English manor-house. Its present sumptuous aspect is due to J. H. Strack, who took over building it in 1845. Today the Schloss houses a museum of the region's prehistory. It sits in a lovely park. Again the initial designs, by Lenné and Schinkel, were English in inspiration, the long drive based on those at Windsor Great Park, but they were later modified by Prince Hermann Pückler-Muskau, who took charge of the park in 1843. A couple of follies, a rose garden, woodlands, waterfalls, lakes, a coach house and a heron fountain make this park a delight. And there is even a bowling green.

Almost due south of Potsdam is a little circle of seductive places, even though the first, Luckenwalde, is also an industrialized town. At its heart is the double-aisled parish church of St Johannes. Built in the fifteenth century and enlarged in the late nineteenth century, it has a curious gable and a late-Gothic tower with a baroque top. Inside are paintings of the second half of the fifteenth century representing St Catherine and St Sebastian.

Ten kilometres further on you reach the village of Kloster Zinna, which grew up around an important Cistercian abbey founded here in 1170. The abbot's house, built in the mid fifteenth century, has an outrageously flamboyant gable. It now serves as a historical museum of the monastery. The monastery church is a Gothic basilica in brick, supported on granite pillars, with choir-stalls of 1360. When the monastery was being restored in 1958, the craftsmen uncovered Gothic wall-paintings.

Jüterbog lies 5 km south-west, a few remnants of its walls as well as three gates (including the double-storeyed Dammtor of 1480) remaining. In 1517, to the fury of Martin Luther, the Dominican preacher Tetzel came here selling indulgences, and the fifteenth-century Dominican church of St Nicholas in which he preached still stands. Its west towers are joined by a little bridge. St Nicholas stands sculpted over the mid-fifteenth-century west door. He appears again in the ambulatory, in five painted panels, set on a gold background, which depict his life, that of St Maurice and that of the Lord. In a north chapel is a reredos from Cranach's workshop, in which the holy women weep at the foot of Christ's cross. From the same workshop comes the winged high altar, depicting the Madonna. Jüterbog's Rathaus is equally captivating, its central gable rising from wide Gothic arches and flanked by little dormer windows with turrets.

The Franciscans followed the Dominicans to Jüterbog, and their church, likewise brick-built, dates from the late fifteenth century. It now serves as a library and concert hall. In the late-Gothic Liebfrauenkirche is a contemporary font, a pulpit of 1575 and a high altar of 1710.

Treuenbrietzen, whose early-thirteenth-century Romanesque basilica has splendid stained glass, lies north-west of here along the F102. The fifteenth-century local-history museum was once a chapel of the Holy Ghost, and apart from its tower of 1756 the parish church of St Nicholas is thirteenth-century late-Romanesque.

Drive northwards from here through Buckholz to Beelitz, where the baroque Alte Post is a former coaching inn and the basically Gothic church has a pulpit of 1656. And from here you can avoid driving on the motorways that circle Berlin by taking a secondary road through the woodland that runs for 22 km north-west to Lehnin.

Cistercian monks from Sittichenbach in Thuringia made this one of the most important monastic centres in the Mark of Brandenburg. The abbey church of Lehnin is a late-Romanesque masterpiece, with parts verging on the Gothic. This three-aisled basilica was begun in 1180 and finished eighty years later under an architect known as Frater Conradus. Its apse is exquisite and delicate. A Gothic reredos of the fifteenth century glorifies the assumption and coronation of the Virgin Mary. Another fifteenth-century altar painting shows the Crucifixion. And here under his stone slab lies Margrave Otto IV, the son-in-law of Rudolph von Habsburg, who died in 1303. Once again, as at Kloster Zinna, the fifteenth-century former abbot's house seems far too splendid for one supposedly dedicated to humility.

Briefly join the motorway, drive west, and take the next exit north for Brandenburg. Lying some 40 km west of Berlin, Brandenburg is not only picturesquely situated on the River

Havel and its lakes (the Plauer See and the Beetz See) but also profits from neighbouring fruit farms and the Götzer hills, which reach heights of 110 m. This is the ancient city that was once the capital of the Mark. Inevitably it suffered enormously during the Second World War, but the historical parts of Brandenburg remain entrancing. Arriving from Berlin and Potsdam, you reach the Neustadt first. Friedens Strasse runs past the Neustädter Markt and Molken-Markt (with its parking spaces) beyond which on the left rises the church of St Catherine (the Katharinenkirche). A brick Gothic building, begun in 1401, its nave and aisles are equal in height and criss-crossed by delicious vaulting. In the luxurious choir, the ambulatory has a font of 1440 on which is sculpted the baptism of Jesus, as well as a double-winged reredos of 1474 by Gerhard Weger.

The cathedral stands on an island, which you reach by taking first Molken-Markt and then Mühlendamm. Just before the Dom, on the right, stands the thirteenth-century chapel of St Peter, which was enriched in 1521 with a reticulated, flamboyant Gothic vault rising from three hexagonal pillars. Then you reach the oldest building in the Mark of Brandenburg, the cathedral of St Peter and St Paul, begun in 1165 and Gothicized in the fourteenth and fifteenth centuries. Its Gothic reredoses are fine, but surpassed in my view by a Romanesque crucifix of 1257, said to have been made in Saxony. The richly sculpted high altar with its painted wings was made in 1517. Another glamorous altarpiece was made by Bohemian masters. The clean lines of the crypt are unforgettable, with ogival vaulting and splendid capitals, as well as a memorial to those Protestant clergy who opposed Hitler and were executed during the Third Reich. The cathedral treasury is also worth a visit, with its thirteenth-century manuscripts, its foundation charter (of Otto I, dated 945) and its Gothic vestments.

Walk on around the cathedral apse, crossing a branch of the Havel to turn left and reach another typical hall church of this region. St Gotthardt was begun in the thirteenth century and finished in the eighteenth, but the overall thrust of its interior remains flamboyant Gothic. An early-thirteenth-century font is borne by the four Evangelists, and the canopy above it dates from 1623. On the north wall is a Gothic tapestry depicting a hunt for a unicorn.

To the north of this church rises a fourteenth-century gateway, the Rathenower Turm, which was enlarged in the sixteenth century and is topped by a stubby stone spike. Three other gateways survive from Brandenburg's fortifications. A second, in the Altstadt, is the fifteenth-century cylindrical Plauer Torturm, while in the Neustadt rise the 28 m high Steintorturm and the 24 m high Mühlentorturm, the former built around 1400, the latter in 1411.

To the east of the Rathenower Turm is the Altstädtischer Markt, with the gabled Rathaus, which was built between 1470 and 1480. Its façade is embellished with intricate Gothic tracery. In front of the Ratskeller stands a stern, somewhat the worse for wear statue of Roland, made in 1474. Five and a half metres high, he seems to be attempting (vainly) to deter one from taking a beer here. To the south, in a baroque house of 1722, at no. 96 Hauptstrasse, is the local-history museum, devoted to the history of the whole Havel region; while further west, along Plauer Strasse, you find the Romanesque Nikolaikirche, which was built between 1180 and 1230. In Klosterstrasse, halfway between the museum and the Nikolaikirche, is the ruined early-thirteenth-century Johannis-kirche.

Brandenburgers are well served with boats plying for hire on the Havel. Drive on due west beside the Plauer lake and across the Plaue to leave the Mark of Brandenburg for the Land of Saxony-Anhalt and the industrial town of Genthin, which lies on the Elbe–Havel canal and boasts a baroque church. Here you turn north-west to reach, after 8 km, Jerichow. The late

Romanesque parish church of Jerichow once belonged to a Premonstratensian abbey. The interior is cool and peaceful. Its finest feature is the crypt, with its splendidly carved capitals.

Beyond Jerichow is Tangermünde. In 1373 the Holy Roman Emperor Karl IV chose this little town as his residence, and Tangermünde flourished enough to become a member of the Hanseatic League. Its Altstadt is still surrounded by superbly preserved late-fourteenth-century walls, which incorporate the Neustadt gate of 1450, the Hühnerdorf gate of the late fifteenth century, and (on the Elbe side of the town) the sixteenth-century Wassertor. Hinrich Brunsberg of Stettin built the magical façade of the gabled and Gothic Rathaus around 1430, while its south wing with its open gallery dates from 1480. Tangermünde also boasts a fortress on the banks of the Elbe which Karl IV enlarged when he decided to live here. Alas, the fortress was badly damaged in a fire of 1640, but it was subsequently restored many times (the last time in 1902). Another fire, this one of 1617, destroyed many half-timbered houses in Tangermünde, so the attractive ones we see today date from the seventeenth and eighteenth centuries. Finally, the parish church of St Stephen, which replaced a Romanesque predecessor in the fourteenth and fifteenth centuries, has fifteenth-century wall-paintings, revealed when the church was undergoing restoration in 1983. Its 94 m high north tower has a baroque bonnet of 1712, and inside is a pulpit of 1619 and an organ made by Hans Scherer of Hamburg in 1624.

A mere 9 km further on is the ample city of Stendal, whose name (slightly modified to Stendhal) was adopted by the French novelist Henri Beyle. Beyle's own attraction to Stendal was due to the celebrated art historian Johann Joachim Winckelmann, who was born here on 9 December 1717, in a cobbler's house which is now a Winckelmann museum. In the middle ages Stendal became wealthy on cloth-making, but was ravaged by incessant wars until Friedrich von Hohenzollern brought peace in the early fifteenth century. The result was an economic and architectural blossoming, and Stendal remained a prosperous member of the Hanseatic League from 1359 to 1518.

In consequence, Stendal has perhaps too many fine medieval churches for the average visitor. The town's oldest, the early Gothic hall church of St Peter, has fifteenth-century Gothic vaulting and a massive rood screen with mid-sixteenth-century sculptures in wood. St James, a fourteenth- and fifteenth-century church, has early-fifteenth-century stained glass which depicts apostles and saints, as well as another rood screen, this one intricately carved in wood.

Augustinians built the superb collegiate church of St Nicholas, brick and in the Gothic style, between 1423 and 1472. Its windows are filled with a complete series of stained-glass windows fired between 1430 and 1460, their 1,200 scenes depicting the life of Jesus and legends of the saints. Here too are preserved sixty-six choir stalls of 1430, and thirteen sandstone statues in the choir, carved around 1240 and intended for a rood screen.

Franciscan nuns worshipped in the late-Gothic church of St Anne, whose monastic buildings are now the town library. As for the early-fifteenth-century church of St Catherine and its contemporary cloister, it now houses the Altmärkisches Museum. Finally, tall pointed spires top the three-aisled Gothic Marienkirche, built between 1435 and 1477. Powerful pillars and columns rise to its vaulted ceiling; its late-Gothic rood screen is sculpted out of wood; and its flamboyant Gothic high altar depicts the death and coronation of the Virgin Mary.

Near by stands the Rathaus, built in the fourteenth century and continually enriched, in front of which is a statue of Roland of 1525. The Ratsstube has wall-paintings of 1462. Stendal's importance at this time is indicated by the hall of justice inside the town hall. Other secular monuments include two solid gateways – the massive Uenglinger Torturm of 1380,

lavishly decorated in the mid fifteenth century, and the Tanger-
münder Torturm, whose base dates from the thirteenth century
and supports storeys added in the next.

From Stendal you can make a gentle excursion towards the
former border between East and West Germany. On the way
to Gardelegen, 36 km south-west, you pass Kloster Neuendorf,
whose former monastic church, begun in 1232, retains
fourteenth- and fifteenth-century stained-glass windows.
Gardelegen itself is guarded by the sixteenth-century
Salzwedeler Tor, with its lovely vault, two enormous round
bastions added in the seventeenth century and its gable, which
dates only from a restoration of 1907.

Gardelegen's Rathaus, rebuilt between 1526 and 1552 after a
fire had destroyed the previous one, has a tower and lantern
added in 1706. The town also boasts some fine two-storey,
half-timbered Renaissance houses, some of them with elaborate
doorways, as well as a late-Romanesque parish church dedicated to Our Lady. First built around 1200, it was later given a
flamboyant Gothic choir followed by a complete transformation of the nave in 1558. The north wall has paintings depicting
the crucifixion and flagellation of Jesus, as well as portraits of
the twelve apostles.

Drive north-west from here to Salzwedel. Although only the
massive keep of its thirteenth-century fortress survives, the
town is still protected by parts of its fifteenth- and sixteenth-
century ramparts, of which five town gates still survive. And in
a baroque house here (at no. 20 Jenny-Marx-Strasse) was
born Jenny von Westphalen, later to marry Karl Marx.
Salzwedel's Altstadt has a fifteenth-century parish church dedicated to Our Lady. Its spacious high altar was sculpted by an
unknown Dutch master in 1410. Its reliefs depict the Madonna,
supported by eight saints, while some thirty other scenes
depict stories of her life and that of her son and his crucifixion.
The altar is lit by stained glass dating from the fourteenth to

the sixteenth centuries. Of the same date as the high altar are six larger-than-life stone statues of Saints; the bronze font was made round 1520; and parts of the Gothic stalls are still here.

Near by is the former priory, half-timbered, with a massive round tower added in 1578. Follow Schmiedestrasse from here to find, at no. 27, a doorway sculpted in 1534 depicting Adam and Eve amongst saints, and at no. 30 the fifteenth-century Hochständerhaus. In the fifteenth century the Franciscans built a church at Salzwedel which is still standing, and in the Neustadt the mid-fifteenth-century church of St Catherine has Gothic stained-glass windows. Salzwedel's former patrician houses include the Ritterhaus of 1596 (at no. 9 Radestrasse); the Rathaus in the Altstadt is a late-Gothic gabled building of 1509.

From here Seehausen on the F189 lies 43 km east, reached by way of the little Arend lake. Seehausen has a late-Gothic church with a Romanesque porch and a baroque tower, and 11 km south is Osterburg, which has a fortified Romanesque–Gothic church with a massive west tower (topped in the baroque fashion).

Running east, the F190 passes through Werben (where if you enter the part-Romanesque, part-Gothic church you will find some late-Gothic stained glass depicting the lives of the Virgin Mary and St Peter), crosses the Elbe and reaches the little city of Havelberg, set as its name suggests on the River Havel. The cathedral here is a must. Like the churches we have just seen, its style is partly Romanesque and partly Gothic. The Romanesque tower seems more like a keep than a church steeple. Its treasure consists of twenty bas-relief sculptures on the roodscreen. Carved around 1400, they depict the Passion and the Resurrection of Jesus, and their style is that of the Parlers, master sculptors of Prague and Nuremberg. Amongst the other sculptures are three in the choir, carved around 1300 for a previous roodscreen. The choir-stalls are Gothic, the font Renaissance.

Our return to the Mark of Brandenburg and to Brandenburg itself skirts the Havel and its lakes. *En route* you pass through Rathenow, which earns its daily bread from optics but also has a parish church which shelters a monument to the Elector Friedrich-Wilhelm – the Great Elector – which portrays him as a Roman emperor with slaves at his feet.

A second delightful excursion from Potsdam circles the Plauer and Müritz lakes. On the way to the lakes you pass through some unprepossessing yet notable towns. I should add that, as I describe it, no one could make this trip in one day. Take the E55 motorway north from Potsdam and branch off left to Nauen, with its museum of local customs and its Gothic parish church which houses a tombstone of 1726. A decent road runs north-west to Wusterhausen, at the foot of a narrow 22 km long lake, plied by motor boats. Wusterhausen also has a three-aisled church, dedicated to St Peter and St Paul and blessed with a late-Gothic crucifix and a pulpit of 1610.

Eleven kilometres further is the little town of Kyritz, which once (though this is hard to believe in such an apparently insignificant spot) belonged to the Hanseatic League. Here the remains of the medieval ramparts haphazardly protect gabled, half-timbered houses, most of them built in the seventeenth century. Those in the Marktplatz are particularly fine, painted in contrasting colours. The Marienkirche dates back to the fifteenth century, and inside is a fifteenth-century Madonna and a sixteenth-century font.

From Kyritz follow the road to Perleberg. This town of some 15,000 inhabitants has an irregular Marktplatz whose half-timbered houses and neo-Gothic town hall are shaded by a church with a mid-fourteenth-century choir and early-fourteenth-century choir-stalls. Turn right here and drive for 24 km along the F189 to Pritzwalk, whose church of St James, built in the second half of the fifteenth century, has a Gothic belfry of 1881. Inside, the font and the high altar both date from the eighteenth century.

Here we temporarily quit the Mark of Brandenburg and visit part of Mecklenburg-Vorpommern by driving north to Meyenburg. At Meyenburg, in a park landscaped in the 1860s, stands a humble Schloss which was made a trifle more pretentious at the same time as the park was embellished. The baroque parish church of 1749 has a tower built a century later. From here a short foray south-east will discover at Freyenstein attractive remnants of a Renaissance Schloss, a flamboyant Gothic parish church and the early baroque Neues Schloss, which is entrancingly set beside water and serves today as a school.

Before we reach Plau am See further north from Meyenburg, the Plauer lake appears on our right, surrounded by woods and with a surface area of some 38 km². Plau am See has a transitional brick church, built in the thirteenth century and, alas, unwisely altered in 1880, but the town's situation alongside the Elbe canal and close to the lake makes up for this. Beside its cobbled streets are half-timbered brick houses, some of them gaily painted. For those who can afford it, I recommend the Seehotel at Plau am See, where you can wash down your fish with Paderborger beer.

Drive beside the Plauer lake as far north as Karow, and there turn right to continue beside the water to Malchow, which stands idyllically between the Plauer See and the Fleesensee. Malchow used to be called the Mecklenburg Manchester, not because the Rivers Irk and Irwell which flow through Manchester remotely resemble these lakes but because both places prospered on the cloth trade. To pursue this comparison, I should add that Manchester's fifteenth-century cathedral is a far finer building than either Malchow's neo-Gothic monastery church, which was rebuilt in the 1880s after a fire, or the local parish church, which dates from the previous decade.

Shortly after Malchow, turn right and drive between the Kölpinsee and the Müritzsee to Waren, whose parish church was rebuilt in 1792 after the old one had been burned down. Waren is the principal town on the Müritzsee, a lake covering 116.8 km² whose eastern borders constitute a protected natural park in which rare birds flourish amongst the conifers. Surrounded by prairies and a 450,000 hectare forest, this is the largest lake between the rivers Elbe and Oder. The pleasure boats of the luxury line, the White Fleet, cruise its waters. The nature reserve of Damerow protects bison. Occasionally stiff winds from the north-west capsize the boats of inexperienced sailors. Even so, small wonder that Waren is a much-favoured holiday resort. The town is over 725 years old, its half-timbered houses delightful, its two delicious churches basically Gothic.

Driving east from Waren and then turning south at Penzlin (where there are remains of a sixteenth-century Renaissance Schloss as well as a fourteenth-century church with a tower added in 1877), you reach Neustrelitz. Its late-baroque parish church, built between 1768 and 1778, has a classical belfry of 1830, built by the Berlin architect Karl Friedrich Schinkel, and popularly known as the butter churn. To my mind the Schloss church, built by F. W. Buttel in the 1850s, deserves a similarly insulting nickname. Near by is a park watered by the Zierke See, with a baroque orangery and a temple of 1891 which once belonged to a now vanished Schloss. Three kilometres further south, turn west and drive past lakes and through conifers to find the Müritzsee again. *En route* you pass through Mirow, whose Schloss is complex. Begun in 1590, the present building retains little of that era save its doorway. The main buildings today are baroque, decorated inside with baroque and rococo stucco.

From here the route winds north-west to Vipperow, and 9 km later turns right to find Röbel, nestling on the south bank of the Müritzsee. Founded in the thirteenth century, Röbel possesses a few reminders of its medieval defences and two Gothic churches, both built of warm brick. The thirteenth-century Marienkirche houses a fifteenth-century Crucifixion group and a sixteenth-century winged altarpiece; the Nikolaikirche is a thirteenth-century late-Gothic hall church with choir-stalls carved in 1519.

Wittstock is some 30 km south and back in the Mark of Brandenburg. Remarkably intact, its thirteenth- and fourteenth-century fortifications encompass the fourteenth- and sixteenth-century Gröper Tor. Wittstock's Marienkirche, built as a Gothic hall church in the mid sixteenth century, has a high altar in two parts. Above is a reredos depicting the coronation of the Virgin created by Claus Berg of Lübeck in 1530; below is another reredos, this one with an early-sixteenth-century Virgin, probably created in southern Germany.

Near by is a motorway, which speedily takes you 33 km south-east to Neuruppin. It lies piquantly beside the 14 km long Ruppin lake, where motor boats moor and you can hire a craft for yourself. Although Neuruppin was founded in 1238, scarcely anything medieval remains in the town, since it was almost entirely burned down in 1787. A lime tree escaped and is said to be over 650 years old. So did the former church of a Dominican abbey, an early-Gothic building of around 1300, which houses an early-fifteenth-century sandstone reredos sculpted with scenes from the life of Christ. Its tower dates only from 1907. But chiefly the heart of the town is grandly classical, ranging from its double-storeyed houses to its spacious Marienkirche which Berson designed in 1804.

Fittingly, this classical town was the birthplace in 1781 of the architect Karl Friedrich Schinkel (though Schinkel was equally proficient as a Gothicist). He and the poet Theodor Fontane (born at Neuruppin in 1819) are celebrated in the regional-history museum at no. 14 August-Bebel Strasse. Here too is a baroque Temple Garden, laid out for the pleasure of Frederick the Great in the 1730s by Knobelsdorff, its baroque 'temple' displaying eighteenth-century sculptures.

Herzberg lies east of Neuruppin, and from it a secondary road runs south through the marshes and the town of Kremmen, with its triple-aisled flamboyant Gothic church (whose choir dates from the thirteenth century) back to Berlin.

The south-east side of Berlin offers an equally rewarding excursion, again one which, with a little ingenuity, avoids motorways. The first stop is beside the River Spree at Fürstenwalde, whose town hall has a Gothic gable of 1511 and a Renaissance gable of 1611. Here the baroque Marienkirche, though begun in the fifteenth century, is in part the work of J. Boumann, whose artistry we have already seen at Potsdam. Beeskow, likewise on the Spree, is 27 km south-east, still surrounded by parts of its fourteenth- and fifteenth-century fortifications. The explorer Ludwig Leichhardt was born here in 1813, and in the late-sixteenth-century Gothic Schloss (which is built of brick) are displayed the spoils he brought back from Australia.

Frankfurt an der Oder is 31 km north-east of Beeskow on the Polish border. Its favourable location on a river crossing made Frankfurt rich, and the city became a member of the Hanseatic League in 1368. Here in 1506 was founded the Mark's first university. Its students included Thomas Müntzer, the Humboldt brothers, and the poet and dramatist Heinrich von Kleist. Kleist was born here in 1777, and the Kleist museum is at no. 17 Julian-Marchlewski-Strasse. Quitting the army in 1799, he devoted himself to writing, producing short stories, including *Michael Kohlhaas*, and a dramatic masterwork in *Prinz Friedrich von Homburg*. But in 1811, the year of its publication, Kleist shot himself.

Much was destroyed here during the Second World War,

and the late-Gothic Marienkirche of Frankfurt an der Oder was particularly badly damaged, but its choir still houses the late-fifteenth-century statues of the Virgin Mary and saints Adalbert and Edwige which once graced its high altar. Just before you reach the Oder bridge is the Friedenskirche, a Gothic building restored in 1890, with a seven-branched chandelier of the last quarter of the fourteenth century. The magnificent Gothic town hall was partly rebuilt in 1610 by the Italian architect Taddeo Paglioni. Its gable is none the less authentically German, and today it houses a gallery of contemporary art. Frankfurt's local-history museum is in Bach Strasse, which is named after one of Johann Sebastian's sons, who for a time ran the academy of singing at Frankfurt.

South of Frankfurt an der Oder is an industrial town built under the Communist regime of the former German Democratic Republic and given the appropriate name of Eisenhüttenstadt. Beyond it is Neuzelle, whose parish church once served a Cistercian monastery and derives its present baroque aspect from seventeenth- and eighteenth-century architects from Italy, Bohemia and Wessobrun in Bavaria. Its interior evocatively recalls the baroque and rococo churches of Bavaria. The high altar carries a tall group depicting the disciples on the road to Emmaus, painted by G. W. Neuherz in 1740, and the treasury of the church possesses a splendid monstrance of 1720.

After Guben the route runs along the River Neisse and the Polish frontier and, passing through the textile town of Forst, arrives at Bad Muskau. Here the ruined Schloss is surrounded by a delightful garden created in the 'English' style by Prince Hermann von Pückler-Muskau between 1815 and 1845. The prince also designed the park around the Norman-style 1860 hunting lodge at the nearby glass-making town of Weisswasser.

Now drive north-east to enjoy Cottbus. In the middle ages this was the most important linen town of the region. In 1701 industrious Huguenots introduced silk-weaving. In the Alt-markt at the heart of old Cottbus the houses of the tanners, linen weavers and cloth workers still stand. These late-seventeenth-century gabled houses in the baroque style are complemented by another classical house. The former Francis-can monastery church is a Gothic building dating from the fourteenth and sixteenth centuries, while the Oberkirche in Sandower Strasse is a striking, flamboyant, Gothic house of God. Cottbus is guarded by the Spremberg gate, which was fortified in the fifteenth century and restored in the nineteenth, as well as by the baroque Schloss Branitz, whose romantic 'English' garden, begun in 1870, is the creation of Prince Hermann von Pückler-Muskau. Now the regional museum, the Schloss displays Sorbian popular art and some of the treasures brought from the Orient by the Pückler-Muskau family, and a room is devoted to the landscape artist Carl Blechen, who was born at Cottbus in 1798. Cottbus also boasts a sinuous art nouveau Stadttheater of 1907.

We are on the edge of the well-watered Spreewald, a kind of landscaped Venice, criss-crossed with streams, dotted with farms and agricultural land. The region is famed for its cucum-bers, horseradishes, gherkins, pumpkins and onions. Here people punt along the shallow waters, as do students at Oxford and Cambridge, save that in the Spreewald the punts are three or more times as long and usually the punters are locals dressed in traditional costumes.

Lübbenau is the capital of the Spreewald, with its orangery of 1820 (which houses the Spreewald museum) and its chancel-lery of 1745, while in the suburb of Lehde is a museum of Sorbian culture, with typical farmers' houses clad in wood. Lübbenau also has a classical Schloss surrounded by an English park. The humbler buildings at Lübbenau are also attractive, some pink, some green, some yellow, some tiled, some half-timbered. The baroque parish church dates from 1744 and has a classical font with an angel designed in 1864 by C. D. Rauch. Beside this church a stele of 1740 gives useful distances, for instance declaring that we are 99 km from Berlin.

Weeping willows flank the Hauptspree as it flows north-west to Lübben. Here an ochre-walled Schloss rises beside the waters, its fourteenth-century Romanesque tower contrasting with the later Renaissance buildings, its sandstone porch bearing the arms of Saxony. Lübben's church is dedicated to the Lutheran pastor and hymnologist Paul Gerhardt. Gerhardt is best known for two hymns – 'O Haupt voll Blut und Wunden' ('O sacred head, sore wounded'), and 'Nun ruhen alle Wälder' ('The duteous day now closeth', to use Robert Bridges's translation) – both memorably set to music adapted by Johann Sebastian Bach. The pastor's career came to a sad end here, for in 1657 Gerhardt was appointed assistant pastor at the Nikolaikirche in Berlin. He unwisely opposed the elector's plan to unite the Lutherans and the Calvinists, and for this principled action was banished to Lübbenau, where he died in 1670.

The Paul-Gerhardt-Kirche at Lübben is a spacious late-Gothic brick building, dating from around 1500, with a noble stone tower and an onion-domed cupola. In front of the tower is a statue of the hymnologist, which naturally depicts him with a book of his hymns in his hand. Around the church porch terracotta tiles spell out a motto that might have comforted him (apart from the fact that these tiles date from the early years of the twentieth century): 'Alles Ding währt seine Zeit, Gottes Liebe in Ewigkeit' (roughly, 'All things pass away save for God's love, which lasts for ever'). Inside, a contemporary portrait of Gerhardt decks the altar, which, like the pulpit and font, dates from 1610. Inside too is a sixteenth-century Gothic Crucifixion scene. I hope to see them one day, but I have returned repeatedly to Lübben and have so far failed to get inside the building, even on a Sunday.

South-west is Luckau. We have seen many gables in this

part of Germany, but the curly ones at Luckau are especially delightful, some of them stuccoed by Italian craftsmen. Inside the brick Gothic church of St Nicholas is a sculpted, painted pulpit made by Andreas Schultze and Christoph Mätzschke in 1666, and an organ case of 1673 decorated with a group of King David's own musicians. Fortresses and Schlösser dot the countryside as you drive north-west to Baruth, whose park was designed by P. J. Lenné in 1838 and whose Gothic parish church has an altar of 1679.

Drive north-west, through Golssen with its eighteenth-century baroque Schloss and early-nineteenth-century classical church, and then through Baruth, with another baroque Schloss and a Gothic church housing an altar of 1679 and a pulpit of 1680, to turn right at Zossen, cross the motorway and reach our last stop before returning to Berlin. Königs Wusterhausen was once called Wendisch Wusterhausen, that is the Wusterhausen of the Wendisch Slavs. King Friedrich Wilhelm I of Prussia, who spent a couple of months here every summer, disliked the name and gave the place its new title. A Renaissance hunting pavilion, modified on his behalf in 1718, still stands here, the sole remnant of a royal holiday-home and the residence of Frederick the Great during his years as Crown Prince.

My final tour of the regions around Berlin takes us north-east of the city and ends on a grimmer note than the other three. A visit to Köpenick, on the eastern side of Berlin, starts the tour. From the centre of Berlin the S-Bahn from Bahnhof Bellevue reaches Köpenick in forty-five minutes. Köpenick is a town of clanking trams. Bahnhofstrasse which takes you to the centre of the town is drab enough, until you reach the grassy area where little stalls sell you a cooked *Broiler* (eastern German for chicken), or even better a *Kartoffelpuffer*. These proletarian delicacies are wonderful, comprising shredded potatoes made into little cakes and then deep-fried till they are golden-brown. You eat them with a topping of apple purée or sugar.

Beyond this tiny parkland, beside the lake, is a monument to the victims of fascism, an upraised fist and statues of miserable victims. Lindenstrasse continues past the Rathaus of 1904, a red-brick *mélange*, it seems to me, of the town halls of Steglitz and Lübeck. You cross the road beside the Alt Köpenicker Bierstube to find around the corner the moated and terraced Schloss, half-baroque, half-classical.

Schloss Köpenick is a museum with a splendid collection of craftsmanship: jewellery, tableware, furniture. One room is almost completely panelled with *trompe-l'oeil* marquetry work. The second-floor exhibition is even more delightful, with an eclectic collection of glass and ceramics (including superb works from Meissen), displayed in a room superbly stuccoed and painted. One treasure on display is a huge biscuit and chocolate holder, made in Berlin for Elector Friedrich III in 1701. The finest exhibits of the third storey are art nouveau treasures. Not all of them were made in Germany. Here is early-twentieth-century work by Émile Gallé of Nancy, and a vase of 1899 by the Rochwood Pottery firm of Cincinnati.

Further east, by way of the limestone quarries of Rüdersdorf, we reach Müncheberg, whose late-Gothic fortifications are almost entirely intact. Here Schinkel designed the tower of the parish church, which was heavily bombed in 1945. Turn left and after 12 km you reach Buckow, which lies at the heart of what the Germans rightly regard as a Switzerland in miniature. Theodor Fontane exulted over its lakes, valleys, gorges, mountains and hills. And at Buckow Bertolt Brecht wrote his *Buckower Elegien* and spent the last four years of his life. His work is here commemorated in the Brecht–Weigel Museum (Helene Weigel being the actress with whom he shared his life and whom he frequently deceived).

North-east of Buckow is a town whose name the post-1945

Communists changed from Hardenberg to Marxwalde. In so doing they indisputably honoured Karl Marx, for Hardenberg is splendid, its original name deriving from the great reforming liberal statesman Karl August, Fürst von Hardenberg, who represented Prussia at the Congress of Vienna and later was instrumental in abolishing serfdom, limiting the privileges of the Prussian nobility and promoting education throughout the kingdom. He also employed K. F. Schinkel to rebuild his village. To Schinkel Hardenberg owes its church of 1817 (and the furnishings, in particular a fastidious font). Schinkel, I think, also designed Hardenberg's mausoleum of 1822, with its Doric portico. He certainly created the classical second storey and the façade of Schloss Hardenberg, while P. J. Lenné designed its English garden in 1821, to which the Prince Hermann von Pückler-Muskau added his own particular nuance.

To reach Eberswalde follow the F167 north-west from Hardenberg, passing through Bad Freienwalde. The spa prides itself on its classical Schloss of 1798. This was the home of the Weimar Republic's foreign minister Walter Rathenau from 1909 until his assassination in 1922. The Gothic parish church of St Nicholas has a late-Gothic font and a pulpit of 1623. As for Eberswalde, its nineteenth-century Gothic church here is a curiosity, its doorways decorated with terracotta.

Now a zigzag route reveals greater treasures. At Kloster Chorin, 10 km north-east, the Cistercians founded a monastery in 1273. When the monks departed at the Reformation this beautiful building was grievously treated. During the Thirty Years' War it was used as a quarry, so to speak, its stones cannibalized for other buildings. Its saviour was Karl Friedrich Schinkel, who insisted that what remained must be preserved and that what had been defaced must be restored. Although parts of the monastery are still in ruins, the early-Gothic west façade of its church is a brick symphony, amongst the finest in the Mark of Brandenburg. The polygonal choir is equally stimulating. Leafy capitals exquisitely decorate the interior of the monastery church. Kloster Chorin is the venue for an annual summer music festival, and even outside this celebration attracts thousands of visitors.

At Angermünde, 15 km on past the Parsteiner See, the Gothic parish church, with its mid-thirteenth-century tower, has a bronze font created by J. Justus in the fourteenth century, carried by three sculpted men.

Drive west to the lakeside village of Joachimstal, whose little baroque church was gothicized in 1815 by Schinkel. This is hunting country, with forests and lakes on which you can sail or water-ski. Winding your way northwards through it along the F109 you reach the lovely town of Prenzlau on the River Ucker, the vestiges of whose medieval fortifications include the thirteenth-century brick Steintorturm, the 40 m high Mitteltorturm of the same date (which shelters the remains of a fourteenth-century chapel of the Holy Spirit) and the mid-thirteenth-century stone and brick Blindower Torturm. A century later Dominican monks built the Nikolaikirche which today serves as Prenzlau's parish church. Inside is an eighteenth-century painting of the Crucifixion which also includes a view of old Prenzlau. The rest of the monastery buildings now house a regional museum. An even finer church is the three-aisled Marienkirche, its ogival windows betraying its early-fourteenth-century date. The church's splendid eastern cornice was sculpted around 1350.

South-west from Prenzlau is Fürstenberg. Its Schloss is charming, built in the baroque style by C. J. Löwe in the 1740s. Delicate carvings enhance its walls and gables. Inside the stuccoed walls are merry with rococo ornamentation. A few wings survive from the former fortress. The parish church was built in 1847 by F. W. Buttel.

Just outside Fürstenberg is a national monument to the atrocities of the Third Reich. More women and children, some

92,000 of them, were executed or died at Ravensbrück than in any other Nazi concentration camp, and today you can see the grim cells in which they were tortured and shot, as well as the ovens in which their bodies were cremated. The Frauen-KZ Ravensbrück, now a national memorial (Nationale Mahn- und Gedenkstätte) to the dead, opens every day save Monday, from 08.00 till 17.00, though in fact I have found that you can walk round it freely on any day. Close by is a tank of the Red Army, which freed the surviving women and children in 1945. Here are mass graves. Lookout towers and the remains of electrified barbed-wire fences merely hint at the evil of this spot. The 'Wall of the Nations' before which the dead were buried lists over twenty countries from which they came to their hideous doom. Roses now grow over their dust, and an eternal flame burns in their memory. Beside the wall is a statue of two desperate, dignified prisoners. Willi Lammert sculpted the statue of a Christ-like figure who holds a woman in his arms, looking across the beautiful lake to the spire of Fürstenberg's church.

Drive south-east to Gransee, a town still preserving some of the white walls of its former fortifications, as well as the bright red Gothic Ruppiner Tor, which dates from around 1430. The mighty parish church of St Mary, with its two quite dissimilar towers, was built between 1370 and 1420, with a powerful façade and an equally impressive apse. Inside are early-sixteenth-century reredoses and a Crucifixion group created around 1500. At Gransee you can also see the Luisendenkmal, a sarcophagus created for the Queen of Prussia in 1811 by Schinkel.

Now the E251 takes us back to Berlin by way of another memorial of Nazi atrocities, for at Oranienburg is the concentration camp of Sachsenhausen. But for this camp, Oranienburg would be delightful. On the right, rising in its park beside the river, is a glamorous white Schloss built by the

Dutch architects Johann Gregor Memhardt and Michael Mathhias Smids in the mid seventeenth century. The town also boasts a baroque orphanage and a neo-Romanesque church designed by F. A. Schüler in 1864.

Whereas the Nationale Mahn- und Gedenkstätte at Ravensbrück is well signposted, at Oranienburg Sachsenhausen concentration camp is scarcely noticeable unless you watch carefully for the directions. Again, however, even if you arrive when it is officially closed, you can usually walk around freely. A well-designed placard explains the layout of the camp in Russian, German and English. A more recent placard reminds you that people have suffered and even died as a result of the recent illegal occupation of this part of Germany by the Soviets.

This concentration camp is notorious for the slogan on its gate: ARBEIT MACHT FREI. The horrid defensive wall with its watch-towers; the barbed-wire fences; the prisoners' barracks (their bunks crammed in up to the ceiling); the huts reserved for Jews; photographs of Himmler and the beasts who devised it all (including Dr Faust of the firm IG-Farben); the roll-call square, with the vicious stone run where prisoners were forced to exercise; the poles on which victims were hung from chains; the earth bunker in which they were buried; everything is here in the hope that such things will never again be seen on earth.

A friend of mine, Pastor Martin Niemöller, who died in 1982, was imprisoned in this concentration camp. He told me how, in solitary confinement, he could hear the screams of other prisoners being tortured outside his cell. It is a relief to drive on from Sachsenhausen, through the lakes of this part of the Mark of Brandenburg, following the signs to Rheinsberg. Schloss Rheinsberg began life as a Renaissance castle and was transformed into a baroque one by G. W. von Knobelsdorff and J. G. Kemmeneter at the request of the future Friedrich II. A couple of round towers and the watered site increase its charm. The park, another masterpiece by Knobelsdorff, is superb, a blend of French and English landscape gardens which incorporates a little mid-eighteenth-century Kavaliershaus. Almost, its beauty cleans the evil taste of Ravensbrück and Sachsenhausen from one's throat.

The eastern Germans have more speedily rid themselves of mementoes of their former communist masters. I think the town of Chemnitz, due south of Berlin near the border with Czechoslovakia best illustrates this. Chemnitz dates back to the mid twelfth century. It rejoices in a Renaissance town hall and the monastery church of Our Lady, whose porch was superbly carved in the late Gothic style by Hans Witten. Impudently, in 1953 the communists renamed the town Karl-Marx-Stadt. As soon as the Russians left, Karl-Marx-Stadt became Chemnitz again.

6

THE BUSTLE OF BERLIN

In 1987, when Berlin decided to celebrate its 750th birthday, Wertheim's elegant department store in the Kurfürstendamm decorated its huge window with thirty-eight different birthday cakes. The largest depicted Marlene Dietrich, seductively dressed as the cabaret singer in *The Blue Angel* and sinking into a succulent cream cake. The two images – sultry Dietrich and rich cream – both sum up this city, at once breathing 1930s decadence and a postwar resurgence that involves rich living in spite of the world's troubles and its own tormented past. As Winston Churchill ironically put it, visiting the city in 1945 after the defeat of Hitler, there was here 'a reasonable amount of destruction'. By 1987 Berlin had been beautifully restored – West Berlin as a modern thriving city and East Berlin a meticulous reconstruction of the magnificence of eighteenth- and nineteenth-century Prussian architecture. Few expected that within half a decade the city would be reunited.

No one really knows whether the city was 750 years old in 1987. Lying at the heart of Europe, some 34 m above sea level, Berlin was created out of eight towns and fifty-nine villages in 1920. The city is of course older than this, but not very old in comparison with many of the other great capitals of Europe. The name itself appears in written history only in 1244 to describe a settlement on the right bank of the River Spree.

Opposite this settlement, on an island in the midst of the river, lay Cölln, which we first hear of in 1237. Inevitably the two places, profiting from the west–east trade route across the Mark of Brandenburg, soon united. Their merchants were rich enough by 1359 to join the Hanseatic League.

Although the Hohenzollerns made Berlin their principal residence, the city remained small, its population in the mid fifteenth century no more than 6,000. Here the Hohenzollerns built a palace and hunting lodges, the former a massive building on the island of Cölln, enlarged by Caspar Theyss in the early sixteenth century. Theyss also designed the hunting lodges at Grunewald and Köpenick.

Like the rest of Germany, during the Thirty Years' War Berlin ceased to flourish. When the Peace of Westphalia brought an end to the conflict in 1648 the city was in ruins, its population once again reduced to 6,000. Eight years previously Friedrich-Wilhelm, the Great Elector, had succeeded to the throne. Determinedly he re-created his capital and country. Berlin was fortified. A canal linked the River Oder with the Spree. In 1675 his troops defeated the Swedes at the battle of Fehrbellin.

Exiled Huguenots, welcomed into Germany by the Great Elector, improved the quality of life in Berlin. These Protestants were both industrious and given to learning. Before the end of the decade they had established at Berlin a French college with chairs of Hebrew, philosophy, rhetoric and the humanities. Savants of the calibre of the mathematician Philippe Naudé, the philosopher Étienne Chauvin and the theologian Isaac de Beausobre were amongst its teachers. By the end of the century 6,000 Huguenots lived in Berlin, and the population of the capital had risen to 30,000.

The Great Elector's successor, Friedrich, ruled from 1688 to 1713; he was aided by his formidably intelligent wife Sophie Charlotte in enriching their capital. For her he built a Schloss at Lietzenburg which, after her death in 1705, became known as Charlottenburg. Meanwhile a school of fine arts was established at Berlin, followed by the Academy of Sciences which was founded by Leibniz.

His successor, Friedrich-Wilhelm I, was a glutton and a tyrant, but as we have seen, by the time of his death in 1740 he had taken care to set the Prussian army on a sound footing. Friedrich-Wilhelm I's unkindness to his cultivated son Friedrich was legendary; but when he succeeded to the throne, Friedrich II, whom we know as Frederick the Great, not only made Berlin the intellectual capital of Europe but also made formidable use of his father's army. Silesia was conquered and Poland partitioned. Berlin grew richer from its textile industry and developed the manufacture of porcelain. Its population grew from 81,000 when Frederick acceded to the throne to 150,000 at his death in 1786. As a francophile he attracted for a time even Voltaire to his court. His favourite architect Knobelsdorff enriched the capital with new buildings: St Hedwig's cathedral, the Opera, a new library.

Not even the Prussian army could stand up to Napoleon Bonaparte, and for two years after the battle of Jena in 1806 the French occupied Berlin. Six thousand Berliners took part in the war of liberation which brought about Napoleon's downfall. But even the short submission of the city to its enemy failed to halt its progress. In 1810 Wilhelm von Humboldt founded the university. Twenty years later he founded the Altes Museum. And Berlin found a new architectural genius in Karl Friedrich Schinkel.

When the German states regrouped themselves in a customs union, Prussia held the dominant position. Her population, 193,000 in 1815, had grown to 400,000 by 1848. Steam power drove the wheels of her factories; but a dangerously unsettled proletariat threatened the stability of the state. When the French lower orders rose in February 1848, those of Germany followed suit the following month. A so-called constitutional assembly was set up, though till 1918 it opposed every single attempt to bring about democratic reform. The working classes of Berlin continued to suffer, living in insalubrious houses and on the verge of starvation.

Politically, however, the country remained one of the most powerful in Europe. Neighbouring communities were annexed to Berlin. From 1871 the German chancellor was Otto von Bismarck; under his leadership Prussia had defeated Denmark in 1864, Austria in 1866 and France in 1871. On 18 January 1871, in the Hall of Mirrors at Versailles, King Wilhelm I of Prussia was declared Kaiser Wilhelm I of Germany. In his capital a column of victory was set up to proclaim the event.

Berlin continued to grow, from more than 820,000 inhabitants in 1870 to 2 million in 1905. The railways brought people and yet more trade. Schinkel's former cathedral was demolished in 1893 to make way for a more grandiose building. A new symbol of German power was the Reichstag. Amongst the artists drawn to Berlin were members of the movement known as Die Brücke. Max Reinhardt's theatre was world-famous.

Social Democrats were also in the ascendant politically. None of them opposed the disastrous moves towards the 1914–18 war. With Germany defeated, Kaiser Wilhelm II abdicated on 9 November 1918, and the Armistice was signed two days later. Politically and economically the country was in chaos, its chancellor, Friedrich Ebert, assailed on all sides. Political assassinations, particularly those of the Spartacist – the extreme revolutionary socialist party – leaders Rosa Luxemburg and Karl Liebknecht in 1919, rocked the nation. Unemployment and inflation paved the way for extremists. The Nazi Putsch of November 1923 proved abortive, but this was but a temporary reprieve.

Yet Berlin remained a glittering artistic capital. Its writers included Bertholt Brecht and Alfred Döblin. Max Reinhardt was still creative, and was joined in the theatrical world by Erwin Piscator. Artists included the savagely satirical Georg Grosz. Furtwängler was directing the Berlin Philharmonic. Alfred Einstein was a professor at the Kaiser-Wilhelm-Institut. Murnau, Fritz Lang and Josef von Sternberg were shooting epoch-making films.

On 30 January 1933, the Nazis came to power. Twenty-eight days later the Reichstag was set on fire, affording Adolf Hitler an excuse to begin a vicious repression of his political enemies. By 14 July only the Nazi party remained. On 20 May under the supervision of Goebbels, 20,000 banned books had been publicly burned on the Opera Platz. Most of Berlin's artistic illuminati left.

Albert Speer was able to indulge his monumental – some would say megalomaniac – style when he became Hitler's chief architect in 1934. In 1936 the Berlin Olympic Games offered Hitler a chance to parade his achievements before the world, games celebrated by Leni Riefenstahl in her brilliant documentary film *Olympia*, a sequel to her *Triumph of the Will* which had glorified the Nazi rally at Nuremberg. In this era novelists also served Berlin well, though often concentrating on its more decadent aspects. Christopher Isherwood's *Mr Norris Changes Trains*, published in 1935, and his *Goodbye to Berlin*, which appeared in 1939, introduced the dangerous flavour of Hitler's Germany to English readers, just as Alfred Döblin's *Berlin Alexanderplatz*, published in 1929 and translated into English by Eugene Jola, had earlier portrayed the hopelessness of life in a great city where men and women were desperately looking for a political saviour.

Hitler's racism displayed itself cruelly with the sacking of the German synagogues on the night of 9 November 1938, though the decision to exterminate Jews systematically was not taken till 1942. By then Germany was at war again. Before the war was over 70,000 tonnes of bombs had fallen on Berlin and the city was in ruins.

After the capitulation of the city to the Russian army on 5 May 1945, Germany was divided amongst the four victorious powers, as was Berlin itself. In West Germany the federal government set itself up in Bonn. The Cold War led to the virtual isolation of the Russian sector of the city and the eventual building of the Berlin Wall. For many years Berlin remained a beleaguered and divided city. It was beleaguered because this part of West Germany lay deep in the heart of the German Democratic Republic, the formerly Communist East Germany. It was divided by the infamous wall, erected in 1961 after the GDR had lost $2\frac{1}{2}$ million (of 17 million) citizens who preferred to live in the West. Squalid, built of grey porous concrete and topped with thick rubber tubing, the wall stretched for about 50 km in Berlin, hampering Westerners who wished to visit East Berlin and preventing recalcitrant East Berliners from escaping. Yet this hideous wall was not without its virtues. When the American poet Robert Frost met the Soviet premier Nikita Khrushchev, he read one of his own poems with the line 'Good fences make good neighbours'; the watch-towers and guard dogs of the Berlin Wall paradoxically eased the tensions between the two parts of the city. Crossing from West to East became progressively easier for the tourist.

Berliners on both sides of the wall remained flippant, tolerant, sharp-witted and always welcoming. The West Berliners especially smiled, since the politicians of the Federal Republic in Bonn continue to pour millions of Deutschmarks into the city to undergird its prosperity. Conscious of their debt to the Western world, they applauded vociferously in 1963 when President John F. Kennedy declared, 'As a free man I take pride in the words "*Ich bin ein Berliner*."' (Their joy was even greater because one of the meanings of the word *Berliner* is 'doughnut'.)

Their isolation ended with the Russian withdrawal in the 1990s and the demolition of the wall, which began on 9

November 1989. And in 1991 the federal government of Germany voted to move half of its ministries from Bonn back to Berlin. Berlin was once again the capital of a united Germany, a city of 3½ million inhabitants once again flexing its political muscles.

So we said goodbye to divided Berlin. No longer were spies exchanged across the Glienicke Bridge. For the first time for over forty years you could walk freely across the bridge into the eastern sector. I flew speedily to the city and took the S-Bahn to Wannsee and then the bus to Schloss Glienicke in Potsdam for my first ever unhampered stroll into the former Communist territory. As it was Saturday, nearly every shop and restaurant in the centre was closed. Virtually every shopkeeper was still resting on Saturdays, the day above all days when their western counterparts were raking in their profits. This eastern lackadaisical attitude, a Berlin banker told me, was typical, for the nanny state had for too long looked after the citizens – whether they worked or didn't. Meanwhile the centre of East Berlin was thronged by West Berliners, simply enjoying a part of their city so long denied them. At least most of the superb art galleries here were open at weekends. Food was still cheaper in East Berlin than in the West. Beer gushed amply forth. In the Friedrichstadtpalast the girls of a Parisian-style cabaret swung their long legs with a precision that rivalled anything the cabarets of the West could offer. Prussian Berlin rose proud again in the newly restored buildings of the Platz der Akademie.

As the day of reunion approached, there were festivities in both sectors of Berlin. The Martin Gropius art gallery in the West appropriately (or inappropriately, some opined) mounted a monster exhibition devoted to the life of the arch-Prussian Otto von Bismarck, nineteenth-century architect of German unity and a nationalist to the core.

The infamous Berlin Wall, which once divided the city, was

not then entirely demolished. For 5 DM per half hour you could hire a hammer from enterprising salesmen and chip away at it yourself. Checkpoint Charlie was the point where the British used to cross to East Berlin, braving insolent guards. On the corner of Friedrichstrasse and Kochstrasse, the Museumhaus am Checkpoint Charlie now has a permanent exhibition of the history of the infamous wall, as well as another devoted to the non-violent struggle for human rights from the time of Gandhi to the present day.

At the former boundary between East and West stands the Brandenburg Gate. For a time, the celebrated Quadriga over this Brandenburg Gate disappeared, for its wreath of honour was damaged by over-enthusiastic Berliners clambering up the gate when they realized that their divided city was once more united. Happily, the monument has now been restored.

No one could guess how many years would pass before the traumas of the collapse of the eastern bloc were played out. The signs of this remarkable collapse were everywhere in the city. I walked along Strasse des 17 Juni. Once the haunt of tarts, each weekend it was filled with rows and rows of buses from Poland. Bringing shoppers across the recently opened border, they returned to their own land with tons of chocolates and crates of beer, the Poles planning to sell them at home to eke out their own meagre standard of living.

I'm glad I was in Berlin when the wall came down. That was a heady week. The long-awaited reunion was celebrated with church services of thanksgiving, with civic high jinks and the assembly of the first united Berlin parliament since the Cold War split the city. The huge window of Wertheim, the luxury store in fashionable Kurfürstendamm, was festooned no longer with Marlene Dietrich in a chocolate cake but with the coats of arms of every Berlin suburb, both East and West.

In the years when their city was divided, enterprising Berliners soon adapted to their perilous status, welcoming tourists who relished the *frisson* of a city where western capitalism and eastern Communism met at a guarded border. The Bristol Hotel Kempinski set (and still sets) the standard for all the luxury hotels in what was then known as West Berlin. First, it was modern, for no ancient hotel survived the Second World War. Secondly, its ambience was old-fashioned and traditional, as if to recall a bygone age, so that a cognac is served slowly and tantalizingly, the glass turned over a flame to make sure its temperature is absolutely right. Thirdly, it stood (and still stands) at the heart of the city, at no. 27 Kurfürstendamm. In the Bristol bar you can sink into rich reproduction armchairs and listen to the pianist. Sated with the excellent cuisine, you can shed weight in the sauna, relax under a masseur, play pool or swim in the indoor pool.

The Schweizerhof, then as now, is almost as opulent, close by Berlin's famous zoo and blessed by Swiss traditions of stylish service. The Steigenberger in Rankegasse was extravagantly built of glass, chrome, marble and brass in 1979 and boasts a mixed sauna and a famed kitchen. In Lietzenburger Strasse are slightly less luxurious hotels than the three major ones, among them the Hotel Arosa, which has skilfully re-created an early-twentieth-century *Weinstube* while not neglecting the obligatory swimming-pool. A similar 'authentic old German' restaurant is incorporated in the spacious Hotel am Zoo on Kurfürstendamm. A survivor of past days is the late-nineteenth-century exterior of the Hotel Kronprinz Berlin at no. 1 Kronprinzendamm, though the interior has been gutted and totally modernized. Outside the city centre the Hotel Seehof in the district of Charlottenburg overlooks the waters of Lake Lietzen, and the Forsthaus Paulsborn and the Schloss-hotel Gehrhus, both in the tree-lined streets of the Grunewald district, seem even more rural; the latter is a delightful survival of 1912, set in its own park and designed as an Italian Renaissance *palazzo*.

Even in the Cold War years, staying in East Berlin was by no means the hair-raising experience that the spy stories of John le Carré might suggest. In the Palasthotel, for example, you found the same luxury, saunas, solaria and massage parlours as in its West Berlin counterparts. The Interhotel Unter den Linden has a style which seems brutal alongside this elegant street, but its service is charming. By contrast the Interhotel Stadt Berlin on Alexanderplatz is so vast that the tourist should instantly make for its Zillestube, named after Heinrich Zille, one of Berlin's most savage caricaturists, where the food (sauerkraut, pigs' trotters, offal and the like) seems almost a caricature of Berlin at its most ethnic.

If you want to taste genuine Berlin food such as the locals relish, expect it to be solid. For me a *Kohlrabi-Eintopf*, a broth of sliced cabbage, diced bits of pork and little potatoes, is often all I can take at lunch (though most Berliners in fact lunch off *Stullen* – two slices of buttered bread with *Wurst* or cheese). *Eisbein* is a pig's trotter, often served with sauerkraut. Goose or roast pork is served with potato dumplings and fried fruit, the whole smothered in a powerful sauce. Berliners have taken to mixing fish with their meats, and *Königsberger Klopse* offers you capers, herring and meatballs. With these overwhelmingly rich dishes Berliners drink a beer enriched with syrup – usually raspberry (*Himbeer*). Another traditional Berlin treat is a haunch of pork, the delicacy served on toast by the celebrated Ermeler Haus at no. 10 Am Märkischen Ufer, with its rococo wine restaurant. It would be a poorer tourist who left Berlin without savouring a savoury *Hackenpeter*, an inexpensive bun filled with minced beef enhanced with onions, or a Berlin pancake (*Pfannkuchen*), not to speak of a *Bockwurst* garnished with mustard and bought at one of the countless street kiosks. Finally, tuck into a potato pancake (or *Kartoffelpuffer*) served with apple sauce and guaranteed to convert the most abstemious.

This is a cosmopolitan city, and the fact is reflected in its food. French cuisine is offered in the Paris Bar at no. 152 Kantstrasse and in the Brasserie on Wittenbergplatz, while even more expensive French food is served in the Hugenotten at the Hotel Inter-Continental; the Alter Krug at no. 3 Potsdamerstrasse is celebrated for its rich Austrian cuisine; and Berlin has a goodly number of fine Italian restaurants run by Italians who have long made the city their home. Some of the staff are not even Italian. Of an evening I like to walk from my usual pad in the Hansaviertel across the Moabit Bridge, which was built in the mid-1890s and, because of two friendly bears sculpted at each end, is known as the Bärenbrücke, past the church of St Johannes to make a left and a right turn across the Kleine Tiergarten to find a not-too-expensive one. Once I asked the waitress if she herself were Italian. '*Nein,*' she replied, '*Berlin ist international.*'

As one might expect, the Kopenhagen at no. 203 Kurfürstendamm serves Danish food, Lee Wah at no. 92 in the same street is a Chinese restaurant, and the Dakotai on the first floor of the Europa Centre specializes in Japanese food. The Alt-Nürnberg, another restaurant in the Europa Centre, offers Bavarian specialities. And one pleasing consequence of many years of Russian occupation is that you can also find Russian specialities in Berlin, such as chicken *tabaka*, cutlets served in the Kiev style and so on, as well as vodka in the Restaurant Moskau at no. 34 Karl-Marx-Allee. Beautifully prepared Hungarian food is the attraction of the Budapest at no. 91 Karl-Marx-Allee.

Easily forgotten is the fact that Berlin lies in northern Europe, and the climate in consequence is variable. Add to this that the Berliners are devoted to central heating and you will perceive the need for warm clothing outside which you can peel off indoors. You need an umbrella even in spring, for a sudden shower or thunderstorm can dampen the most delightful visit. It surprised me to find men and women wearing formal dress at the opera and in theatres. And apart from the student snack bars, Berlin restaurants are filled with guests smartly dressed either in jackets and ties or in chic dresses.

Getting to know the city is easy. First explore the Kurfürsten-damm which runs south-west from the Kaiser Wilhelm Memorial Church for 3½ km as far as the Halen Lake. Berliners habitually shorten its name to the Kudamm. Laid out by the Prince-Electors to reach their hunting lodge at Grunewald, it was transformed into an elegant avenue on the orders of Bismarck. By the late nineteenth century the Kurfürstendamm was lined with exquisite art nouveau houses of which only six (nos. 29, 50, 60, 78, 172 and 188) survived the Second World War. Today the Kudamm is shaded with three rows of trees and crammed with shops, theatres, pavement cafés, cabarets, night clubs, cinemas, bars, hotels and department stores. There are also two useful banks here which, unlike every other bank in Berlin, open on Saturdays: that in Wertheim's store and the one at no. 24 Kudamm. Take a coffee and a cream cake at the celebrated Café Kranzler, whose name derives from the café founded in Unter den Linden in 1825 by the famous Austrian confectioner Johann Georg Kranzler.

Near by is Breitscheidplatz, the commercial centre of Berlin, always packed with students, tourists, passers-by, businessmen and businesswomen, shoppers and, outside school hours, school-children. Here buses, the Underground and the S-Bahn, and the railways converge. Here are hotels and shops. And here, curiously enough, is the Berlin Zoo, its entrance in Hardenberg-strasse. When it opened in 1844 the site was far from the centre of Berlin and indeed lay beside one of the city gates. The first group of animals belonged to the royal house, but the zoo soon established itself as one of the major animal collections in the world. By the end of the Second World War only ninety-one animals were left. Today there are over 11,000, representing 1,500 species. Incorporated in the zoo is Berlin's aquarium, which opened in 1913. If you have not time to see every one of the 400 beasts in this zoo (not to mention the 8,300 inhabitants of the aquarium and the 1,500 species of bird), don't miss the elephant quarters. Indian and African elephants, separated from the spectators by an alarmingly narrow dry moat, lumber through their acrobatic paces in the mornings and then spend the afternoons leaning against trees, politely ignoring the rhinoceroses which share their pad.

Pelicans here rejoice in their own pond, while coots, tufted ducks, mallards and herons swim placidly on nearby lakes. Here live great apes, baboons and a troop of rare orang-utans (of which fewer than 2,500 survive throughout the world). The first orang-utan to be born in captivity saw the light of day in this zoo in 1928. Here too are bred crocodiles, which are fed on fish and rats. Another favourite beast is Knautschke, the hippopotamus, born here in 1943.

Turning right from the zoo's exit, walk along Hardenberg-strasse and turn left again into the Tiergarten. Some 3 km long and 1 km wide, this park was laid out by the brilliant European landscape gardener Peter Joseph Lenné (who lived from 1789 to 1866). One of its features are gas lamps of yesteryear, those across the lock on the Landwehr canal brought from Britain, Brussels, Dublin, Zurich, Leiden and Copenhagen. Another series, on Tiergartenufer, are on one side all German, their soft lights coming from Düsseldorf, Hanover, Munich, Nuremberg, the Krumme Lanke housing estate and Frohnau, those on the other side from Budapest, Chemnitz, Dresden, Würzburg and Leipzig. Near by is a plaque marking the spot where the murdered bodies of Rosa Luxemburg and Karl Liebknecht were thrown into the canal in 1918.

The park is filled with *Liegewiesen* – areas where no one is allowed to disturb your peace with ball games. Its lakeside Café am Neuen See is an excellent place to recover after a session in a rowing boat. And Liechtensteinallee is the former diplomats' quarter of the Tiergarten, still lined with statues of hunters and their prey sculpted by Carl Begas in 1904.

On the western side of Breitscheidplatz rise the ruins of the Kaiser Wilhelm Memorial Church (the Kaiser-Wilhelm-Gedächtniskirche). This neo-Romanesque church was built between 1891 and 1895 in memory of Kaiser Wilhelm I and his minister Otto von Bismarck, the architecture chosen to draw a comparison between the new German empire and the old Holy Roman Empire. The year 1943 saw its ruin as the Allies bombarded Berlin. Instead of rebuilding it, the Berliners decided to preserve the church as it stood at the end of the war. As a result, this church is virtually the sole reminder of the horrific destruction of the Second World War. Its once great rose window is a shattered hole. Inside what remains of the church is a permanent and moving exhibition depicting the history of this doomed church from its beginnings in the 1890s to the flames of 23 November 1943. Here is a memorial to Kaiser Wilhelm I who died in 1888, and mosaics glorifying the Hohenzollerns as well as heroes of the Reformation. But this exhibition also displays the new spirit of Berlin, for it includes a call for reconciliation. Here is a cross made from nails collected from the charred beams of Coventry Cathedral in Great Britain, a cathedral which German bombs reduced to rubble in 1940. An inscription near by reads 'Forgive us our sins as we forgive those who sin against us.'

The architect Egon Eiermann was commissioned to design a new church to stand next to the Kaiser-Wilhelm-Gedächtniskirche and serve for worshippers and for concerts. His decision to build it out of 10,001 blocks of blue glass from Chartres was brilliant. The new church, opened in 1961, complements the old memorial church without remotely copying or competing with it.

Between the Kaiser-Wilhelm-Gedächtniskirche and the Europa Centre a fountain dedicated to the terrestrial globe was set up in 1983. Refusing to go along with such a pompous title, the Berliners have dubbed it the 'water meatball'. Water pours from the mouths of animals and humans, and in the hot summer days children cool themselves in it. Usually you can enjoy street theatre here.

As for the Europa Centre, which is surmounted by the three-pointed star of a Mercedes, its twenty-five levels were created in the early 1960s to house offices, shops, boutiques, cafés, cinemas, bars, a theatre, a cabaret and the city's main tourist office. The Swiss chain Mövenpick has installed one of its up-market fast-food restaurants here. Another complex waterworks, this one designed by a Frenchman, Bernard Gitton, in 1983, serves as a clock, the hours and minutes delineated by green-coloured water in a maze of transparent pipes. Arrive at 1 p.m. to watch it gurglingly empty itself, to fill up again for another twenty-four-hour cycle. Then make your way to the top floor, 86 m above ground level, for a panoramic view of Berlin.

Beside the Europa Centre two massive sets of steel chains decorate the entrance to Tauentzienstrasse, set here by the sculptors Brigitte and Martin Matschinsky-Denninghoff in 1987. The shops and department stores which line Tauentzienstrasse run south-west from the Europa Centre. Of these stores the most famous is undoubtedly the KaDeWe (the Kaufhaus des Westens) whose six storeys of stalls occupy 43 m² and whose top-floor food hall is famous. Its coffee bar offers *Irish Coffee mit Irish Whiskey*' (or *mit* any other liqueur), and its cheese stall offers ten English varieties.

Tauentzienstrasse soon runs into Wittenbergplatz (whose Underground station is especially glamorous) and at the other side becomes Kleiststrasse, which runs as far as Nollendorfplatz. In a former theatre which still stands here Erwin Piscator produced revolutionary plays in the 1920s. But the greatest attraction at Nollendorfplatz is its flea market, set in turn-of-the-century railway carriages in the S-Bahn. Even more attractive to my mind is the Heinrich Zille museum in this station. Zille's view of working-class life in turn-of-the-century Berlin is as affectionate as it is occasionally cruel. In his paintings soldiers proposition ladies up alleyways. A fat woman seeks help from her doctor. With one hand another massive lady raises her scrawny husband over her head. Cloth-capped men goose their womenfolk. Couples make love, frequently with their children in bed with them. Four members of the same family cram themselves into one bed.

The museum is enlivened with photographs of the Berlin of Zille's era. Exhibits chronicle his life. Another photograph shows the grey-bearded Zille with his unruly shock of hair in his studio in the 1920s, and here too is his death-mask of 1929. The artist grew ruder with age. Here are his erotic lithographs, published under the pseudonym W. Pfeifer around 1913. He loved to draw fat women and fat models. In his later paintings the women take to goosing their menfolk, looking wickedly over their shoulders at us and sometimes, to make the scenes even naughtier, with their drawers and trousers down. Why a woman kneeling down to unblock a stove is naked is anyone's guess.

Walk north from Nollendorfplatz, and you find yourself halfway along Kurfürstendamm. If you continue back to and past the Kaiser-Wilhelm-Gedächtniskirche and then follow Kantstrasse almost as far as the Theater des Westens, you can explore another building from the same epoch by turning left into Fasanenstrasse to find nos. 23–5, part of which now serves as a museum housing the works of Käthe Kollwitz. (Perhaps because she was a native of Berlin, her own portraits of local life are kinder than those of Heinrich Zille.) In Fasanenstrasse is also the Jewish Community House, which stands on the site of a synagogue burnt down by the Nazis in 1938. As might be expected, its restaurant serves kosher food.

Return to Hardenbergplatz to take bus no. 54 (in the direction of the airport) to visit Schloss Charlottenburg. This elegant, basically eighteenth-century palace was begun by the Elector Friedrich, who became King Friedrich I of Prussia in 1701. It is named after his second wife, Sophie Charlotte. Architects of the calibre of Arnold Nering, Eosander von Göthe, Georg Wenceslaus von Knobelsdorff and Karl Gotthard Langhans enriched the building, each one respectful of his predecessor's achievement. As a result nothing is out of place, nothing jars. Many contributed to the allure of this Schloss; but ultimately, it seems to me, this is Frederick the Great's finest gift to Berlin. His bounty created the rococo interiors with their tapestries, chinoiserie and fragile porcelain.

No one today would believe that much of Schloss Charlottenburg was completely burnt out by the end of the Second World War, for contemporary architects' drawings and later photographs have enabled much of it to be restored to its original condition. Only the Chinese porcelain was irrevocably lost in the war. Stucco ceilings have been reconstructed. Eighteenth-century marble fireplaces, tapestries and rich carpets are back in place. Carved and gilded console tables, another table patterned with a chessboard and Friedrich I's insignia (the Prussian eagle), French chandeliers, allegorical paintings, portraits of the Prussian royal family, their friends and other European monarchs have been restored. The porcelain room has been fitted out with a new collection. The east wall of the chapel has an early-eighteenth-century painting of the assumption of the Blessed Virgin Mary, depicted to resemble the recently deceased and much mourned Queen Sophie Charlotte, and the royal box here is richly sculpted and surmounted by the Prussian eagle and crown. Chinoiserie from the time of Frederick the Great and meticulous replicas of eighteenth- and nineteenth-century wallpapers and damasks enhance the succession of rooms. The Golden Gallery gleams again, its green stucco marble and its painted ceiling all restored by 1973. In Frederick the Great's bedchamber is a bust of Voltaire, although he eventually quarrelled with the monarch; outside, the Schloss is guarded by a magnificent equestrian statue of the Great Elector by Andreas Schlüter.

The garden of Schloss Charlottenburg is one of the most complex and yet satisfying parks in the whole of Berlin. The Elector Friedrich III commissioned the Schloss in 1695 as a summer residence for his second wife Sophie Charlotte, who passionately adored gardens and envied above all the one created by Le Nôtre at Versailles. Charlotte brought Le Nôtre's pupil Siméon Godeau to Berlin and set him to work. Bounded on two sides by the River Spree, the site was admirable, offering wide vistas and the possibility of constructing canals and waterfalls. On Sophie Charlotte's instructions Godeau cut down part of the Jungfernheide forest to create a yet more extensive view. Four rows of alleys lined the centre of the garden. Richly planted borders were created, leading to a reservoir filled from the river by a canal.

Wandering in this lovely garden, one can imagine the gaiety created here by Sophie Charlotte, who was known as the philosophical queen (queen because her elector husband became King Friedrich I of Prussia in 1701). She brought to Schloss Charlottenburg some of the leading savants of Europe, in particular her friend Leibniz who founded the Berlin Scientific Academy. Philosophy for her did not conflict with pleasure, and these gardens were the scenes of balls and fireworks, beginning with the elector's birthday celebrations in 1699 and continuing throughout the remaining six years of Sophie Charlotte's life. Their coronation in 1701 was marked by celebrations (or 'merry doings', as they called them) lasting for six months and including Italian opera. Another time the crown prince, but thirteen years old, fought and defeated a pseudo-Turkish pirate ship sailing up the River Spree. The contest was of course rigged, and afterwards a French opera company performed in the crown prince's honour. After Sophie Charlotte's sudden death Leibniz wrote, 'I tell myself that I have lost one of the greatest blisses in the world, which I had hoped to enjoy for the rest of my life.'

The garden did not remain untouched in subsequent centuries. First the Swedish architect Eosander von Göthe created an orangery here. Next Frederick the Great planted several thousand lime trees. The taste was now for 'natural' rustic styles in gardening, and a fashionable landscape gardener named Eyserbeck was summoned to Berlin to remodel in part the garden at Charlottenburg. Happily he did not attempt to destroy Siméon Godeau's geometric designs. Instead he enlarged the garden, scattering more flower-beds around the Schloss, incorporating irregular meadow lands and a romantic hermitage in the distance. Carl Gotthard Langhans designed a green and white baroque belvedere, and a couple of fishermen's huts were built beside the Spree as a rustic touch. Another royal death brought a new feature at the beginning of the nineteenth century, the mausoleum for Queen Luise, built like a Greek temple by the widowed King Friedrich-Wilhelm III in a dark alley of pines which the melancholy queen had loved and which, opined her husband, 'might soon unite us again'. He himself sketched the first design, and K. F. Schinkel brought it to perfection. The king was laid to rest beside Luise in the mausoleum in 1840. His son's heart was laid at his parents' feet. Here too lie Kaiser Wilhelm I and his wife the Empress Augusta.

New landscape artists added their skills to the garden. A talented gardener named Steiner was employed by Friedrich-Wilhelm III to lay out a winding path to the carp pool and create an island dedicated to Luise and scattered with statues, including her bust. In 1816 Friedrich-Wilhelm III also brought to Berlin Peter Joseph Lenné, who replanted the wide section between the Schloss and the reservoir. Restored after the Second World War, this is the astonishing garden you visit today, with a children's play park and a picnic area close by.

Opposite Schloss Charlottenburg stands Berlin's Bröhan Museum, dedicated to Jugendstil art of the turn of the century, the twenties and the thirties. Take the bus back to Bahnhof Zoo, looking out for the art nouveau town hall of Charlottenburg on the way. Then take a taxi past the 67 m Victory Column, put up in 1873 to celebrate Germany's military prowess, as far as the Brandenburg Gate. The route passes the Second World War Russian war memorial, which is flanked by two Russian tanks.

Carl Gotthard Langhans designed the Brandenburg Gate for Friedrich Wilhelm II, taking as his model the Propylaia of the Acropolis in Athens. Opened in 1791, this gate, whose Doric columns and entablement are decorated with scenes from classical mythology, was the first neoclassical building created in Berlin. On top of the gate is a group sculpted by Johann Gottfried Schadow, the goddess of victory in her chariot, which is drawn by four horses. Napoleon Bonaparte carried it off to Paris in 1806, and the celebrated *Quadriga* was not returned to Berlin until after Marshal Blücher's victory of 1814. The sculpture suffered grievously in the Second World War, and when the west Berliners restored it they left out the Prussian eagle and the Iron Cross which had decorated the lance of the goddess since 1814. Rightly, in my view, they have now been put back.

On the other side stretches Unter den Linden, and to walk through the gate now, just as to walk through what was once Checkpoint Charlie, makes one conscious of the new freedom. I shall never forget pausing on the former eastern side of the gate to admire its proportions, after I had taken coffee with and learned much from the sagacious Bishop Albrecht Schönherr of Berlin (who lived in the eastern sector), only to find an

East German policeman hitting the top of my car with his truncheon and forcing me to move on. A minor matter, no doubt, but it made one conscious of the petty restrictions which that heinous regime imposed upon the Germans themselves.

Pariser Platz stretches east of the Brandenburg Gate. Until the Second World War, this was the heart of political Berlin. Bismarck had established his Chancellery here in the Radziwil Palace in nearby Wilhelmstrasse (which the Communists re-named Otto-Grotewohl-Strasse); the French embassy was a rococo palace. The British embassy stood near to the Ministry of Foreign Affairs and, after 1933, Adolf Hitler's Chancellery. Undoubtedly in those days the Hotel Adlon set amongst these offices was the most luxurious and famous in Berlin. Further down Unter den Linden, where it crosses Friedrichstrasse, three celebrated cafés, the Bauer, the Kranzler and the Victoria, served *Schnitzeln* and coffee. Only the Bauer survived the Second World War; the other two have been replaced by the Grand Hotel. A lucky survivor of the bombardment of 3 February 1945 is the Haus der Schweiz, on another corner of this crossing.

Unter den Linden was originally designed to link the Schloss of the Prince-Electors to the Tiergarten. The first lime trees, from which it gets its name, were planted by the Great Elector in 1647. Soon buildings grew around the road, and the suburb, while still rural in its aspect, took the name Dorotheenstadt in 1673. The palaces which flank Unter den Linden began to be built only during the reign of Friedrich II. Restaurants and cafés came later.

In 1851 Christian Rauch created the equestrian statue of Friedrich II in the middle of Unter den Linden. His horse proudly snorts, and his hand is imperiously laid on his hip. The base of the statue is worth more than a cursory look, for it is sculpted with members of the royal family as well as with scholars and artists. The statue marks the beginning of a section of Unter den Linden which was greatly enhanced under the impetus of this particular monarch and formerly known in consequence as the Forum Fredericianum. It includes, on the corner of Bebelplatz, the Altes Palais, once the home of Kaiser Wilhelm I and now part of the Wilhelm von Humboldt University. The son of the architect of the Brandenburg Gate, Carl Ferdinand Langhans, built this palace between 1834 and 1836.

It stands close by the Alte Bibliothek, a former library popularly known as the *Kommode* because of the curve of its Viennese baroque façade. Boumann built it between 1774 and 1780 to house the royal library, and a plaque records that one of the readers in 1895 was Lenin. Only the exterior was rebuilt in the original style after the destruction of 1945. In the same square stands St Hedwig's cathedral with its green dome and classical pedimented entrance, built by Boumann and Legeay between 1747 and 1773. Inspired by the Pantheon in Rome and, it is said, built thus on the express order of Friedrich II, it serves the Catholics of Berlin.

The final architectural masterpiece of Bebelplatz is the Staatsoper. Knobelsdorff built it between 1740 and 1743, a symbol of the new monarch's determination to be a patron of the arts after he had escaped the tyranny of his father Friedrich Wilhelm I. The Staatsoper was severely damaged by a fire in 1843, but Carl Gottfried Langhans faithfully restored it, and it was restored again after the Second World War. To the east of the Staatsoper, in a little square, stands the Opera Café, a restaurant set up in what was once the Prinzessinnenpalais (or Palace of the Princesses). From it a colonnade leads to the Crown Prince's Palace, built in 1857. Four statues by Christian Rauch, representing the victorious generals of the war of liberation against Napoleon, embellish the square. Scharnhorst, in front, seems to be quietly brooding.

The other side of Unter den Linden from Bebelplatz is equally entrancing. Beside the National Library, with its pretty courtyard, is a palace built by Boumann for Prince Heinrich, the brother of Friedrich II and, as the statue of Wilhelm von Humboldt outside it indicates, this is now the Humboldt University. Wilhelm, sculpted by R. Begas in 1882, wears homely knee-breeches and silk stockings. A second statue represents von Humboldt's brother Alexander, a geologist and naturalist. You can't see the statues in winter, since they are housed in wooden boxes to protect the marble. In the courtyard behind them is a 1990s statue of the superb historian Theodor Mommsen, who published some 920 separate works. Oddly enough, he doesn't seem too busy. And whereas Lenin read in the Alte Bibliothek, it was here that Karl Marx studied between 1836 and 1841.

Next to the Humboldt University rises the Neue Wache, the new guardhouse which Karl Friedrich Schinkel built between 1815 and 1818 on the model of an ancient Greek temple. Today the Neue Wache is one of the most moving buildings in Berlin, transformed in 1960 into a monument to the victims of fascism and militarism. Inside an eternal flame burns beside the tombs of an unknown soldier and members of the resistance to Hitler.

Beyond the Neue Wache is the former arsenal of Berlin, the Zeughaus. This is not only the oldest building in Unter den Linden but also architecturally one of the most complex. Four successive architects worked on it from 1695 till its completion in 1706, namely Arnold Nering, Martin Grünberg, Andreas Schlüter and finally the Frenchman Jean de Bodt. For the interior courtyard Andreas Schlüter designed masks of dying warriors. After it ceased to serve as an arsenal in 1875, the building became a military museum. Today it houses museums devoted to Berlin and to the history of Germany. On the east side of the Zeughaus is a welcome restaurant. I recommend its *Kräuterquark 'Berliner Art'* (a fresh white cheese with green herbs served with oil and peeled potatoes) and its

Brandenburgische 'Bommel Pfanne' (two small beefsteaks with sauerkraut and *Bratkartoffeln*).

It is time to cross Unter den Linden again to explore another building by Schinkel, the Friedrichswerdersche church which stands in Friedrichswerdersche Markt. Built out of brick and in the neo-Gothic style between 1824 and 1830, the church is now the home of an exhibition devoted to classical Berlin and its classical sculpture. Here are outstanding sculptures by Schadow, Rauch, Tieks and Drake. I find its own architecture even more delightful than the exhibition, for Schinkel devoted much care to the interior décor and the stained-glass windows. The gallery fittingly contains an exhibition on his life and work.

Schinkel was also responsible for building the Schlossbrücke, the bridge which crosses the Schleusenkanal at the end of Unter den Linden. Finished in 1824, it carries martial statues celebrating the war of liberation, carved by pupils of Christian Rauch in the mid-1850s.

Here, on an island created by the River Spree and its arm the Schleusenkanal, is one of the richest collections of art in the world. Berlin's Museumsinsel is the site of an ensemble of museums built between 1823 and 1930 and almost all restored after the Second World war. The Altes Museum, with its majestic Ionic colonnade and splendid rotunda, was the creation of Karl Friedrich Schinkel. Opened in 1830, this was Berlin's first museum, and Wilhelm von Humboldt assisted Schinkel in selecting its first exhibits from the royal collections.

Today the Altes Museum displays a permanent collection of German sculpture and painting, amongst these modern Western art from the Ludwig collection. Do not miss a side entrance by the cathedral which leads to the Kupferstichkabinett, a collection of 135,000 copperplate engravings.

In Bodestrasse behind the Altes Museum is the Alte National-galerie. Designed by J. H. Strack in the form of a Corinthian temple and opened in 1876, its collection consists of nineteenth- and twentieth-century art. Amongst the sculptures are works by Schadow, Rauch, Thorwaldsen and Canova. Adolph von Menzel (1815–1905) is a neglected artist well represented here, not solely by his paintings of the court of Friedrich II but also by more homely works. French impressionists are matched by the lesser-known German ones: Max Slevogt, Lovis Corinth and Max Liebermann. Kokoschka, Nolde, Kirchner, Pechstein and Otto Dix lead the German expressionist painters, matched by the sculptures of Georg Kolbe.

In this art gallery I feel relieved not to have been painted by Otto Dix. His 1926 portrait of the poet Iwar von Lücken stitches the poet up, displaying his mended trousers, his black- ish fingernails and a couple of white roses in a beer bottle. Even the odd perspective hints at the poet's craziness. In the same room of the gallery is another savage portrait: Christian Schad painted Ludwig Bäumer in 1927 with a slit in his left cheek and some overblown flowers. But this was the glaringly truthful fashion of the Neue Sachlichkeit movement; on the opposite wall hangs a work of 1928 in which Georg Grosz painted himself with devastating honesty: gloomy, anxious, with grey face, hair and clothing. On the next wall, a painting completed in 1923 by Rudolf Schlichter ruthlessly exposes a half-naked woman.

From the Kupfergraben quayside you enter the Pergamon Museum, which stands behind the ruins of the Neues Museum. The Pergamon Museum, which was finished only in 1930, consists in fact of five museums, of which the finest are the collection of antiquities and the museum of the Near East. In the first is exhibited the superb Pergamon altar, fragments of which were discovered successively from 1878 and patiently put together. The altar was built in honour of Zeus by the citizens of Pergamon in Asia Minor after their successful war against the Galatians, which lasted from 180 to 160 BC. Its stunningly beautiful frieze depicts the mythological conflict between the gods and the giants. Another frieze displays the life of the Greek hero Telephos. The rest of this part of the museum is almost as impressive, with the superbly restored market gate of Miletus, dating from the second century AD; 28.92 m wide, 6.86 m deep and 16.68 m high, its sheer size overwhelms you. Pediments are piled high on columns, with a broken pediment in the middle.

In a north wing of the Pergamon Museum is a collection of Greek sculpture, mostly collected for Friedrich II.

The Museum of the Near East (the Vorderasiatisches Museum) boasts a collection of Mesopotamian and Assyrian art spanning 4000 years and housed in fourteen separate galleries. Here is the splendid Ishtar Gate of Babylon, built for Nebuchadnezzar II (604–562 BC). Reliefs of lions and goats are picked out in yellow against a blue background. Bulls and fantastic beasts (evidently created out of the fiercest bits of real animals) defend the city of the great king. The museum's greatest treasures include in gallery 2 the central portal of the citadel of Sam'ai, in gallery 3 the stele of Asarhaddon, in gallery 5 the façade of the temple of King Karaindack II (c. 1415 BC), amongst much else excavated at Uruk, and in galleries 10 and 11 the ninth-century-BC reliefs of the palace of Assurnasirpal II, found at Kalhu.

In 1903 Sultan Abdulhamid gave to Kaiser Wilhelm II the façade of the Islamic Omayyad castle of Mchatta, which dates from the seventh century AD and forms the core of the exhibition in the Islamic Museum. The two final museums in this part of the island are less spectacular, namely the East Asian collection and the museum of ethnology.

The half-dozen collections which constitute the Bodemuseum make up for this slight falling-off in quality. Initiated in 1904, the Bodemuseum occupies the whole of the northern corner of the island, and its name honours Wilhelm von Bode, director-general of the museums of Berlin from 1905 to 1920. Its Egyptian collection ranges from 5000 BC to the beginnings of the Christian era, and has rooms devoted to papyrus and to Egyptian funeral art. The most celebrated work of art in the early Christian and Byzantine gallery is a sixth-century mosaic from the apse of San Michele, Ravenna. A collection of sculpture offers a wealth of medieval Gothic and flamboyant masterpieces, alongside baroque and rococo works sculpted in Berlin and in Bavaria. Here too are displayed a series of prophets which once graced the church of Notre-Dame at Trier, a limewood altarpiece from Augsburg, and stone sculptures by Tilman Riemenschneider. From outside Germany there are some outstanding sculptures of the Italian Renaissance; the picture gallery is equally fecund, with works by both Cranachs, by Filippino Lippi, by Poussin and by Ruysdael. Finally the gallery includes a collection of more than 500,000 coins, medals and ancient seals.

Amongst his other stunning buildings Karl Friedrich Schinkel designed a Protestant cathedral for Berlin. In 1893 it was demolished to make way for a new, far more megalomanaic cathedral designed by Julius Raschdorff and clearly meant to glorify Prussia as much as the deity. The style itself is Wilhelmenian, with a ponderous dome and four weighty cupolas.

The road stretching north-east from the Protestant cathedral crosses Spandauer Strasse to reach Alexanderplatz. Near by is the 365 m high television tower with its bar, café and an observation platform which turns a full circle in the space of an hour. Set up in 1969, its architects were Fritz Dieter and Günter Franke. In the vicinity is the town hall and the Marienkirche. The former, built of red brick between 1861 and 1870, bears a frieze depicting the history of Berlin. From either side you can make your way into the Ratskeller. And today this town hall is the home of the municipal government of the reunited city. A couple of statues in front of the town hall serve as reminders of the postwar nightmare that was Berlin. One, the *Trümmerfrau*, is a woman clearing away the rubble; the second, the *Aufbauhelfer*, depicts a volunteer helping with the reconstruction of the city.

Another statue in this square, of Karl Marx and Friedrich Engels, sculpted by Ludwig Engelhardt in 1986, is a reminder of the more recent past. And a finer sculpture than any of these graces the Neptune Fountain which R. Begas created in 1871. It rises between the town hall and the Marienkirche, where once stood Eosander von Göthe's Hohenzollern Schloss. As for the church, this brick Gothic hall church, of a kind common in the Mark of Brandenburg, was built in the late fourteenth century, with a tower dating from 1418. Langhans added the crown of the tower in 1789. The interior has a fifteenth-century painting of the *danse macabre* and a baroque pulpit of 1703 by Andreas Schlüter. In the churchyard to the north of the building, a lifesize bronze statue of Martin Luther by Paul Martin Otto turns his back on the church to expound the scriptures to the world outside.

By taking Spandauer Strasse, which runs beside the town hall, you reach one of the oldest parts of the city and its oldest church. On the Spreeufer of the Nikolai quarter of Berlin, a massive bronze equestrian statue of St George slays a dragon. Ahead of him along Probpststrasse rise the twin towers of the Nikolaikirche. This church was begun in 1230, though all that remains from that era is the granite base from which rises the present late-Gothic brick church, which was finished in the fifteenth century. Its Gothic choir dates from 1379, while its two spires were designed by Hermann Blankenstein in 1877. Rising for four storeys, their warm stones, their round, blank windows, their simple Gothic windows, are restful and harmonious. Inside the white pillars from which painted arches rise shelter a museum of religious art as well as one depicting the history of Berlin and Kölln from their beginnings till 1648. A notice tells you that between 1657 and 1666 the hymnologist Paul Gerhardt worked here. Outside, in the church square, the Berlin bear sits on a fountain.

Around this church clusters a series of little streets with cafés and unpretentious houses, while on the corner of Mühlendamm and Poststrasse is the sole rococo house in Berlin, the Palais Ephraïm, ornate with Tuscan columns, wrought-iron balconies, urns and putti. The Palais Ephraïm was built between 1761 and 1766 for Friedrich II's jeweller and banker Nathan Veitel Ephraïm, and today serves as a museum of the history of the Mark of Brandenburg. The museum spills over into the nearby Knoblauchhaus (which is in Poststrasse), while in Mühlendamm is the Berlin Handwerk Museum. Next to it is the house in which Gotthold Ephraim Lessing wrote his *Minna von Barnhelm*.

The tiny Eiergasse runs from the apse of the Nikolaikirche to Molkenmarkt, where a market had established itself even before the union of Berlin and Kölln. Here stand two fine houses, no. 1, built in 1935 with a reproduction of a late-eighteenth-century frieze designed by Heinrich Gentz, and no. 3, a genuine eighteenth-century home designed by Jean de Bodt. From here runs Jüdenstrasse, in which rises the neoclassical Stadthaus built by Ludwig Hoffmann between 1902 and 1911 as an overflow chamber for the town hall, its dome rising to 101 m. Still further east in Parochialstrasse stands Berlin's oldest baroque church. Arnold Nering and Jean de Bodt built the Parochialkirche between 1695 and 1714, today yet another museum of religious art. Continue to the end of Parochialstrasse to find the restaurant known as Zur letzten Instanz ('In the last instance') because of its proximity to the tribunal. Inside is a celebrated *Kachelofen* (porcelain stove), and Berliners claim that this is their oldest surviving restaurant.

Close by are rare remains of Berlin's thirteenth-century

fortifications, and north along Littenstrasse you come upon the remains of a Gothic church built for the Franciscans in the same century. In the church square are two other memorials to bygone Berlin: a couple of capitals, dating 1706 and 1713 from Eosander von Göthe's Hohenzollern Schloss. Across the street rises the tribunal, in part neo-baroque, in part art nouveau, built at the beginning of this century to the plans of Thoerner, Schmalz and Mönnich.

We are close to the birthplace of Berlin. Walk back along Littenstrasse to cross Stralauer Strasse and reach the bank of the Spree. By walking left here you reach a bridge; cross over and find in the Köllnischer Park the Museum of the Mark. Built in 1908, it is dedicated to the artistic and cultural life of Berlin. One of its most popular rooms is devoted to Heinrich Zille (1858–1929), the satirist of working-class life, and in the park is a monument which depicts Zille crayon in hand. On this bank of the Spree, at no. 10 Am Märkischen Ufer, stands the eighteenth-century Ermeler Haus, its rococo interior sheltering a café and restaurants whose food I have already recommended. From Märkischer Platz walk along Wall-Strasse and turn right into Neue-Ross-Strasse to cross the branch of the Spree and reach the Fishermen's Island. Here the settlement of Kölln was first established. Breitestrasse, which is the continuation of Neue-Ross-Strasse, has four gabled Renaissance houses.

From it Gertraudenstrasse will take you south-west to the Spree canal. Dutch navigators dug it, and its embankment has a Dutch-sounding name, Friedrichsgracht. By following Friedrichsgracht north-west from the statue of St Gertrude, the patron saint of travellers, you come to the charming Platz der Akademie in which rise two cathedrals and a classical theatre. The Französischer Dom and its German equivalent the Deutscher Dom were built in the early eighteenth century for French Protestants and German Protestants respectively. Both cathedrals were enlarged in the early 1790s by Gontard and

Unger, who added their characteristic domes. Today the Fran-
zösicher Dom is a Huguenot Museum and also has mementoes
of the anti-Nazi martyr Dietrich Bonhoeffer. As for the theatre,
it was built by Karl Friedrich Schinkel in 1821 to replace one
which had burned down four years earlier. Today it is used as
a concert hall, and houses an organ of seventy-four voices
built by the Dresden firm of Jemlich.

Berlin is by no means exhausted by this tour. Amongst its
museums is the Bauhaus archive at no. 14 Klingelhofstrasse,
which displays works by Walter Gropius, Paul Klee, Lyonel
Feininger, Wassily Kandinsky and László Moholy-Nagy. The
Brücke Museum is yet more entrancing, with masterpieces by
Ernst Heckel, Karl Schmidt-Rottluff and Ernst Ludwig Kirchner. In Berlin-Zehlendorf the Museumsdorf Düppel has re-
created a medieval village.

Nor have I mentioned every palace of the city. On the banks
of the Grunewald lake stands the Renaissance hunting lodge
which Caspar Theyss built in 1542 for Elector Joachim II.
Schloss Tegel was begun in 1550 and transformed in the early
1820s for Wilhelm von Humboldt by Karl Friedrich Schinkel.
And Schloss Britz is an eighteenth-century Prussian home,
rebuilt in the early 1880s and set in a superb park.

I also particularly recommend three excursions. From Bahnhof
Zoo, line 1 of the U-Bahn (in the Ruhleben direction) will take
you to the 1936 Olympic Stadium of Berlin. Here Hitler hoped
to impress the world by staging the Olympic Games and is
said to have been deeply discomfited when the American negro
Jesse Owens insisted on winning four gold medals. In truth,
film of the event reveals the Führer placidly congratulating
Owens on his success. A swimming-pool, a hockey pitch, an
open-air theatre seating 20,000 and an equestrian stadium have
since been added to the magnificent bowl which Werner March
designed in 1936. The great Olympic Bell of 1936 was cracked

in the Second World War and is now displayed by the southern gate, embellished with the German eagle clutching the Olympics rings and the legend 'I summon the youth of the world' ('*Ich rufe die Jugend der Welt*').

The youth of Berlin certainly gather here, for hockey, racing and training for every kind of sport. Berliners still like to be the best in the world, and their athletic zeal is displayed above all on the last Sunday in September, when some 30,000 people take part in the Berlin marathon.

Berlin's Pfaueninsel (Peacock Island) is my second recommended excursion. To reach it take S-Bahn 1 from Bahnhof Zoo to Wannsee, a journey which traverses the Grunewald woods. Before boarding the bus to the harbour, literary-minded folk should look for the sign directing them to the grave of the poet Heinrich von Kleist, who killed himself on 21 November 1811, because, he said, 'There is no one left on earth to help me.' His tombstone is engraved with his own words: 'O immortality, you are wholly mine.' At the Wannsee harbour the ferry plays merry traditional songs as it transports you to the island. A passionate hunter of snipe and ducks, Friedrich-Wilhelm II bought this island in 1793 to pursue the sport. He commissioned the court carpenter, Johann Gottlieb Brendel, to build on the island a barn, a dairy, a hen coop and a peacock pen (which was to be disguised as a haystack). Today the island is a protected nature reserve, where dogs and smoking are prohibited. Peacocks still perch in the trees. Here is a Kavaliershaus designed by Schinkel, as well as Friedrich-Wilhelm II's bizarre Schloss.

The third excursion is to Spandau, taking U-Bahn line 7 towards Rathaus Spandau and alighting at Zitadelle. Spandau's most celebrated resident was Elector Joachim II of Brandenburg, and Cranach painted his stern face with its double-pointed beard. The portrait is reproduced on a wall of the railway station. The second most celebrated resident of this spot was the Nazi Rudolf Hess, imprisoned here after the Second World War until his death in 1987. The citadel itself is an entrancing Italian building, for the most part designed in the late sixteenth century by the Venetian architect Chiamello de Gandono. Inside the citadel you can eat in a historic *Gaststätte*, before venturing forth along pedestrianized Breitestrasse, to find the handsome and strong Nikolaikirche. Built of pink bricks, with a wide tower topped by a cupola, it shelters a high altar of 1572.

But to me Berlin's ambience is found not in its mighty palaces and galleries but, above all, in its suburbs, where life goes tranquilly on as if the cataclysmic events of the twentieth century had never taken place. The suburb of Schöneberg is just such a spot, even though the authorities here seem to have done their utmost to remind the citizens of recent history. Schöneberg's flag-bedecked, monumental town hall (its art deco walls softly illuminated at night) rises in John Kennedy Platz, and inside are portraits of such leading postwar Berlin figures as presidents Theodor Heuss, Heinrich Lübke and Konrad Adenauer. Here too is a painting of the US General Lucius D. Clay, American military governor in Germany after 1945.

Yet behind the town hall of Schöneberg delicious old Berlin reasserts itself, with a most glamorous park and fountains playing beside the Carl Zuckmayer bridge. On Tuesdays and Fridays, market stalls are set out around the town hall, selling sausages, cheeses and all sorts of bread till one o'clock in the afternoon. And of course the town hall has a Ratskeller. In the Kleine Ratsstube I once ordered a beer and found the waiter staggering over with five flowing Steins, claiming they were all for me, before taking four of them behind me to be quaffed by four other guests. As Bertolt Brecht put it in 1920, 'Berlin is absolutely stuffed with bad taste; but on what a scale!'

INDEX

INDEX

INDEX